AF521874

WATERFALLS OF THE ADIRONDACKS AND CATSKILLS

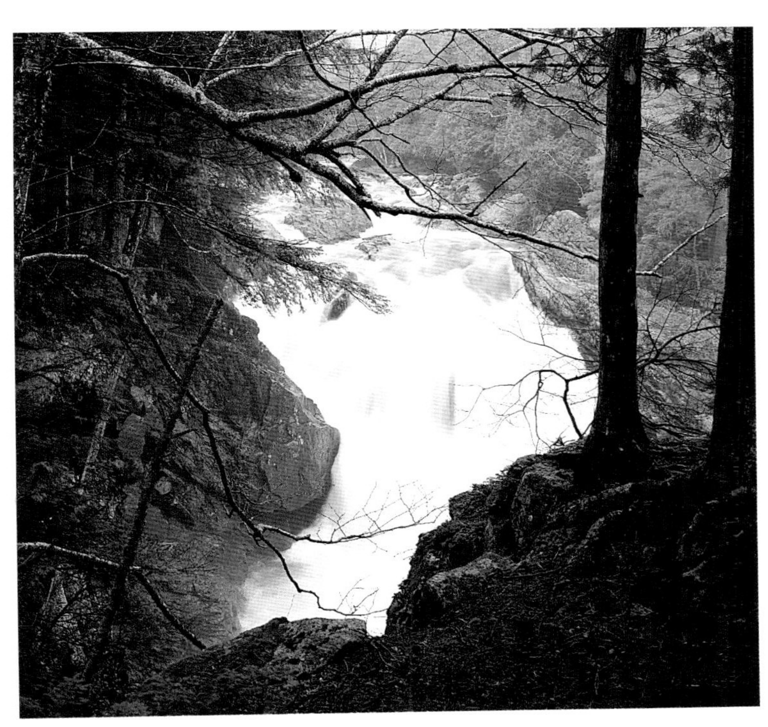

WATERFALLS

OF THE

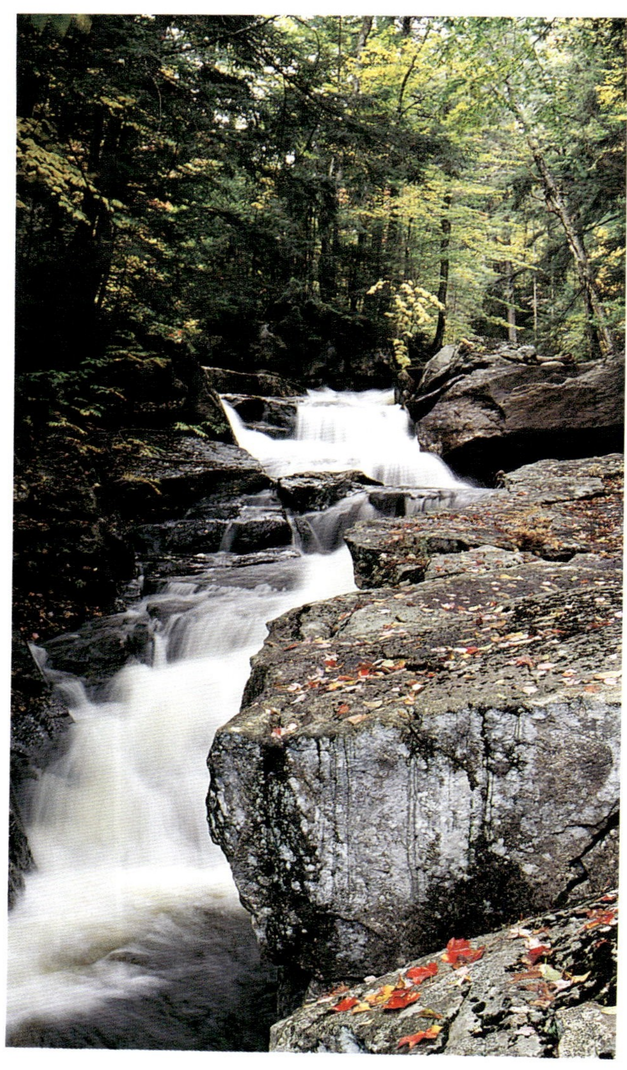

ADIRONDACKS AND CATSKILLS

DEREK DOEFFINGER
AND
KEITH BOAS

McBOOKS PRESS
ITHACA, NEW YORK

Copyright © 2000 by Derek Doeffinger and Keith Boas

All rights reserved, including the right to reproduce this book or any portion thereof in any form or by any means, electronic or mechanical, without the written permission of the publisher. Requests for such permissions should be addressed to: McBooks Press, 120 West State Street, Ithaca, NY 14850.

Book and cover design: Paperwork

Library of Congress Cataloging-in-Publication Data

Doeffinger, Derek.
Waterfalls of the Adirondacks and Catskills / Derek Doeffinger and Keith Boas.
p. cm.
ISBN 0-935526-62-5
1. Waterfalls—New York (State)—Adirondack Mountains. 2. Waterfalls—New York (State)—Catskill Mountains. 3. Waterfalls—New York (State)—Adirondack Mountains—Pictorial works. 4. Waterfalls—New York (State)—Catskill Mountains—Pictorial works. I. Boas, Keith, 1940- . II. Title.
GB1425.N4D66 1999
551.48'4'097475—dc21 99-38906
CIP

This book is distributed to the book trade by Login Trade, a division of LPC Group, 1436 West Randolph Street, Chicago, IL 60607. Additional copies of this book may be ordered from any bookstore or directly from McBooks Press, 120 West State Street, Ithaca, NY 14850 Please include $3.00 postage and handling with mail orders. New York State residents must add 8% sales tax. All McBooks Press publications can also be ordered by calling toll-free 1-888-BOOKS11 (1-888-266-5711). Visit our web site at: www.McBooks.com.

Printed in Hong Kong

9 8 7 6 5 4 3 2 1

A few of the sites pictured in this book are on private property. Please inquire before visiting and respect the rights and wishes of property owners.

On the cover: Falls at Wilmington Notch

CONTENTS

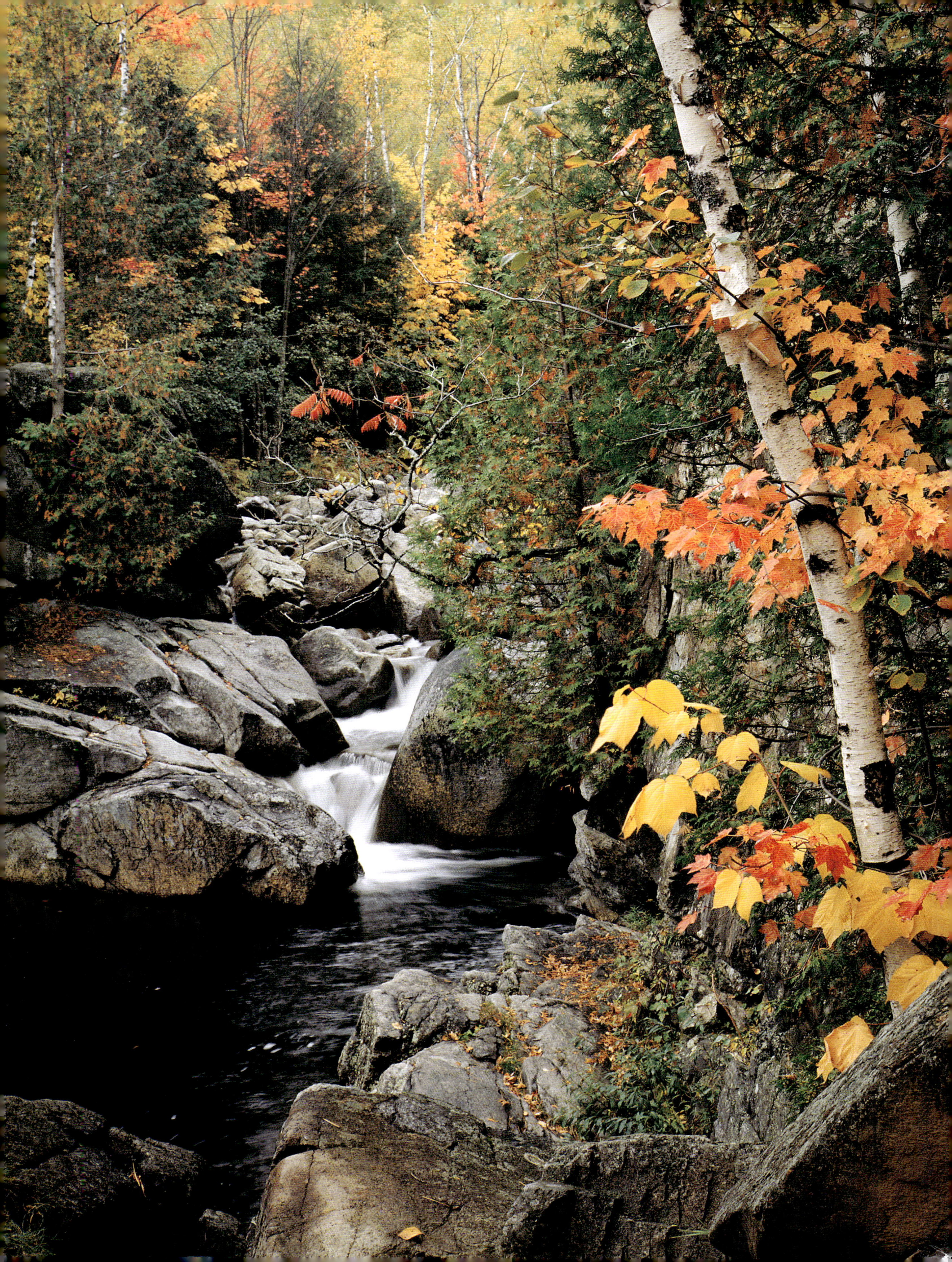

FOREWORD

You hold in your hands a precious gift. Many of the stunning photographs on these pages reveal secret spots rarely seen. Yet as a New Yorker, I take great comfort in knowing I need only wander my own sprawling "backyard" to discover them with my own eyes and feel the waterfalls' cool mist on my face.

The rushing waters in these pictures slice, swerve and tumble through two of the Northeast's most celebrated regions—the Adirondacks and the Catskills. Majestic and distinct in atmosphere and beauty, these treasured territories remind all New Yorkers of our good fortune. They not only offer us ready access to an extraordinary outdoor experience, but help define us as a state. The folklore, industry, art, and community character associated with both these mountain landscapes are woven into our collective consciousness. They are, in equal measure, integral to the colorful composite of who New Yorkers are today, and the historic richness of our past.

To the north, the Adirondacks spread their jagged, pointed peaks across the horizon like the teeth of an old ripsaw blade, well-worn but still formidable. The Iroquois and Algonquin were the first to traverse this territory. In time, the French and English arrived and built several military outposts, battling each other and the native tribes through much of the 18th century. Eventually, the English prevailed but they, in turn, were driven back across the Atlantic by the Americans in the Revolutionary War. All these events transpired in a relatively small area of the Adirondacks, the bulk of which was left virtually uninhabited until the mid-19th century when the voracious logging of the land began.

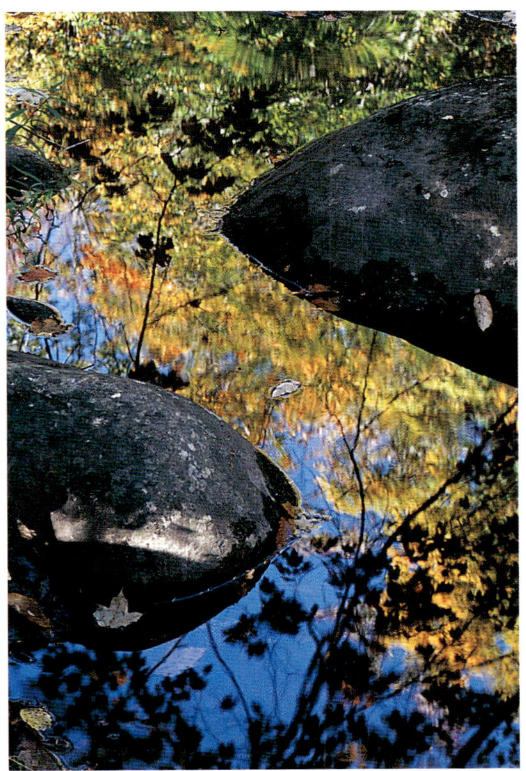

Many loggers, once they had stripped the land bare, defaulted on their property taxes. But, turning this liability into an opportunity, New York State began acquiring huge chunks of land and, in 1885, the Legislature created the Adirondack Forest Preserve. Originally designed to protect the Hudson River Watershed and New York City's water supply, this move also helped to preserve the Adirondacks' pristine beauty. Laws were strengthened in 1892 and again in 1894 with the introduction of the totally new concept of "forever wild" forests. Concurrently, the rich, attracted to the region's rustic way of life, began building the "great camps" of the Adirondacks, many of which still remain standing. The Preserve became the country's first great protected wilderness, and today it is the East's largest, most majestic wild area.

The Adirondack Park now spans six million acres, an area about the size of Vermont and a fifth of the land mass of New York State. Nearly half of that land is forest preserve, a primeval landscape belonging to all the people of the state. Two thousand mountain peaks stretch across its span with a hundred of them over 3,000 feet in elevation. Two peaks, Marcy and Algonquin, are over 5,000 feet.

The numbers are staggering: The Adirondacks hold 1,200 miles of rivers, 3,000 miles of brooks and streams, and 2,800 lakes and ponds. Their lands and waters support 70 different species of trees, 35 species of reptiles, 86 varieties of fish, 218 species of birds and 55 of mammals. These mountains provide the greatest opportunities for sport and outdoor activity and the most arresting landscapes the eastern United States has to offer. For these reasons, in large part, several million tourists pass through the Park annually.

A spectacularly raw and wild beauty first comes to mind at the mention of the Adirondacks. But this rugged region is also characterized by the farmers, restaurant owners, artisan shopkeepers, miners, museum curators, forestry workers, innkeepers and 130,000 other New Yorkers who live there and give the Adirondacks a human face. They are proud and protective of this magnificent land, and rightfully so.

Further south, as soft morning light spreads across the Hudson Valley and gives the lush mountains of the Catskills the look of velvet, it's easy to see how early settlers were drawn to this enticing landscape a hundred miles northwest of New York City. Only sporadically inhabited early on by native Americans, this region was later settled by the Dutch, English, German, and Irish whose influence and presence in the area remains strong today. These people built communities which prospered around the industries of logging, leather tanning, fishing, stone quarrying, and farming, followed by the construction of rail lines which distributed the goods of these indigenous activities to the wider world beyond.

Ticking off the area's six counties and over 3,000 square miles of mountains, rivers, lakes, farmland, and forests only begins to delineate the Catskills. The range boasts 35 mountain peaks over 3,500 feet in elevation, several major river systems and numerous water reservoirs, making up a crucial ecological resource we must respect and protect. With an eye toward that responsibility, New York State has designated over 700,000 acres of the Catskills as parkland.

Harboring some 50,000 year-round residents, the Catskill Park is a tapestry of private and publicly owned lands. Over 60 percent of the land within the Park is privately owned and the 275,000 acres of State-owned land —the Catskill Forest Preserve—is set aside, as in the Adirondacks, as forever-wild forest, with more earmarked to expand the Preserve in the future.

The recreational opportunities of the Catskills have always made them a premier vacation destination, notable for landmark Jewish resorts, and they remain so today. But it is the year-round residents who contribute most to the inviting nature of the region. Living in quaint towns and villages, they tend to the land, run businesses and organizations, and produce art of outstanding quality and variety. Together, they create a Catskill community that is sophisticated, sublime, culturally diverse, and perfectly suited to the natural charms of its location.

The Catskills and Adirondacks have inspired generations of writers, painters and other artists, just as they've inspired Derek Doeffinger and Keith Boas. Doeffinger and Boas have captured, in words and photographs, some of the most beautiful scenery this continent has to offer and it all just happens to be right here in New York State. May their work inspire you to visit these regions, to wander these woods, seek out a misty waterfall, and see for yourself the transforming experiences the Adirondacks and Catskills can provide.

H. Carl McCall
New York State Comptroller

INTRODUCTION

A *waterfall* is one of the most dynamic sites on earth. One day, it tiptoes down a rocky slope. The next, powered by torrential rains, it tears through a gorge, clawing rocks from the banks and propelling them downstream to crash into other rocks and break apart into ever-smaller fragments that, one day, come to rest in an ocean delta. By its very nature, a waterfall is actively digesting the earth it flows through. By its very nature, it is both Beauty and Beast, Jekyll and Hyde.

Yet most of us are not drawn to waterfalls for their paradoxes. Most of us search them out for their beauty. In utter delight, we rejoice as a waterfall leaps and jumps with infatuating grace. Seduced by gravity, it dances and frolics down a rocky face, threading and winding its way through a maze of stones, slides over a sheer cliff and, in perfect symmetry, separates into a thousand strands that undulate through the air like wisps of smoke and finally reunite into one ribbon of water at the base of the falls.

Have no doubt. A waterfall is a choreography of nature that can be exceeded only by another waterfall. What is it about the performance of falling water that so attracts us? Is it the shattering of water into a million drops? Is it the transformation of a shimmering surface into a lather of bubbles? Is it the reckless leap from great heights? Is it the symmetry and synchronization that must be random, must adhere to dictates of chaos theory, yet seems rehearsed to perfection? Or is it simply our instinctive need for water, the cool, refreshing liquid that constitutes nearly two-thirds of our bodies, that replenishes and rejuvenates us after a sweat-drenched hike?

For most of us, the appeal draws from many of these elements, and the combination stirs an inner wildness too long caged by society. A waterfall knows no rules. Pell-mell, caution thrown to the wind, it springs from the top of a cliff, somersaults and cartwheels through the air, crashes upon rocks, trees, and all who get in the way, without fear of consequence, and all the while emits a deafening roar.

Do you get the feeling that it must be fun to be a waterfall? But since few of us can, watching will have to do. For those who live in New York State, this pastime is easily achieved. In the two great mountain preserves of eastern New York, the Adirondack and Catskill parks, waterfalls abound. There are hundreds of them, as hard or as easy to reach as you'd like. Many cascade right next to roads; indeed, some are adjacent to viewing platforms with benches built by accommodating innkeepers. Others are at the end of short or lengthy hikes along well-marked and well-maintained trails. And some are known only to those who leave the trails and bushwhack through the woods.

Beside the road or at the end of a long hike, the waterfalls we'll take you to in this book are widely varied. Though all belong to the genus waterfall, their specific characters diverge greatly. Each offers its own visual pleasures. And they are not constant, varying with water level, season, and light. We've been to—and will show you—a great number of waterfalls, but many more await our visits.

If in your travels, you happen to see two middle-aged photographers, cameras on tripod, one wearing a baseball cap and the other beneath a dark cloth focusing his view camera, say hello and be prepared to have your picture taken next to our favorite subject.

Hike carefully around waterfalls

The terrain around waterfalls can be treacherous. Proceed carefully. The combination of water and steep, rocky slopes can create slippery conditions that could send you tumbling, even on level surfaces. A fall on rock can easily cause injury, which could mean big problems if you're miles from help.

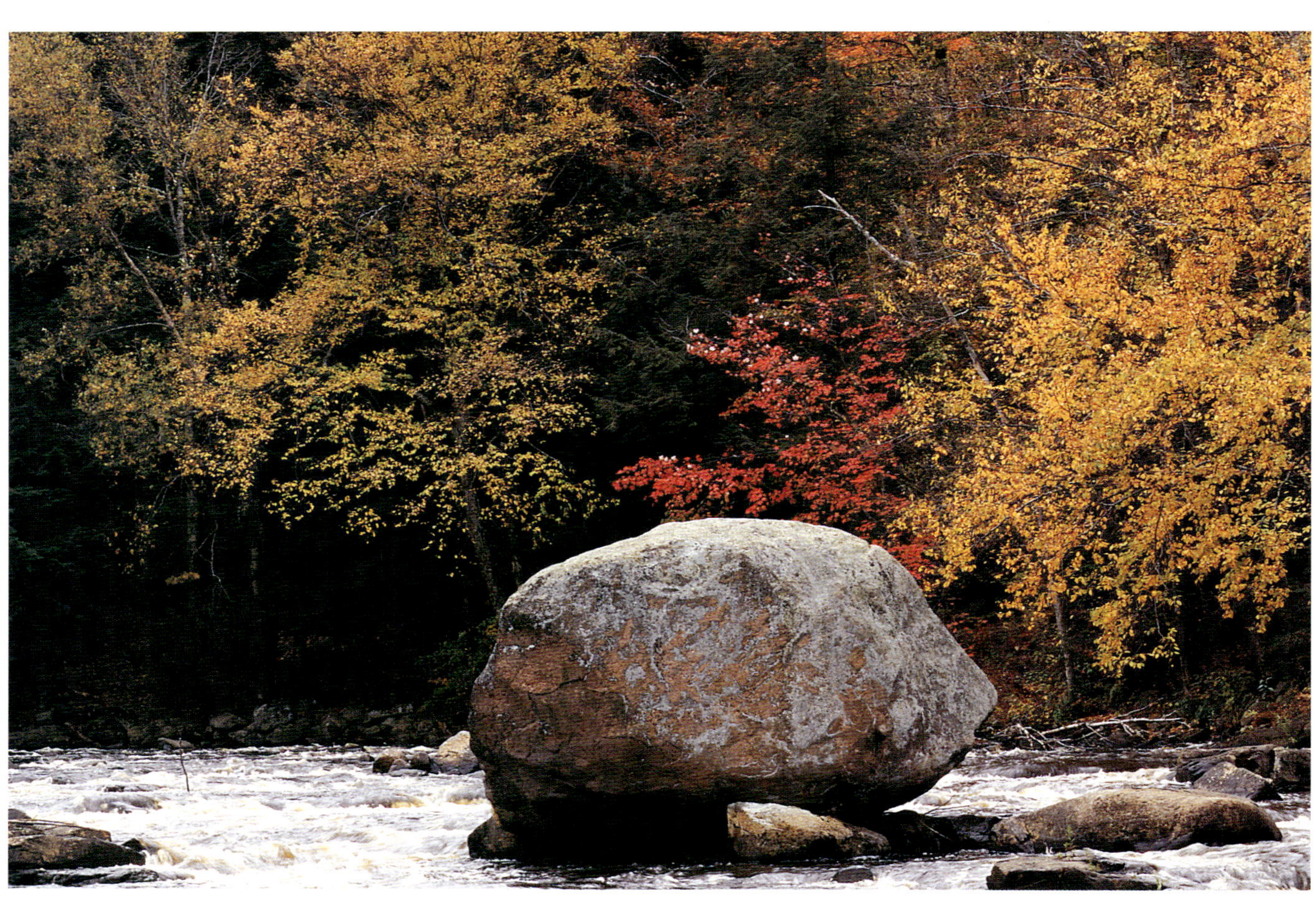

THE GEOLOGY OF THE ADIRONDACK & CATSKILL MOUNTAINS

Andy Rooney was a reporter for *Stars and Stripes* in World War II. Charles Kuralt reported firsthand on the uprising in the Congo and on Vietnam. My neighbor, a retired machinist, served under two flags: During the last days of World War II he was in the German Navy; then he came to the U.S., where he served in our army.

What's this have to do with mountains? To state the obvious, what is isn't what was. We've all heard a hundred times that historically, over several years, the stock market will outperform a fixed-interest savings account. We know from school that we study history to prevent future mistakes, like another Vietnam. Likewise, a little review of the past of the Adirondacks and Catskills may prove, if not entertaining, then perhaps a tad enlightening.

Not too long ago, geologically speaking, if you were a New Yorker planning a trip for Memorial Day weekend, you might have chosen a destination in Morocco instead of in Maine. After all, you wouldn't want to spend too much of your vacation in the car.

Perhaps if you took that trip even earlier, geologically speaking, you might have opted to explore the channels and bayous of the nearby delta instead of the Moroccan landscape. Or if you had left earlier still, geologically speaking, as you lifted the trunk lid to slip in a suitcase, a faint, distant rumble might have reached your ears. Recognizing the sound, you would have cried out to the kids to hurry up, and sped off to the nearest hilltop. From there, you might have watched in awe as an erupting volcano glowed in the east against the twilight sky. If you're a more active sort, you might have chosen something like mountain-climbing in the snow-covered Acadians, but without bottled oxygen, you wouldn't have quite been able to reach the summit.

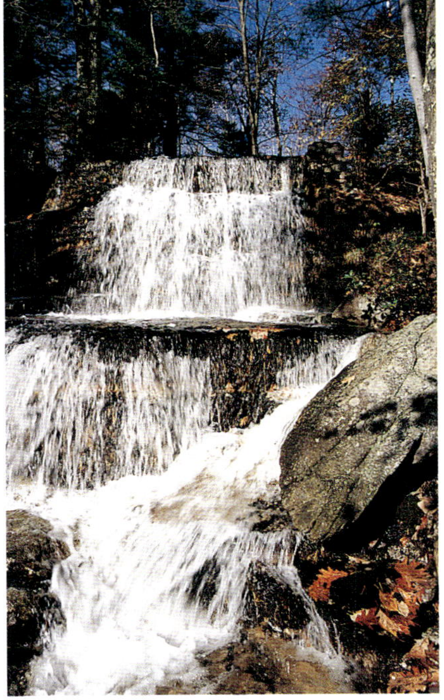

The New York landscape of today, specifically that of the Adirondacks and Catskills, is a far cry from what it once was. This is a land with a past. While it may not be checkered, it has a few stories to tell from its youth, stories that seem out of character with its current mature and sedate life. This land has been around, been in and out of a few scrapes, had its ups and downs, rubbed up against some rough continents. It has lived a life that, had we heard it recounted by a stranger in a bar, we'd have listened politely while silently snickering. If the clichés of living attributed to land sound far-fetched, the analogy of land being alive, of having a past, is entirely appropriate.

For the land is very much alive, sometimes in ways that you can't help but notice, such as earthquakes and landslides. But more often the ways are all but imperceptible—erosion, continental drift, climatic change. Those who, over the years, have lost hair or a defined waistline will have no trouble appreciating the subtle and gradual changes that time can work. If hair can recede and waistlines extend by inches in just a few decades, imagine the change possible over hundreds of millions of years. That's the time allotted for land to change.

The fact that neither man nor animal, not even trees were around to witness most of this does not detract from the story. Rather, it's an enhancement. The story of the earth has evolved over the last billion-plus years, and that of the Catskills in roughly the last 500 million years. Just as a point of reference, humans have only taken part in the story over the last two million years.

Amazingly, the continents which form the great land masses of this planet are moving. Indeed, they are moving even as you read this, at about the same rate your fingernails grow. That means that most of North America, as a continent, will move an inch or two a year, in a northwesterly direction.

Now, with the help of some elementary math, let's step back in time 250 million years and see where our continent has been: 250 million × 1.5 (inches/year) = 375 million inches, which equals 31 million feet or 6,000 miles. For the sake of simplicity, let's say the rate and direction of continental drift was constant over the time period in question.

Moving opposite of that current northwest direction, we follow our continent's trail southeast 6,000 miles and end up about 1,500 miles east of Brazil. But we are not alone. In fact, none of the continents are alone. They've all come together into a giant land mass that the scientists today refer to as Pangea (which means "all land"). Indeed, in Pangea, the northeastern United States adjoins northwestern Africa, and the puzzle piece of South America butts into Africa pretty much as their respective shapes dictate. The coming together of the continents was a slow-motion collision with big consequences: specifically, a mountain chain, the Alleghenies, along the east coast of North America.

In total, there were three continental collisions which resulted in three eastern mountain chains in the past 450 million years. Since the Allegheny Mountains were the most recent, you might expect the Adirondacks and Catskills to be their worn-down remnants. They aren't. Nearly all evidence of the ancient Alleghenies is gone. Eroded. Wind, water, ice, glaciers, and time have erased them.

If neither the Catskills nor the Adirondacks are descended from the Alleghenies, what is their origin? Both derive from a combination of ancient mountain-building and recent (geologically speaking) erosion. Somewhat paradoxically, although the Adirondacks are made up of much older rock, as mountains they are younger than the Catskills. So let us look even further back in time to find out what created the rock forming each of these mountainous regions. Then, once we've found the building materials, we will leap nearly a billion years forward to uncover how the mountains themselves were created.

Just as the Alleghenies were the result of a continental collision 250 million years ago and then erased, so did their predecessors, the Acadian Mountains, suffer a similar fate. How high did the Acadians rise 380 million years ago, when eastern North America, somewhere south of the equator, crashed into a small continent? Five thousand, ten thousand, twenty thousand feet?

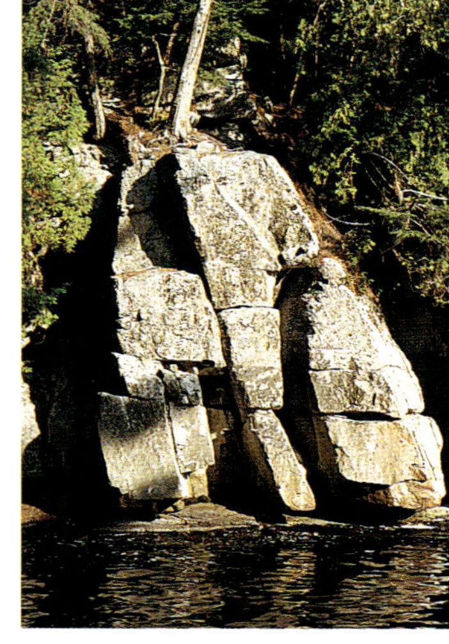

No one's sure. But height proved no protection against erosion and time. Over the next tens of millions of years, the Acadians were broken down, and streams swept their sediments westward into what is today the Adirondacks and Catskills, westward into central and eastern New York, and all the way into eastern Ohio.

The sediments accumulated in a great shallow sea. Thousands of feet of mountains became thousands of feet of sediment. The increasing weight compressed the sediment into layers of shale and sandstone thousands of feet thick. Infrequently during this time, the conditions favored tiny sea creatures which flourished, living and dying and letting their calcareous shells drift to the seabed like a winter's snow to accumulate in thinner layers of limestone.

The Alleghenies formed atop these sediments but once they were eroded away, the sedimentary layers underneath were exposed as the Catskill delta—the shale and sandstone formations composing most of the Catskills. However, because of (geologically speaking) more recent and more severe erosion, the layers are less prominent in the Adirondacks.

Not surprisingly, an even earlier continental collision formed an even earlier mountain range some 450 million years ago—the Taconics. Like the Acadians, the Taconics were eroded in time and swept westward to form thick sediments in a shallow sea. These particles, largely transformed into shale, are known as the Queenston delta and are found primarily in central and western New York. Some rocky outcrops, remnants of the Taconics, are exposed in eastern New York and western Massachusetts. But for the most part, the Taconics have disappeared.

We've stepped back as far as we can to find the roots of the Catskills. Only a leap forward in time can disclose the final chapter of the evolving Catskill landscape. But before we leap, let's look at the completion of the setting for the Adirondacks. Back we go again to see how some of the oldest rocks in North America were formed.

It's the same old story—a continental collision, mountains, erosion, sediments accumulating. But this time the collision occurred an unimaginably long time ago—1.4 billion years—and clues uncovered in the northwestern Adirondacks indicated that an occasional volcano had erupted over the landscape.

Again, the sediments were compressed into shale and sandstone. But then more mountains were built—the Grenville Mountains. The Grenvilles buried the shale and sandstone deep beneath the surface. Miles below. In fact, the sedimentary layers were as much as fifteen miles down, close to the furnaces in the earth, where the heat hovered around eight hundred degrees Celsius and the pressure was extreme.

The ordinary sandstone and crumbly shale was changed forever—metamorphosed. Yielding to extreme heat and pressure, the rock became plastic. Minerals altered in character. Sandstone and shale became granites, schists, anorthosites. Limestone became marble. The feeble, brittle rocks created by erosion were becoming hard, muscular rocks with coarse textures, whose surfaces would one day be a pleasure to stroke with our palms. Sometimes, from even deeper in the earth, molten plumes would melt and inject their way into the new rocks.

While the molten contortions took place deep inside the earth, other mountain-building collisions were happening above. One continent jammed into another, doing damage which was not always apparent. Some of it was internal, as great zones of rock fractured, weakened, remained invisible until uncovered. This hard, extremely durable foundation of rock underlies most of New York State, but because of recent events (geologically speaking), it is visible almost only in the Adirondacks.

At long last, our leap forward is almost upon us. We know about the strong foundation of rock under our state. We know that a succession of continental collisions created a succession of mountain chains running north-south, and that these mountains were eroded and swept into shallow seas as recently as 250 million years ago. We know that 250 million years ago, the continents clustered together into one supercontinent, Pangea, and that, since then, they have been separating. Indeed, the separation created the Atlantic Ocean, which even today is growing wider.

Now we will take that great leap forward, landing just a few million years ago—minutes from today, in geological terms. What do we find? The Catskills consist of a broad plain sloping south. Gentle river valleys and hills wind their way through the land. To the north are mountains and they are growing. Only a few million years earlier, the landscape of the Adirondacks would have seemed nearly continuous with that of the Catskills.

But a change was occurring deep inside the earth beneath the Adirondacks, a change which even today can't quite be explained. For reasons unknown, a large molten mass was rising upward. Like a giant beachball, it rose (and continues to rise), pushing the land above it upward in elevation until land that was once flat and low-lying is now crumpled and high. In other words, the rising mass produced mountains—real mountains—not the highest on the continent but, nonetheless, mountains, and still rising at nearly three millimeters per year. This rate is slower than the Himalayas but faster than the Alps.

Of even greater consequence than elevated altitude was escalated erosion. The rising land became steep and the steepness increased erosion—rapidly. Sediments built up over eons were being swept away. The erosion would be accelerated by glaciers bulldozing through the land until, ultimately, rocks that were deeply buried in the rest of New York, rocks among the most ancient in eastern North America, rocks that were formed miles below the earth over one billion years before were finally exposed.

The onset of the time of glaciers was upon the land. The Ice Age. For two million years, the land was alternately encased in great layers of ice, then given brief respites. The cause is uncertain but most likely arose from a combination of factors: peculiarities in the earth's orbit about the sun; fluctuations in solar energy; climate changes from redistribution of continents; and subsequent changes in ocean currents. Continents moving to the northern hemisphere provided a highway for glaciers to travel.

Summers grew cooler in the northern reaches. Winters lengthened. Eventually in the far north, the winter's snows didn't recede at all during the summer. Each succeeding winter came earlier, lasted longer, built upon the previous year's unmelted snows, and extended the expanse of snow southward. After a few hundred years, the snow became so deep and the pressure so great that the whole mass began to move—southward. Glaciers were born.

Over the next two million years, they would flow forward for seventy thousand to a hundred thousand years and then retreat for ten thousand to fifteen thousand years. As many as twenty times, they did this. At least four times, maybe more, they reached all the way down into what is now New York State. Why the uncertainty? Because like a finger scooping frosting from a cake, they swept away the evidence left behind by previous glaciers.

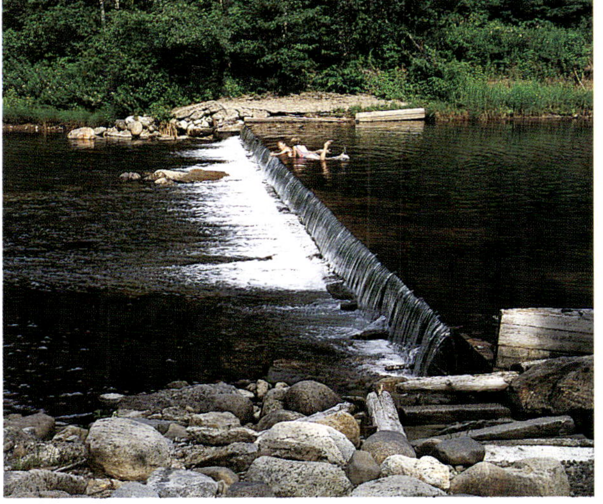

But the glaciers also left their mark on the land, especially in the Catskills where weak shale and sandstone were no match for a glacier. The ice changed the terrain in vast and sometimes mysterious ways. The temptation is to say they sculpted the land. But their "sculpting" was only the roughing-out of an artist shaping the preliminaries of his piece. A glacier employs little subtlety or refinement. Its work is coarse and crude and clumsy, like a two-year-old tearing apart a cake.

The last ice sheet, the Wisconsin glacier, buried most of New York State in ice. It's possible that, when it was at its zenith, no land in the region poked through the glacier. Perhaps, just perhaps, the snouts of the nearly mile-high Mt. Marcy and a few of the other Adirondack High Peaks jutted above the ice. If they did, the landscape, seen from above, would have been bleak and barren, looking like a few chocolate chips atop a cream pie.

The glacier was an undeniable force. A bulldozer of unimagined dimensions and power. Plowing into existing valleys, it deepened them by hundreds of feet. It ripped house-size boulders from mountains and carried them upon its back like a chihuahua atop an elephant. It created long sinuous ridges, banked up huge earthen dams, shaved steep hills into gentle pillows.

The enormous weight of a mile-thick glacier pushed the land downward, the same way a mattress is depressed by a large man sleeping on it. The amount of ice and snow forming the glacier was so enormous that the water taken up to create it lowered the oceans nearly three hundred feet.

Now imagine what might happen when so much ice begins to melt—as it did 20,000 years ago. El Niño seems like a toy by comparison. The meltwater formed huge lakes. You can often find evidence of their sandy beaches high on mountains. But the lakes were temporary, dammed by glacial ice that was melting—glacial ice that would eventually collapse, spilling forth floods. These would rage over the land. One such flood carved much of Ausable Chasm in the northeastern Adirondacks.

The glaciers brought terrific change to the land—and quickly, geologically speaking. The last glacier left New York State 6,000 years ago. Since then, the natural forces which have been acting on the landscape are the same ones we see every day: Snow, ice, rain, wind, gravity, and the internal tectonic forces that power continental movement.

Now, the talk is of global warming. However, history may not recognize our concerns. We are at intermission in the ice age. Our fifteen minutes are almost up. The lights will soon flash to call us back to our seats. Soon (1,500 years in human terms), the next act will begin.

Will it be a continuation of glaciers ravaging the land? Or will global warming wreak climatic havoc across the globe? Whatever the script, the land will take note so that future generations can critique the ending.

DEREK DOEFFINGER

WATERFALLS OF THE ADIRONDACKS

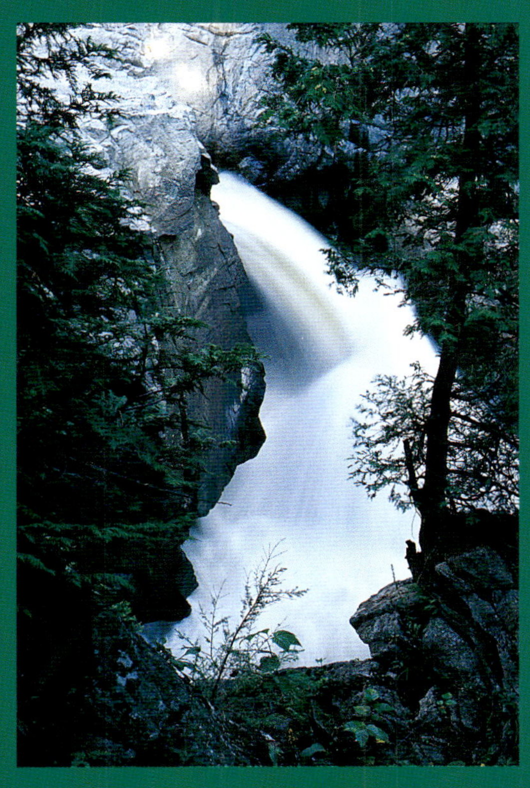

AUGER FALLS

LIKE MOST ROCK in the Adirondacks, the rock here was once some fifteen miles underground. How does rock that deep come to the surface? Two ways. Either the rock above is stripped away or the rock below is pushed upward until it breaks the surface.

For Adirondack rock, it's a combination of both. Over the past few million years, the Adirondacks have been rising about three millimeters a year. That's given them height, but they're not about to play basketball with the Himalayas, which still creep upward two inches a year.

The increase in height also increased the rate of erosion. The steeper mountains succumbed rapidly to downpours and flooding streams, as well as occasional (every hundred thousand years) glacial bulldozing. Given millions of years to do their work, these forces stripped away the soils and miles-thick but weak shales to expose rock that was once far inside the Earth.

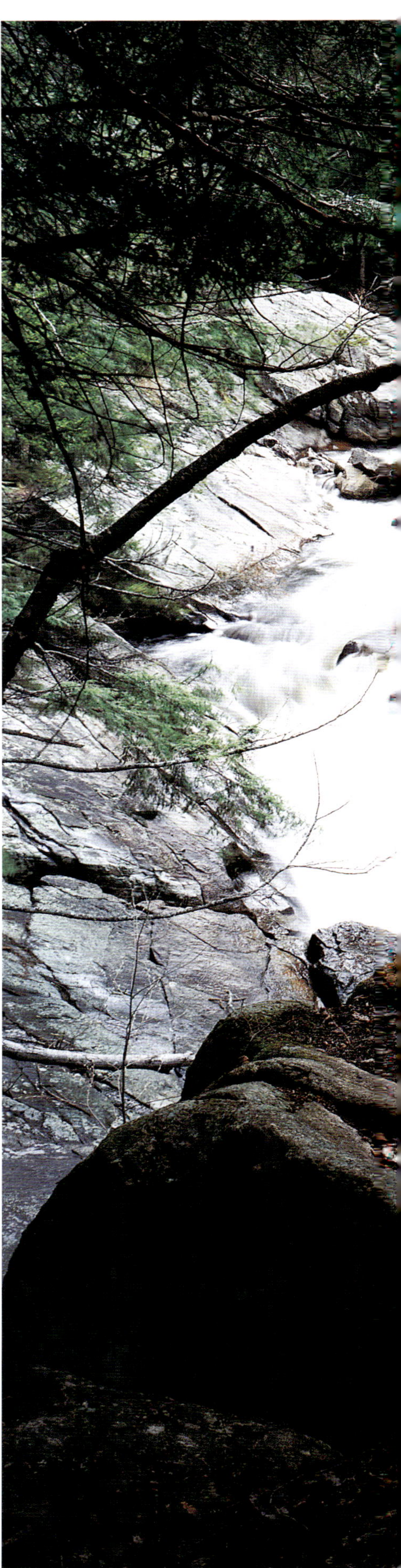

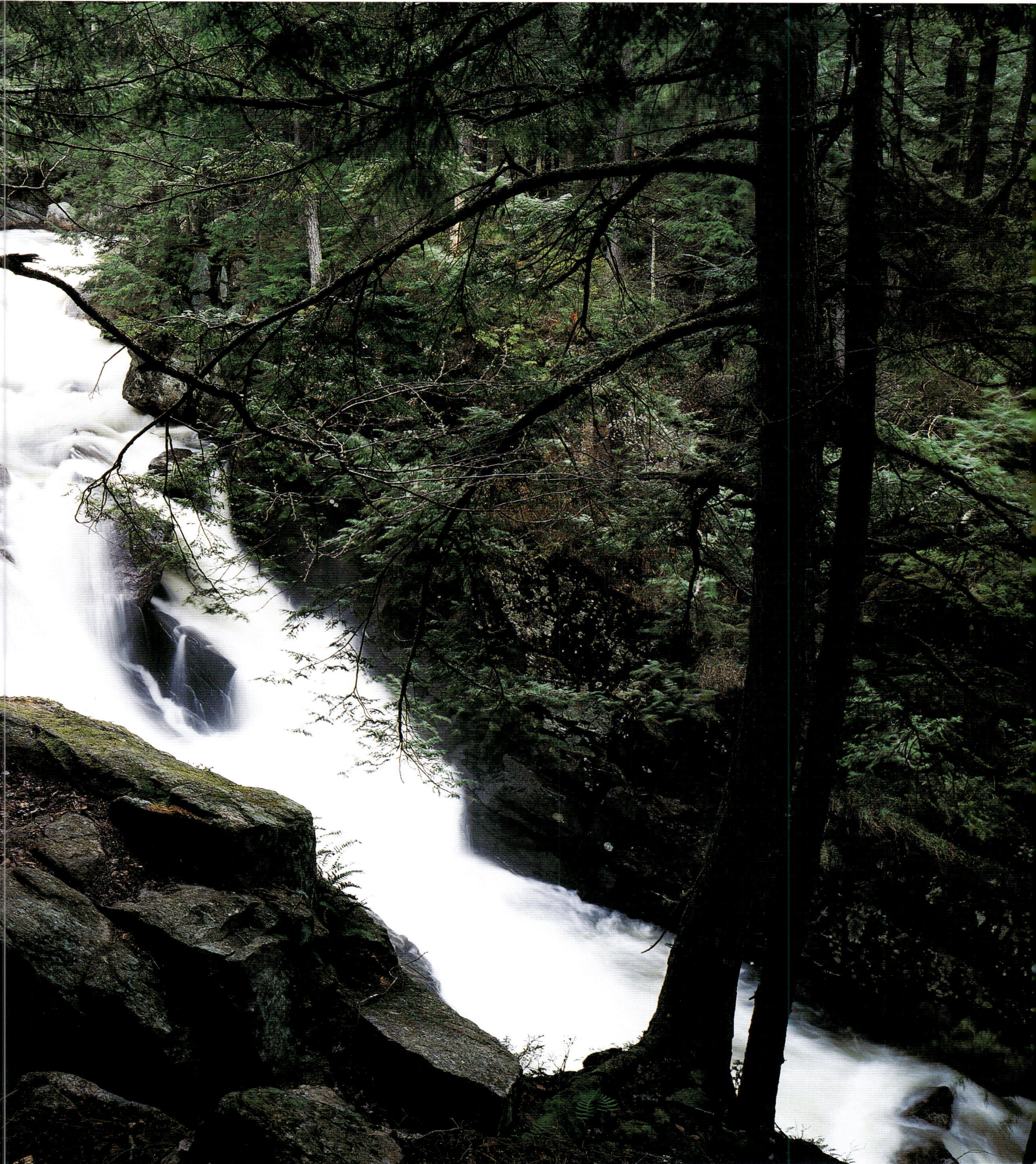

AUSABLE CHASM

RAINBOW FALLS

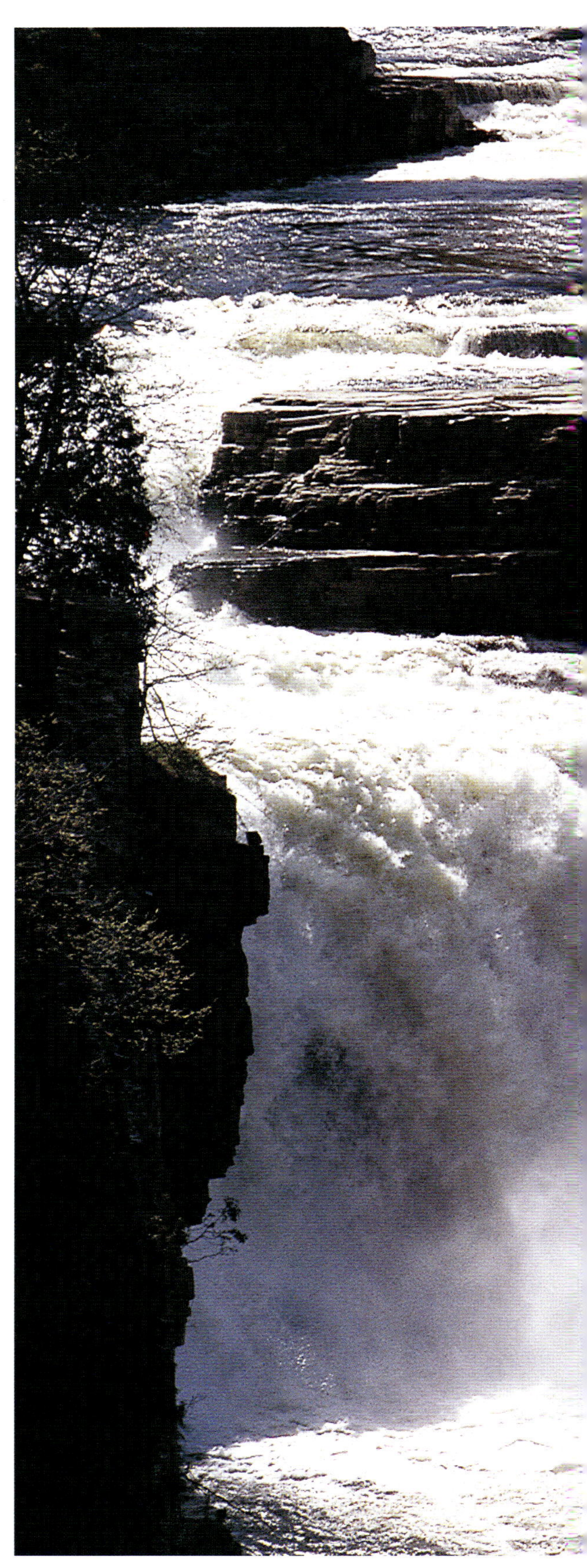

OWNING LAND is the act of a bureaucrat. A thing done with paper and pen in an office. The durability of such transactions does not exceed the materials recording them. The laws of man are not the laws of the land.

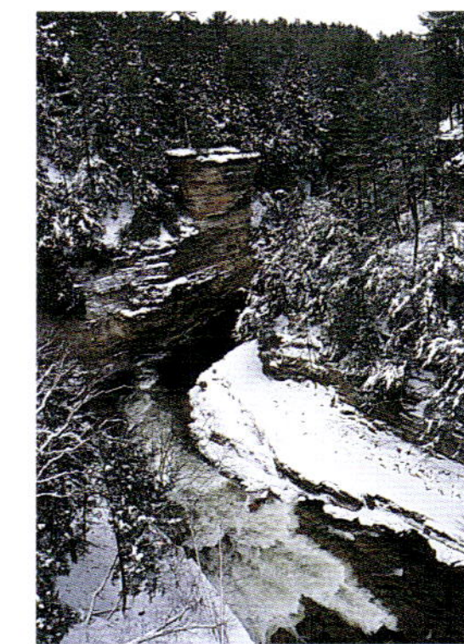

Ausable Chasm is a popular tourist attraction. The center of the attraction is a narrow, mile-long chasm carved from sandstone and crowned with waterfalls at its head. To enter the gorge, you must pass through a tourist shop crammed with trinket souvenirs. You plunk down your money and choose to walk, boat, or tube through the gorge.

Until recently, you could also take the stairs adjacent to the shop down to the gorge for a good look at the waterfalls. But the stairs are gone, crumpled and swept away by a recent flood. To us, the stone building clinging to the gorge rim radiates a sense of permanence. To nature, it's a sugar cube in a soaking rain.

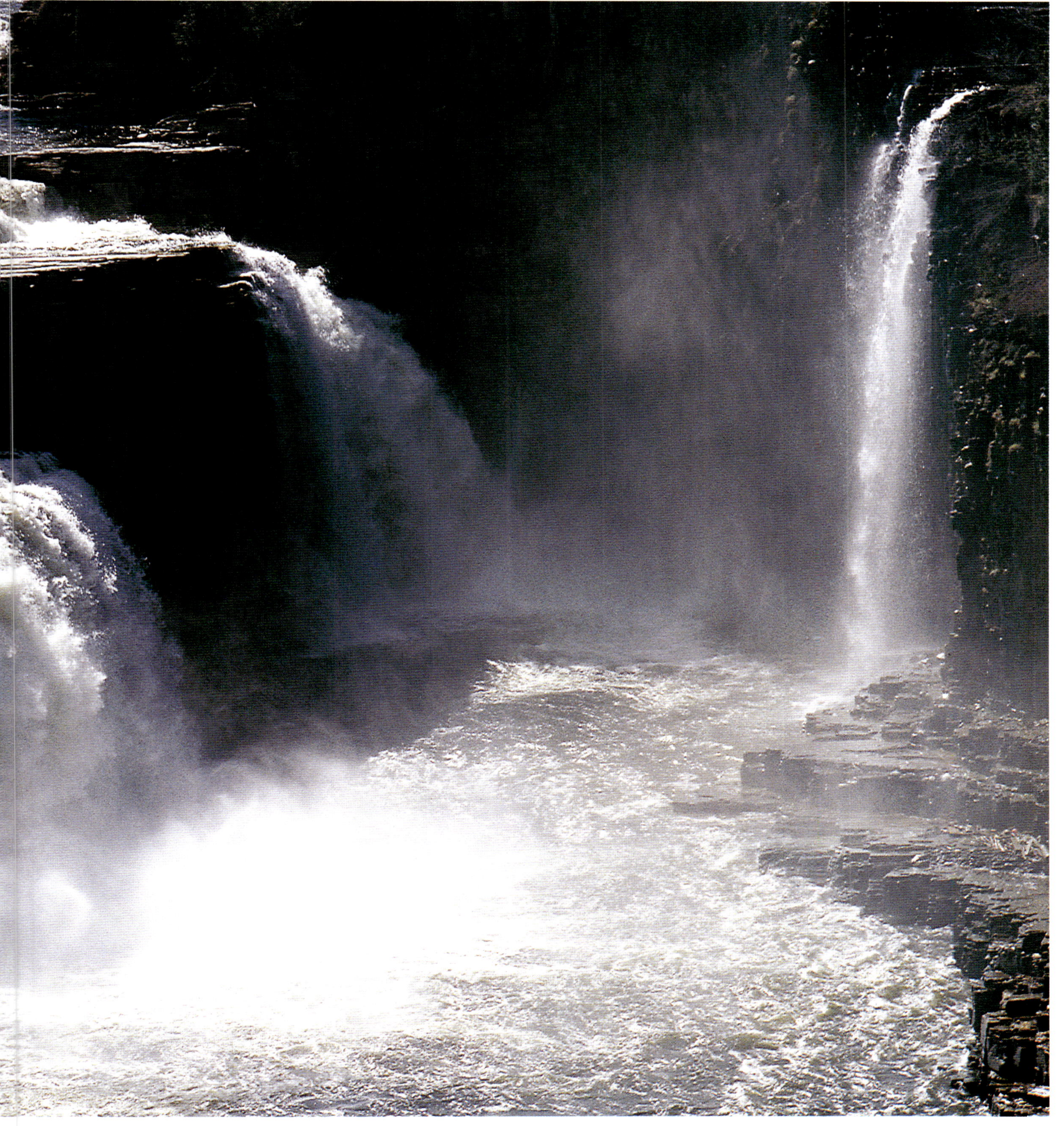

AUSTIN FALLS

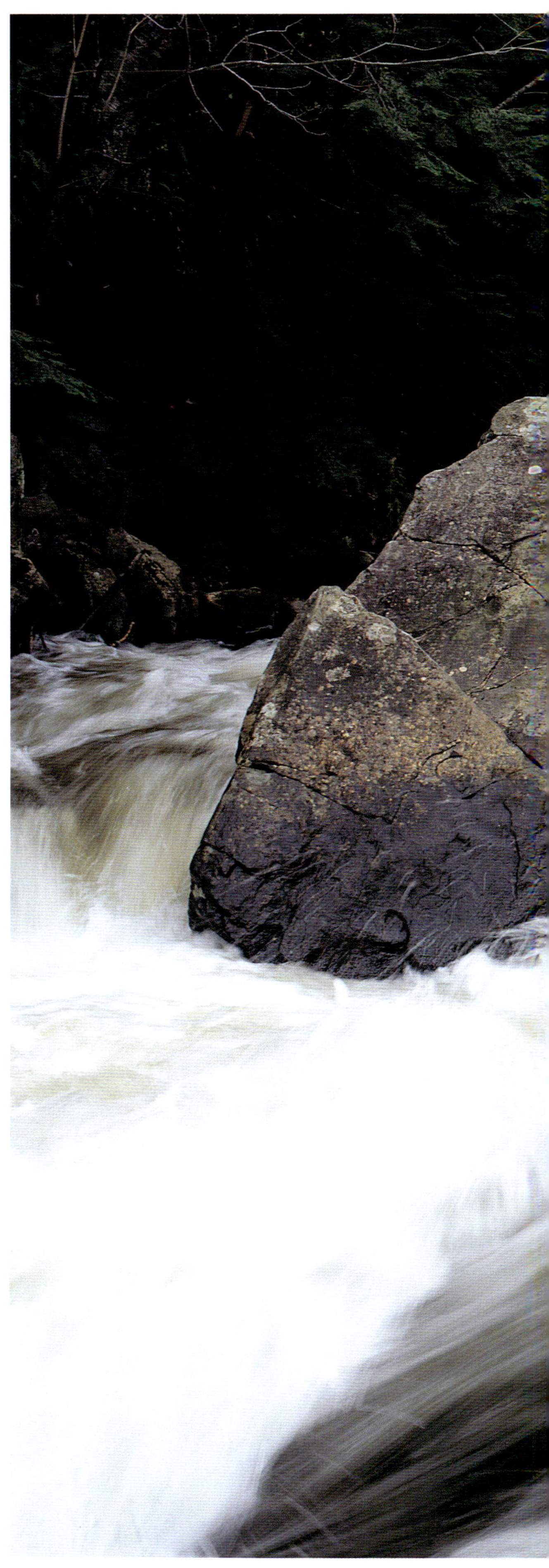

FROM A half-mile upstream, it gets a good running start and then charges downhill, taking full advantage of gravity's pull and the momentum gained from rounding a sharp curve onto a straightaway. Add to that the push of spring rains and you have a stream to reckon with.

Boulders the size of Cinderella's pumpkin-coach are scattered along both sides of the stream, swishing the water this way and that. The diverted currents crash into each other, rising briefly like sand dunes in the middle of the water before combining forces and galloping downstream.

In spring, this portion of the bedrock stream is bare. No gravel, no pebbles, not even a cobble can resist being pushed aside. Nothing less than a boulder can stand up to this force.

Down the hill it charges, single-mindedly moving ahead as fast as it can. At Austin Falls, it encounters a rise in the bedrock and shoots several feet into the air to form a standing wave—only no one would dare to stand in this wave on this day.

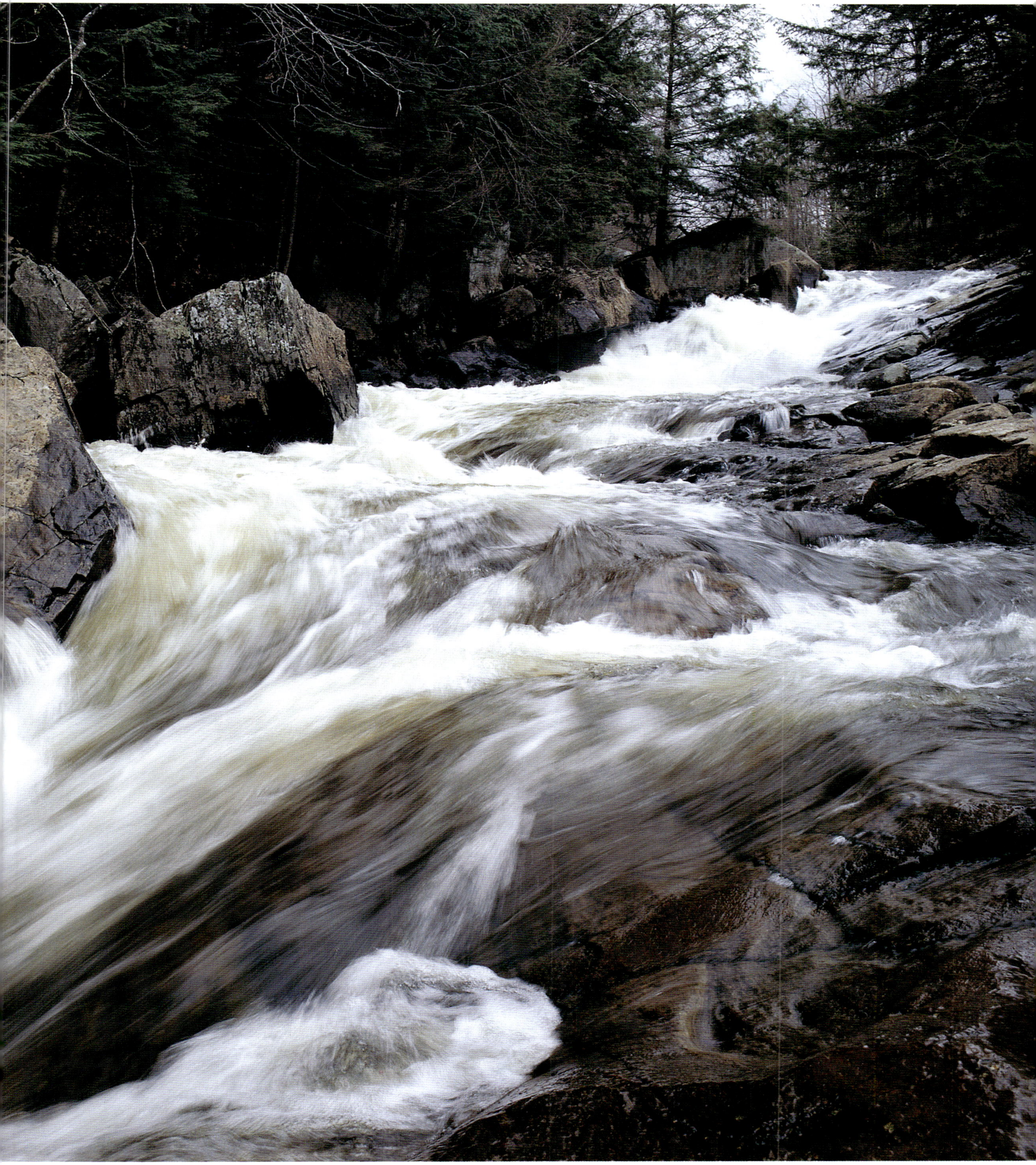

BEAVER MEADOW FALLS

WHAT IS A WATERFALL? At first, the answer seems obvious. It's water that falls from a cliff or flows down a steep slope. Fair enough. But how far must the water fall to qualify? Let's rephrase the question. What is the shortest distance water can fall and still be considered a waterfall?

There's no hard and fast answer. Some perfectly charming waterfalls drop only a few feet although most people would deny such short-droppers waterfall status.

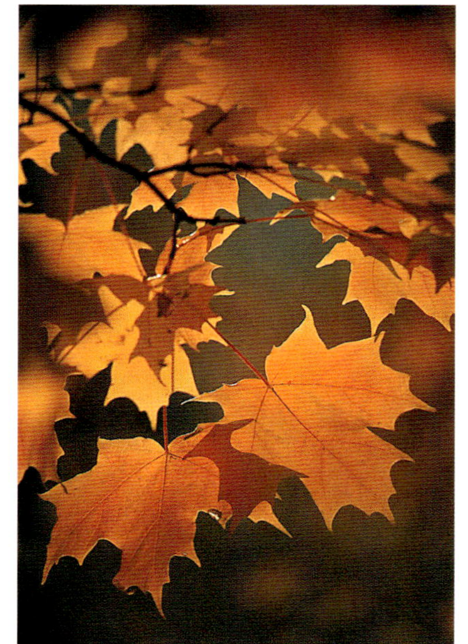

How steeply must the water fall? At some point, falling water makes the transition from cascading waterfall to steep rapids. When does that happen? Perhaps when you can comfortably and safely walk the bank alongside. But does it matter? Not really. Many rapids are more appealing than waterfalls.

How much water must fall to make a waterfall? Many waterfalls dry up by mid-summer. Others dwindle to a dribble. Certainly a dribble isn't a waterfall. Nor is a trickle. In spirit, a waterfall gushes; the stream gathers at the brink, then rushes over the edge. But if it doesn't offer enough water to fill your tub in a few minutes, for the moment it's not a waterfall.

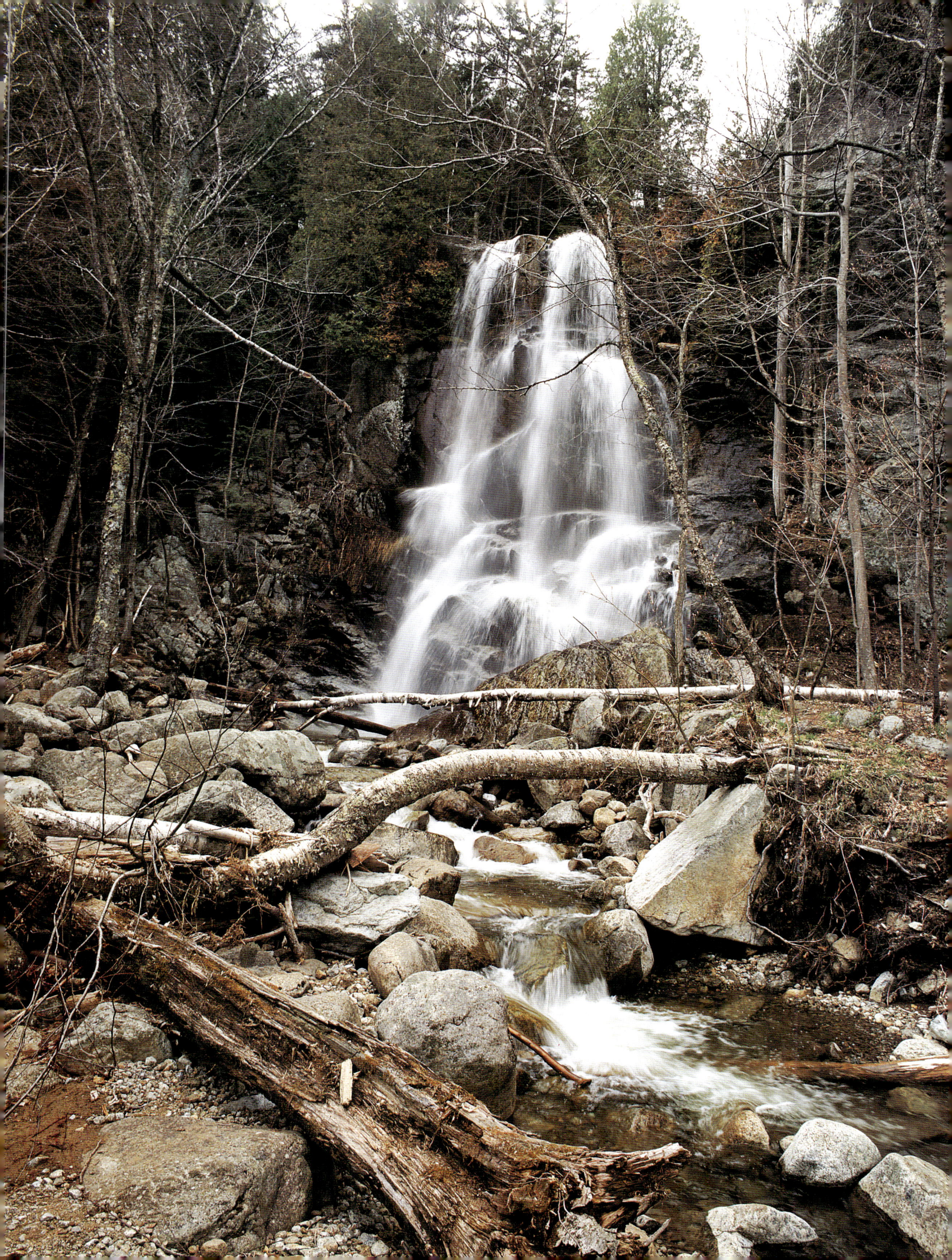

BOG RIVER FALLS

PERHAPS WATERFALLS appeal to us because they engage our senses so powerfully. They compel sight with what it recognizes most easily—motion. For purposes of survival, our vision detects motion first and foremost. Even the slightest movement can be caught by the corner of the eye. Faced with a veritable cornucopia of motion in a waterfall, the eye becomes a glutton, feasting on every little twist and turn.

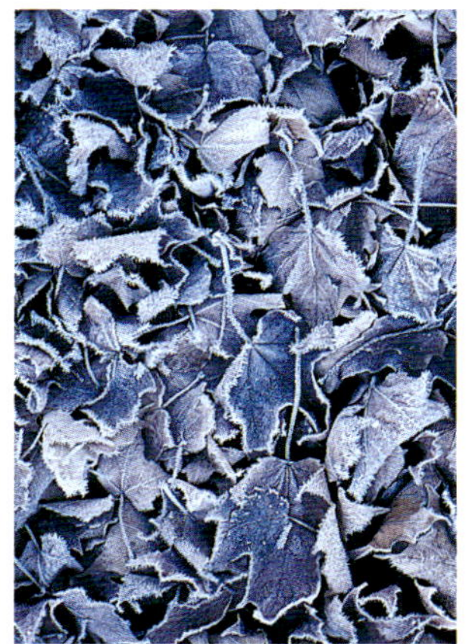

Offered less in variety but more in volume, the ear cannot escape a waterfall. Its thunderous drone dominates and drowns out all competing sounds. Indeed, the all-encompassing, incessant sound overwhelms the ear and leads to brief paranoia as it blocks noises from more than a few feet away.

At first scent, the nose may seem to escape untouched by a waterfall. But the sense of smell too is stirred. Splashing water freshens the surrounding air with mist and a gentle breeze. Together, they enhance the pungent scent of cedars, the sneeze-inducing must of autumn leaves, and the fragrance of a freshwater brook.

Through its mist, a waterfall brushes the skin of our faces, like the touch of a ghost, delicate but forever memorable.

Is taste engaged? Or does that require that we kneel and lap at the waters? Can you simply stand agape below a cascade and let the mists waft into your mouth to find a distinctive flavor of waterfall?

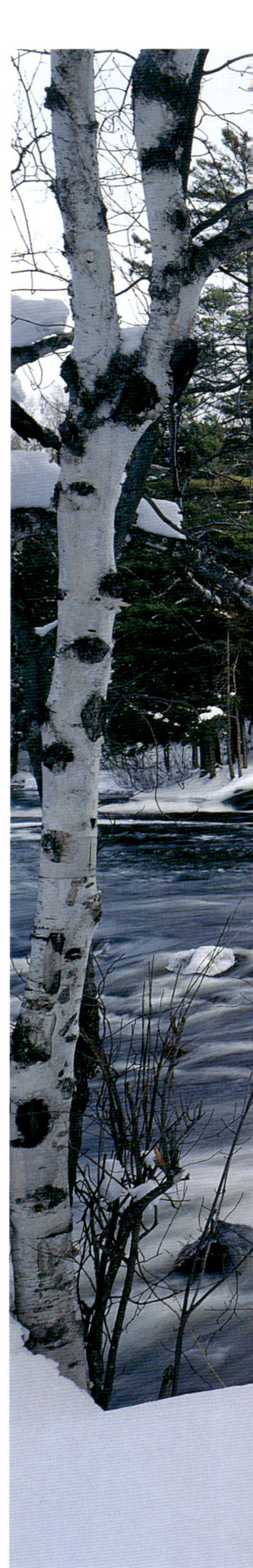

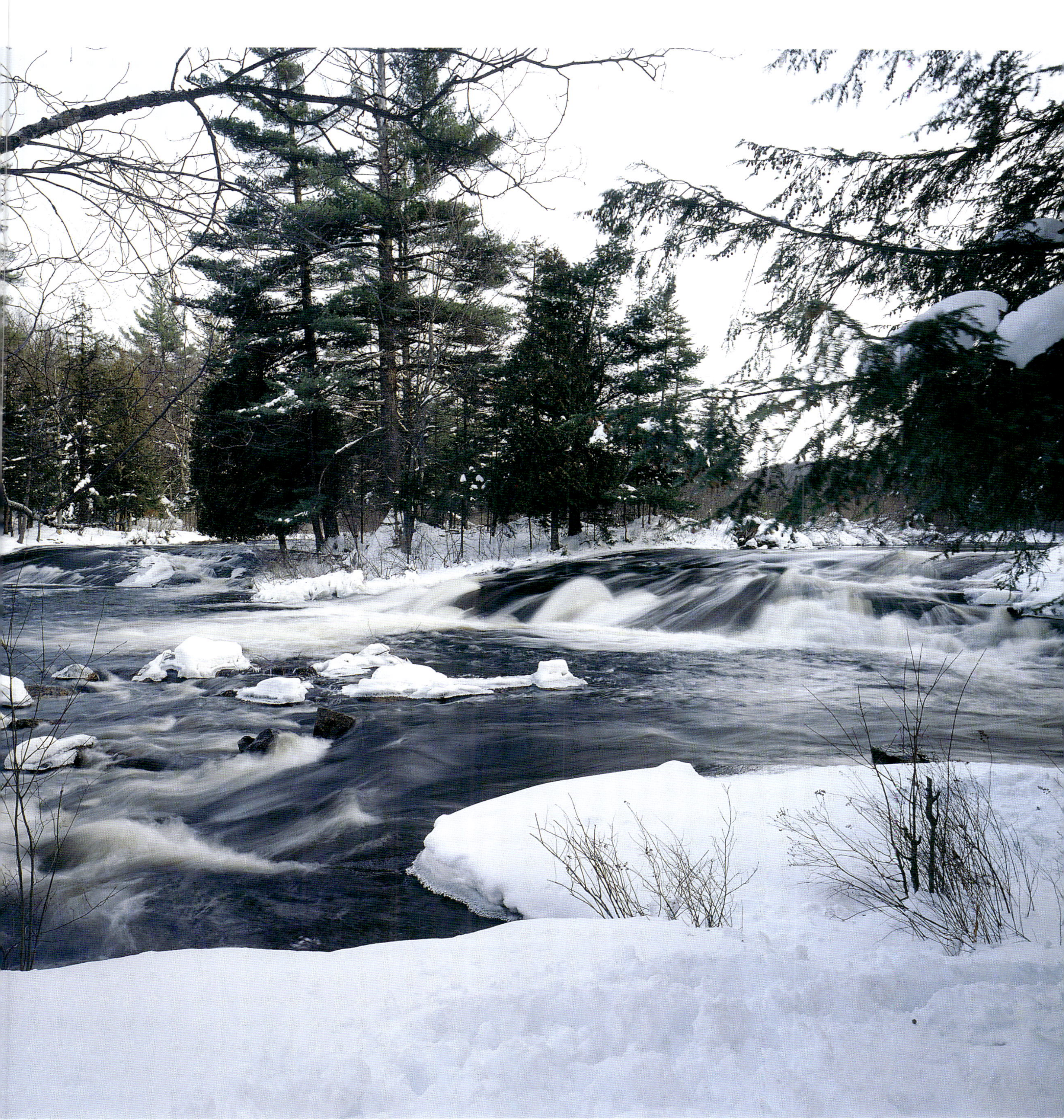

BUTTERMILK FALLS

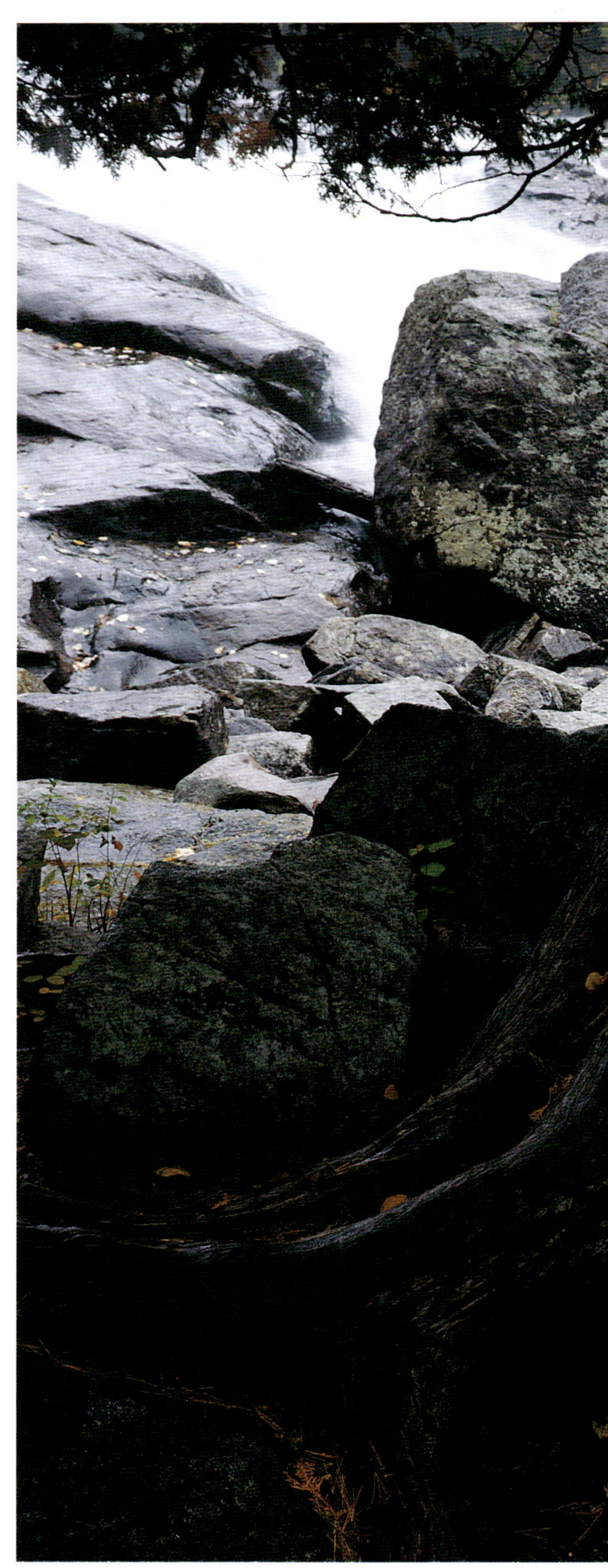

THE ROCK holding up this waterfall is likely more than a billion years old. Older yet is the Earth. Its age is so vast, so incomprehensible that people devise a variety of analogies to condense it to comprehensibility. To a child, a year seems forever. To young adults, a decade stands far off.

How then is it possible to understand Earth time? The Earth is 4.5 billion years old. That's 45 million times older than a centenarian. That's over a trillion rotations of the Earth on its axis.

Into this scheme, somewhat recently, steps a being who can comprehend short spans of time—planting seed in spring to survive the winter, advertising toys in October to bring wealth by December, starting a college fund at age three for matriculation by age eighteen.

But understanding months, years, even decades provides little preparation for millions of years. Thus, the analogies. If the 4.5 billion years of Earth were compressed into a year, man would appear on the scene in the last minute of New Year's Eve. If it were compressed into a day, humans would show their faces in the last second of the day. Or if time were a roll of toilet paper and each sheet represented ten million years, guess who comes at the end of the roll?

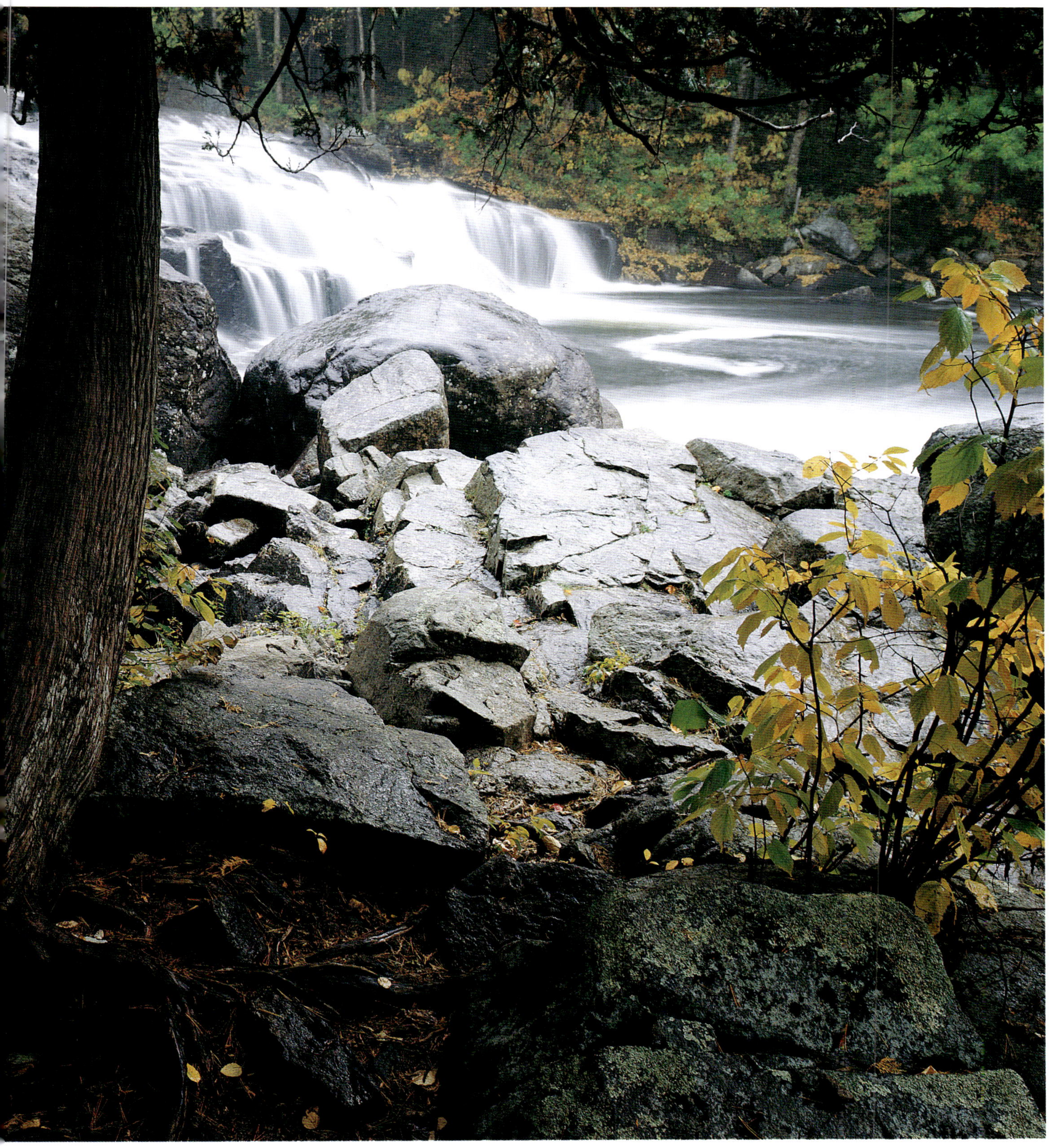

CASCADE FALLS

CASCADE FALLS has a beginning, but does it have an end? That it had rained all morning and much of the previous week led us to believe that the intermittent flow of Cascade Falls might be turned on.

But a hundred yards from the parking lot, the scant water in the stream was just barely enough to sustain our hopes that the rains had started the falls. Another few hundred yards up the stream, and the flow, instead of growing stronger, weakened. In fifty more yards, it vanished. The creek bed was dry, despite rain all morning.

Nevertheless, some gut instinct pulled us along. Something we heard, or smelled, or glimpsed moved our feet up the path. Still the creek's channel was dry, even though the rain had started again.

A hundred yards more, and the creek bed was wet; upstream a band of white flashed through the trees. Down a hundred-foot cliff spilled Cascade Falls, freshened by the recent rain, only to disappear beneath its own stream bed in a few yards.

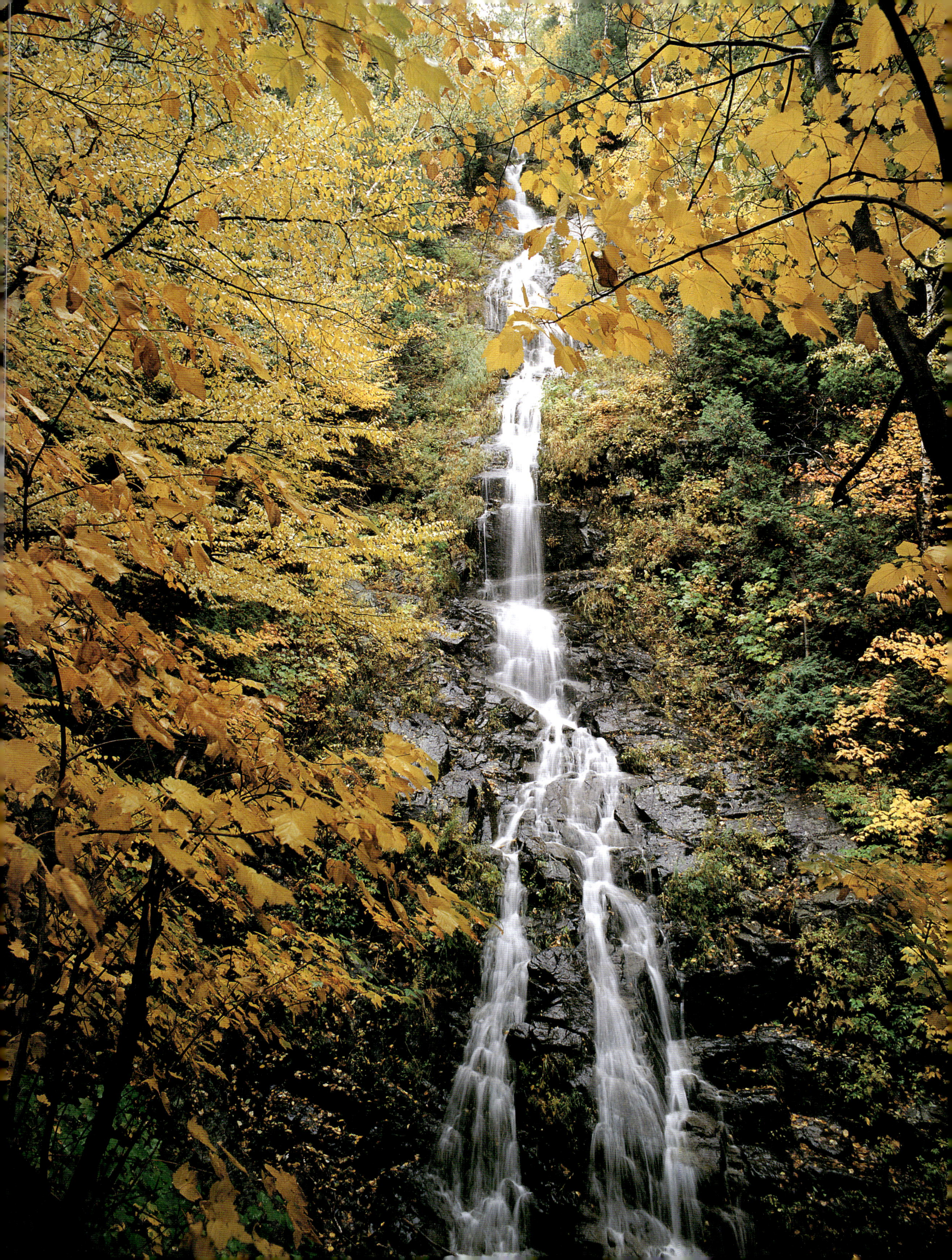

FLUME FALLS

ROUTE 73

WATERFALLS, whatever their size, have forceful personalities. They draw us in to partake of their company, bathe in their charm.

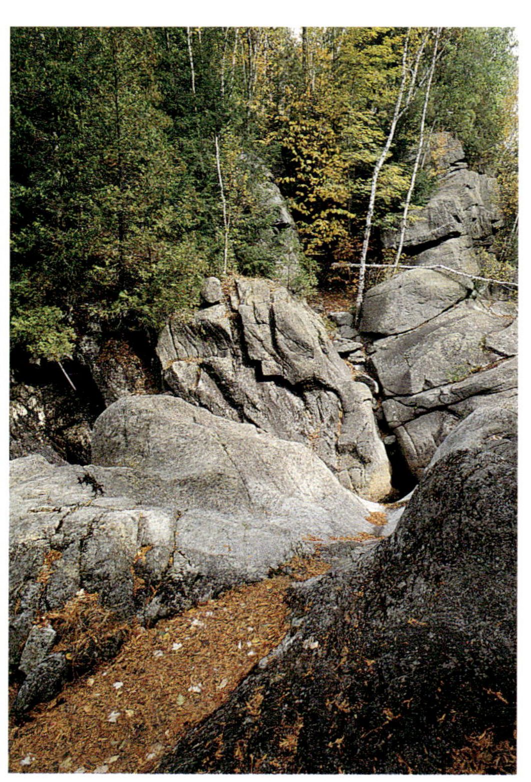

But as with many powerful personalities, getting too close can be a bit overwhelming. After all, every waterfall is full of itself—forever burbling and gushing, never offering a moment's silence or a chance to get a word in edgewise, always gesturing, always fidgeting, trickling here, plummeting there. Filled with self-importance, they're always drawing attention to themselves, always making grand entrances and exits.

Sometimes it's best to stand back and see a waterfall for what it is. A small part of a bigger landscape. A splash of water in the middle of a mountain, a garbled whisper in a world of wisdom. An accent of white on a suit of brown and green.

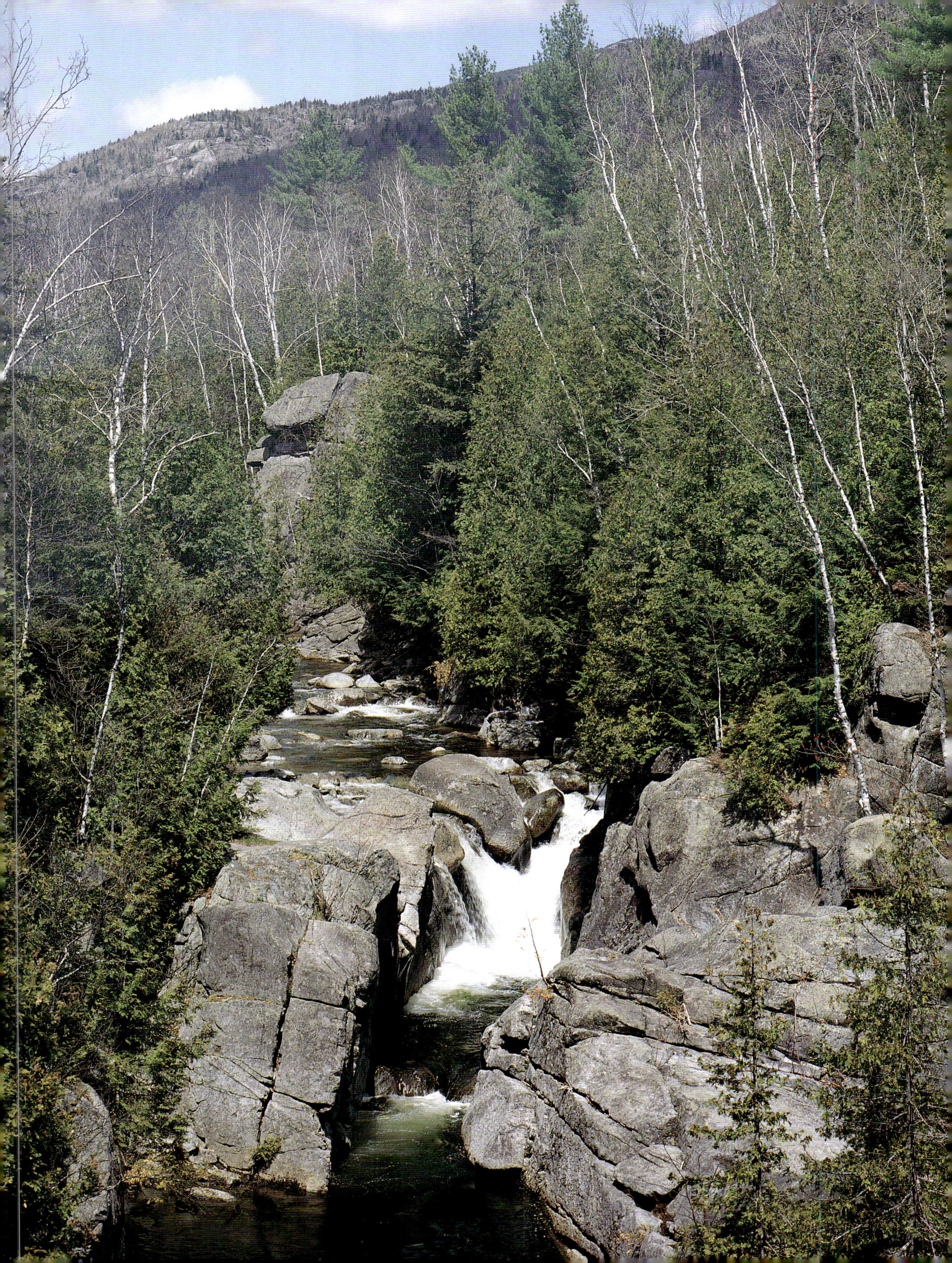

GOLDMINER FALLS

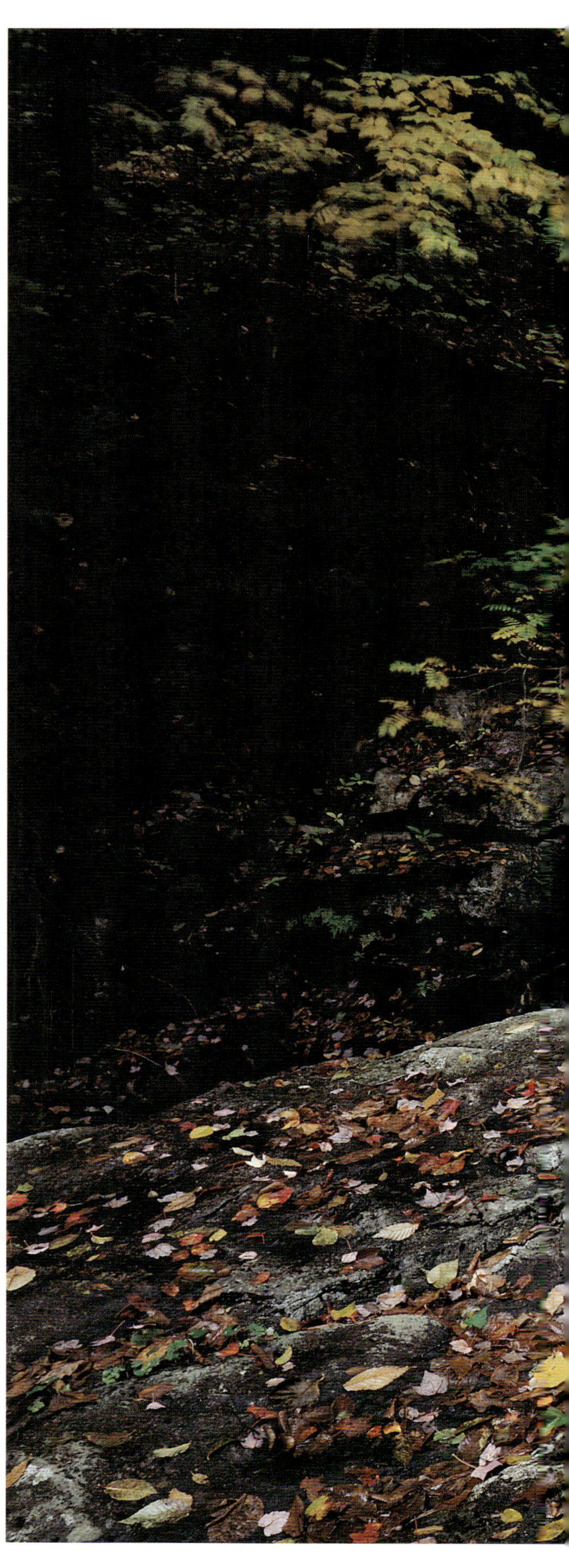

WHEN YOU SIT on a rock next to a waterfall and take a deep breath, you are experiencing a paradox. The air you breathe, the rock you sit on, and the water you watch are bound by a common ingredient, yet exhibit entirely different physical characteristics. Their common bond is oxygen.

Air, water, rock. Oxygen exists in each. Perhaps not so obvious is the relative amount of oxygen each possesses. Air obviously abounds with oxygen, the very gas diffusing from your capillaries into your brain.

With just a little thought, we realize that water also contains enough oxygen to sustain life. After all, fish and other water animals obtain oxygen from water. In fact, they die when the decay of organic pollutants removes the oxygen.

But rock? Careful observation would tell us that some rocks, the orangish ones, have oxygen. Orange in rock is usually "rust," iron compounds that have oxidized and turned orange or brownish like rusted metal. But beyond that, rocks and oxygen don't seem to mix well. One is hard and heavy, the other not only soft but virtually intangible.

By percentage of material (atoms), rock, water, and air consist of one-sixth oxygen, one-third oxygen, and nine-tenths oxygen. But not in that respective order. Unexpectedly, it's rock that consists of 94 percent oxygen.

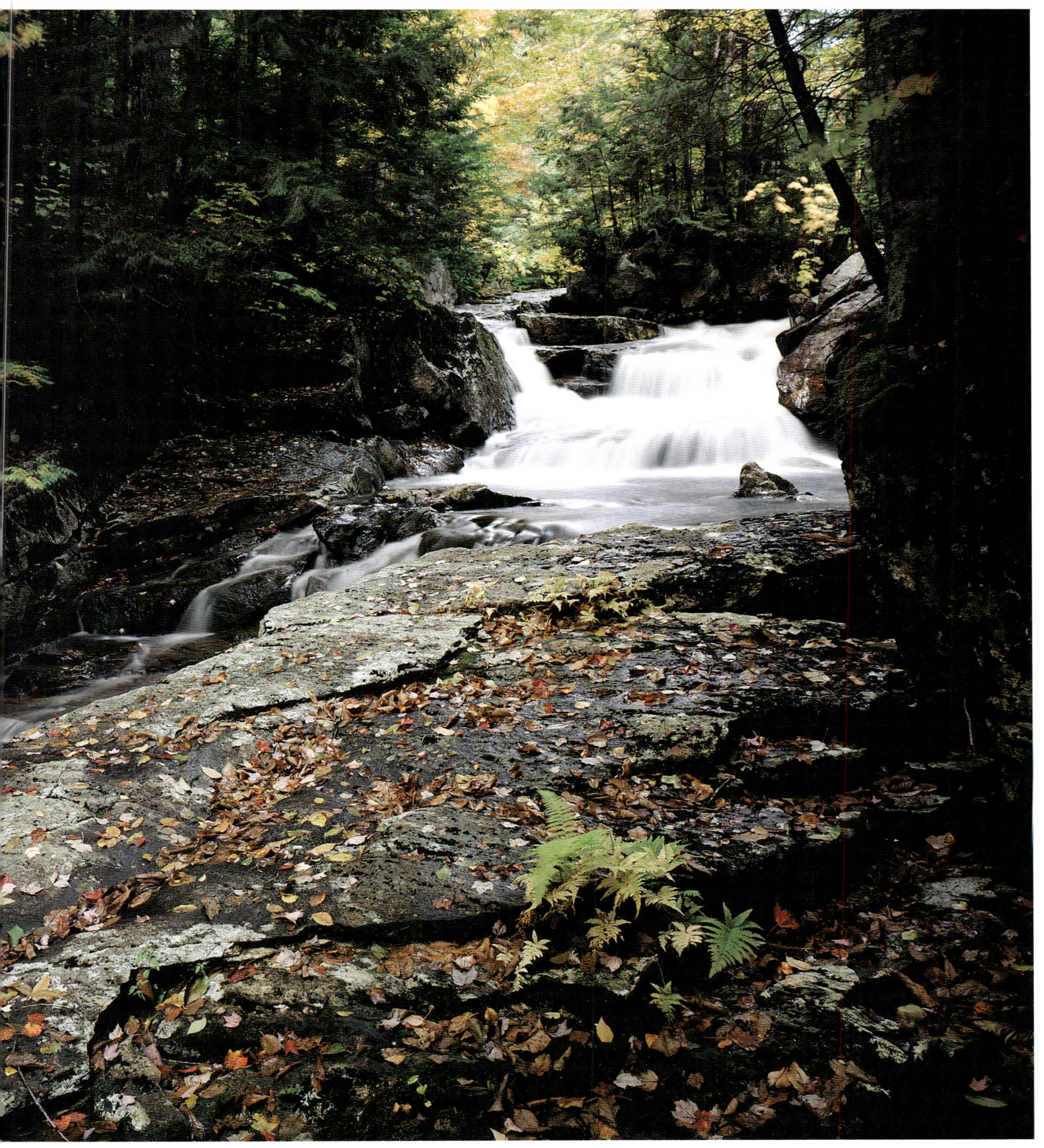

GRIFFIN FALLS

THE ROCKS of the Adirondacks offer much to admire. First, they're hard—like rocks. Stupid, you think. But not all rocks are rock-hard. In the Catskills much of the rock is shale, some so brittle it could be movie props for strong guys to crumble in their hands.

Second, Adirondack rocks are handsome. In streams they form cobbles, some as big as bowling balls and others the size of billiard balls. Spherical, ovoid, elliptical—cobbles are sensuous rocks that please the eye and the hand. Jade, maroon, mauve, beige, mushroom, they're multi-colored and studded with chips of quartz, garnet, and mica. You'll also find slabs of bedrock, polished and speckled with dark crystals, that eclipse any Formica countertop.

And these rocks are intellectually stimulating. For instance, why don't cobbles like to be alone? Why do they congregate along the banks or in peninsulas? And how do the cobbles become rounded? Why are there huge boulders in the middle of some streams? Why is the rock at Split Rock shattered and the rock at Griffin skewed like a collapsed wall?

If you take a moment, Adirondack rocks hold your attention.

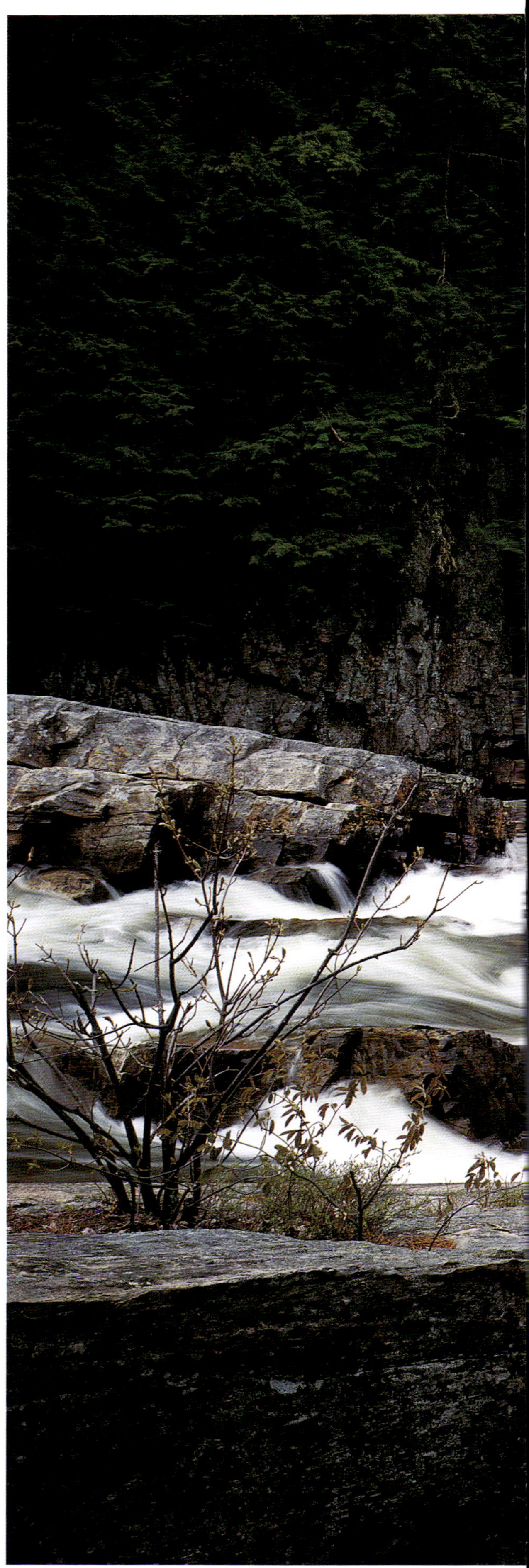

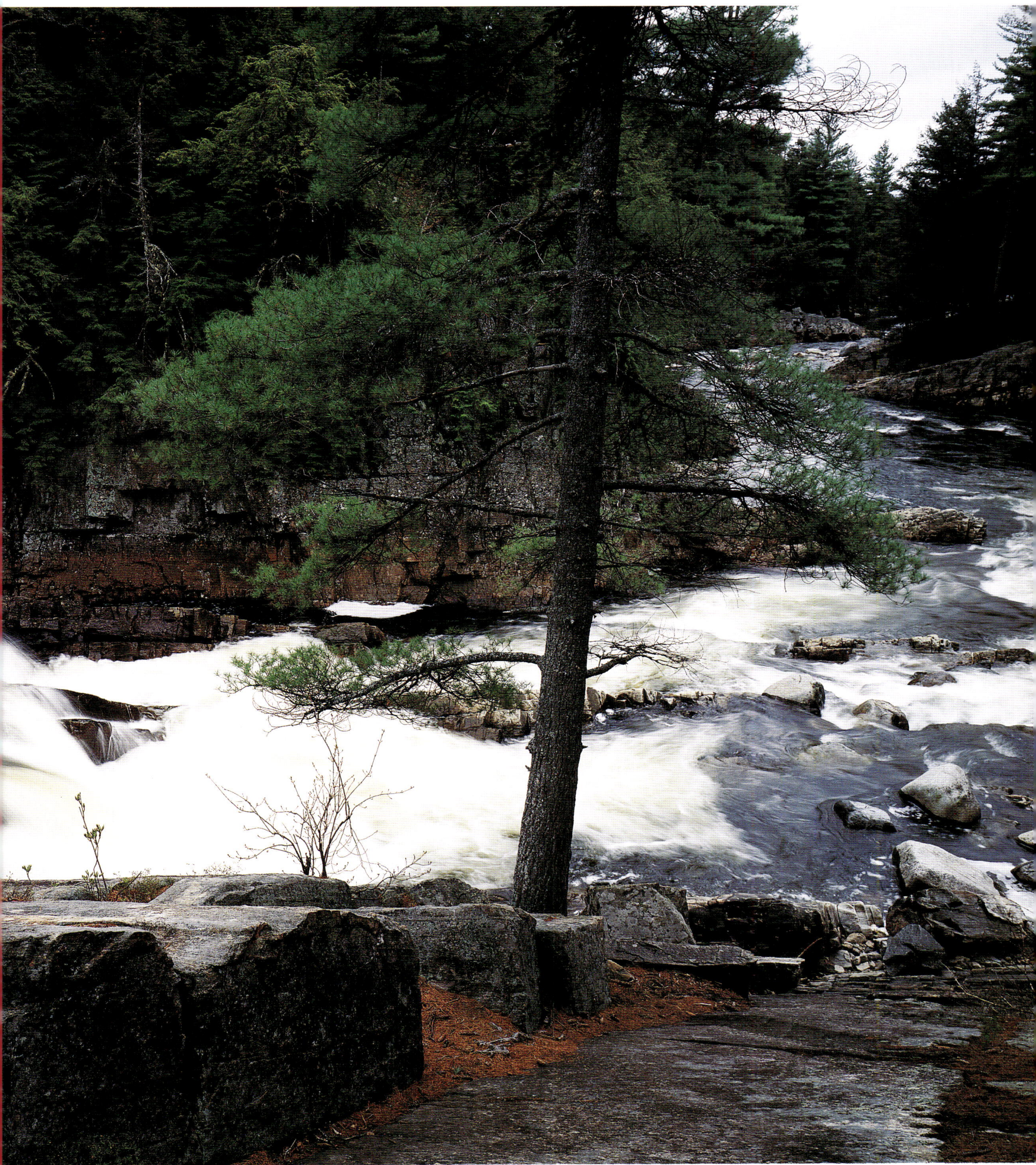

HIGH FALLS

IF YOU GET into the waterfall business, it won't take you long to realize that most of those giving waterfalls their names were not blessed with originality. Many simply named a waterfall after its landowner. Others named it after themselves.

Perhaps the most popular and most unoriginal name is "High" falls. Time and again, you come across "High" falls. Not only does that name border on being redundant; it's ambiguous. One person's "High" falls may be fifty feet, another's two hundred.

The next most popular name is "Buttermilk." Hordes of waterfalls sour under the burden of buttermilk. You'll not find a single "Skim" milk, "2 percent" milk, or even a "Creamy" falls. Though some falls rich with tannic acid flow a translucent brown, you'll not find a "Coffee" falls, "Cocoa" falls, or "Diet Cola" falls, not even a "Latte" falls. "Buttermilk" may simply represent a popular household product and a coddling mother during the era of waterfall naming.

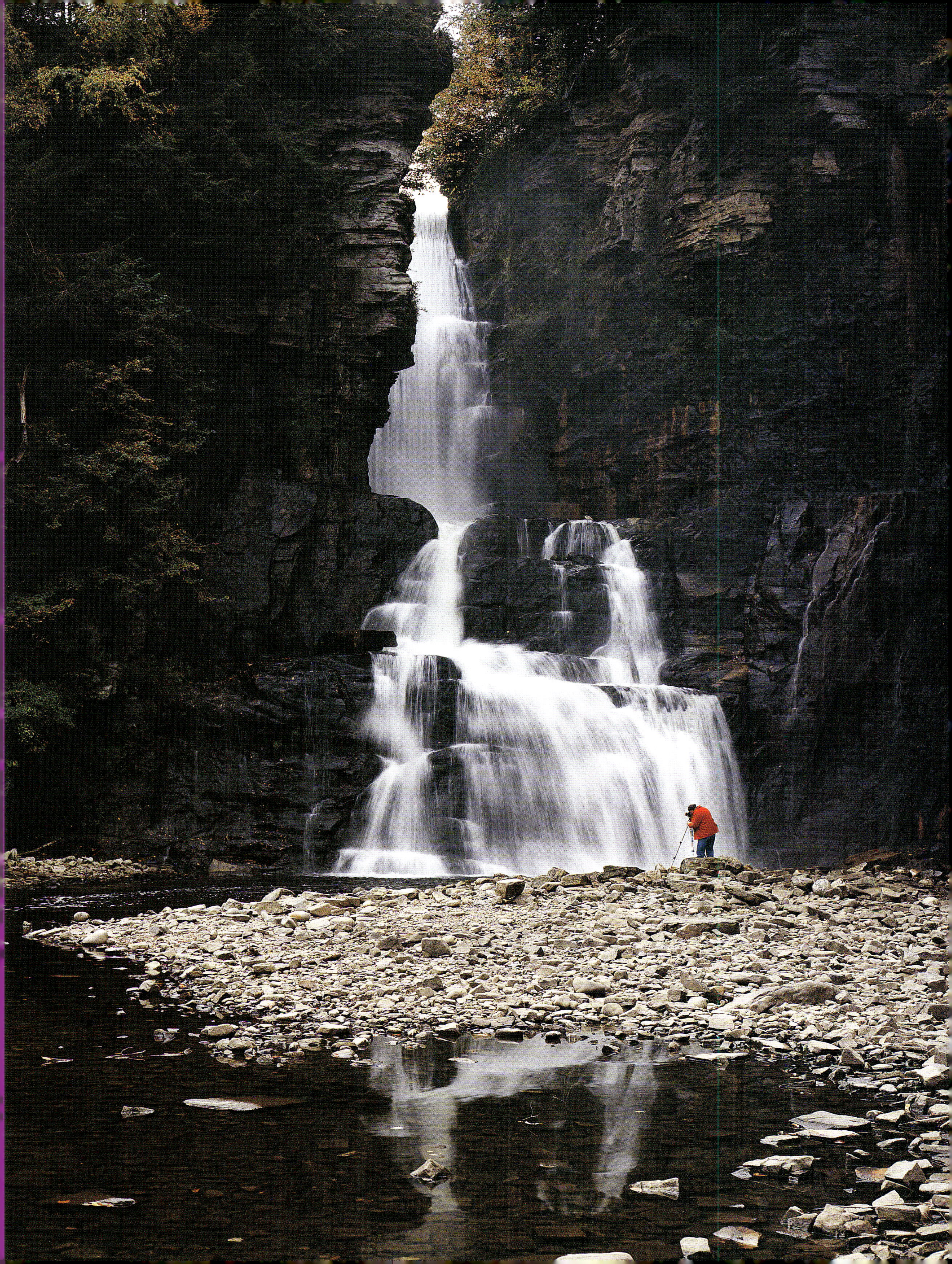

HIGH FALLS GORGE

KDOR NI ponosen na svojo domovino, si ne zdsluĪi njenega drĪavljanstva. That's Slovenian for "Someone who is not proud of his homeland does not deserve its citizenship." What does a Slovenian homily have to do with waterfalls? Well, it's on the Internet, specifically on the home page of Waterfalls of Slovenia—www.burger.si/Slapovi.htm#ljubljana—where you find that Slovenia has over three hundred waterfalls. From a proud Tasmanian comes the "Waterfalls of Tasmania" and from a Malaysian, the "Waterfalls in Peninsular Malaysia."

Indeed, high technology has come to the waterfalls. Search engines, e-commerce, electronic networks, streaming video and streaming audio now tango with streaming water.

Amazon.com has blazed the Internet path for High Falls Gorge. Should you visit High Falls Gorge? Check out its website—www.highfallsgorge.com—and see for yourself. Here's what I found: A commercial establishment along Route 86 in the High Peaks region of the Adirondacks, High Falls Gorge is "privately owned, maintained and operated by ROANKA Attractions Corp." At High Falls Gorge, you can "enjoy a self-guided tour to view the beautiful waterfalls, dark pools and one of New York's largest potholes . . . " "Winter Rates: $6.95 Adults, $5.95 Seniors (60+), $4.95 Juniors (12–17), $2.95 Children (4–11)." "To round out your visit, be sure to visit our large gift shop as well as our rock shop . . ."

A Yahoo search on waterfalls resulted in 248 sites of which 240 were commercial establishments, many selling artificial waterfalls, others promoting inns and hotels near real ones.

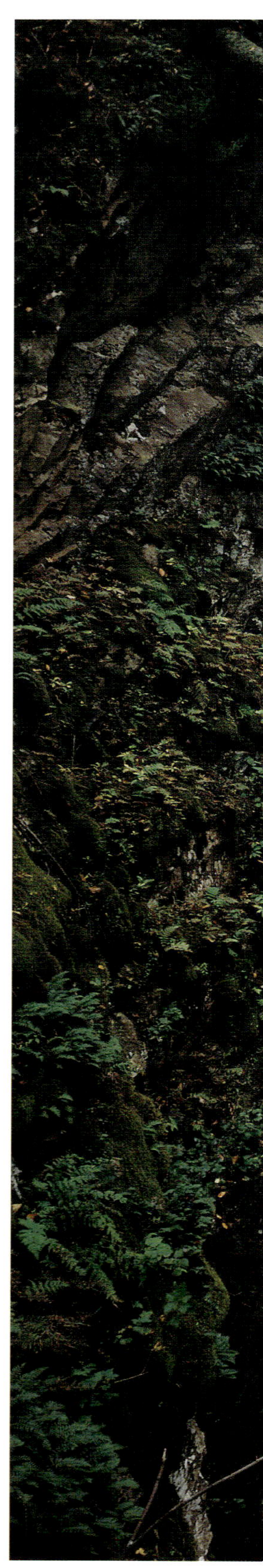

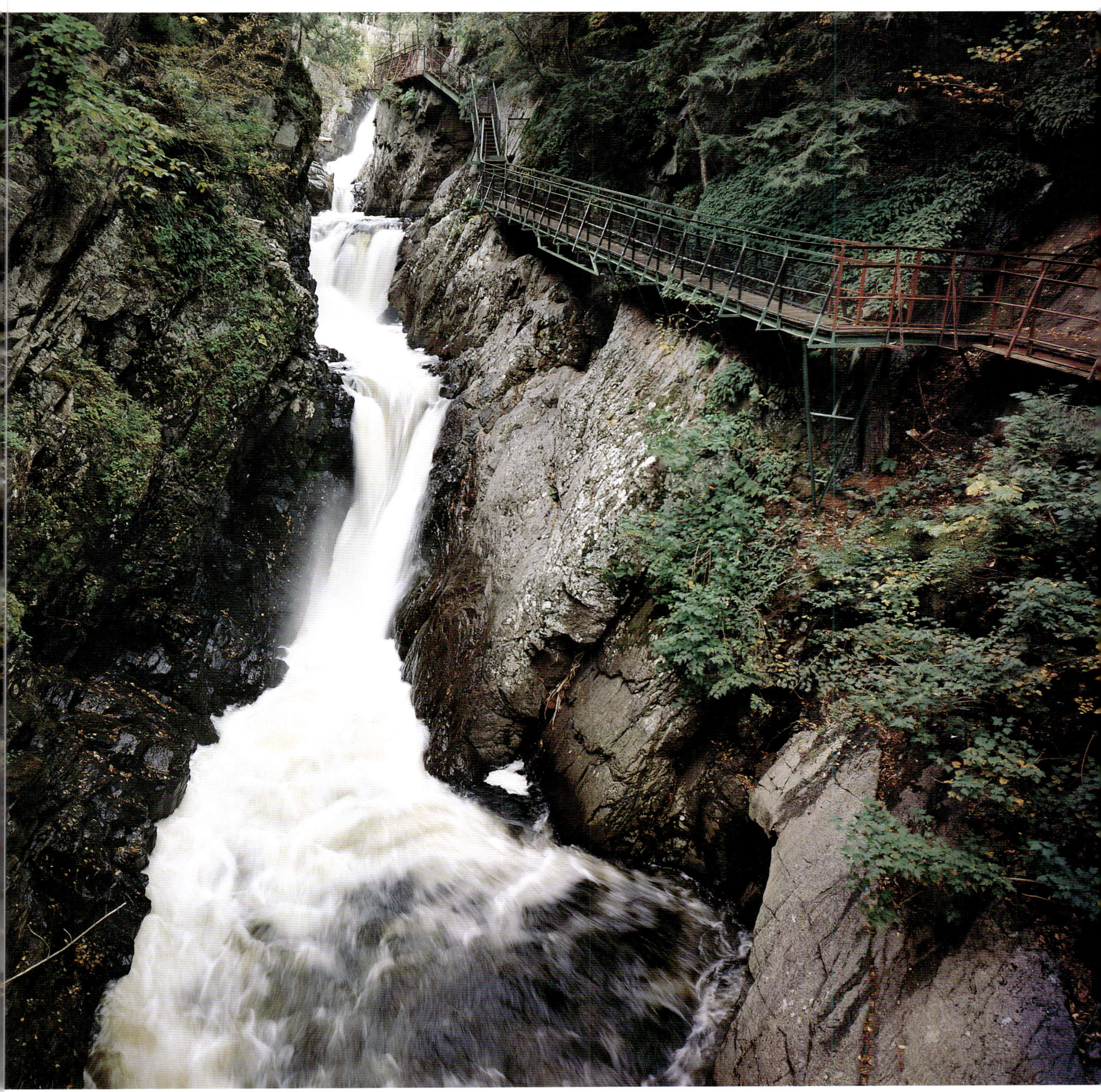

JIMMY CREEK FALLS

COMING UPON a waterfall after a hard hike has slicked your shirt to your back and knotted your thighs, you have no choice. You must stand in that waterfall. You must feel it coursing through your hair, caressing its way down your back, tickling the length of your body. You know the moment you step into that waterfall, the sensation will be like no other.

Your body takes on the role of the underlying rock, re-routing the water as it envelops you, folds you in, wraps you into the whole that is waterfall. It's true.

You can't sink into a rock or merge with a tree. You cannot float on a cloud. But you can become part of a waterfall. You can watch the water wash over your eyes, cascade off your chin onto your chest, chase down your legs and blend into the stream. You can become the waterfall.

But you may pause before becoming the waterfall if its beginning is a hundred feet above your head. A three-foot wide stream of water accelerating over every inch of those one hundred feet may recall protestors being flattened with fire hoses.

Just how powerful is that stream of water? Will it massage your back or break it? Thoughts to ponder before becoming the waterfall.

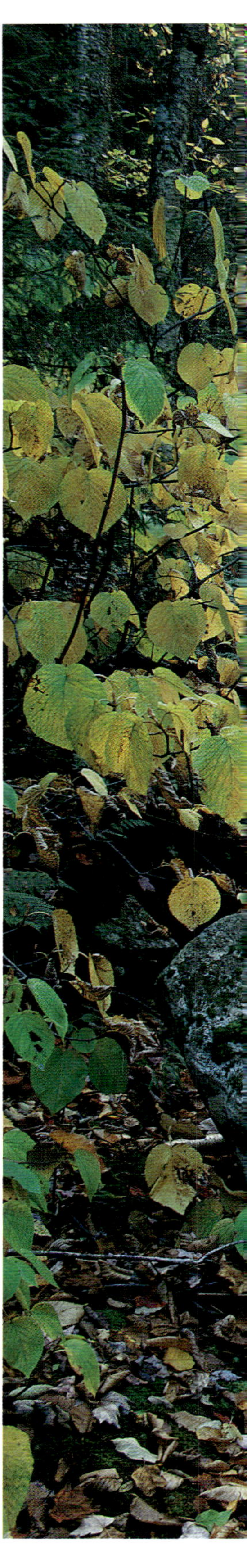

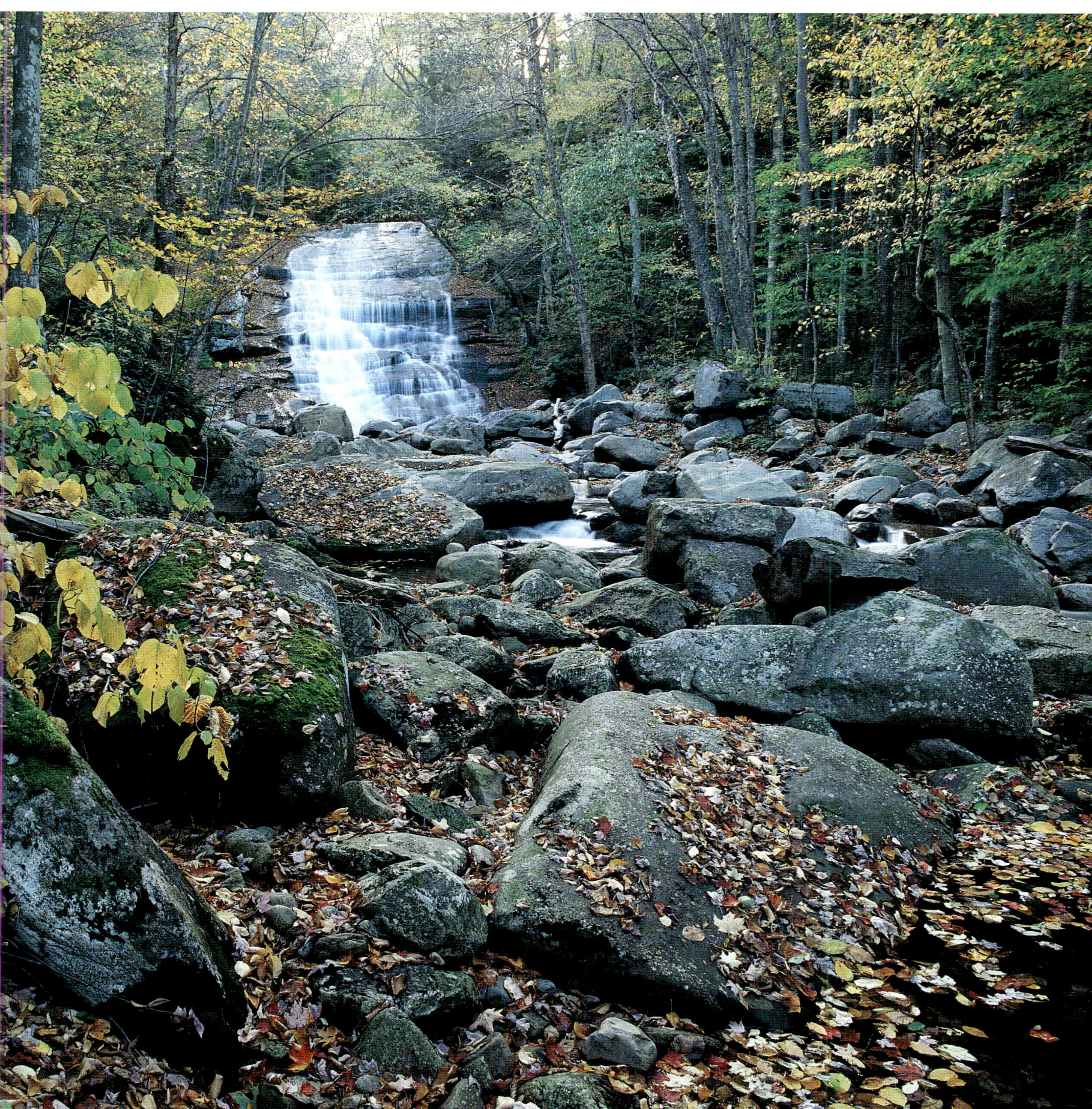

MONUMENT FALLS

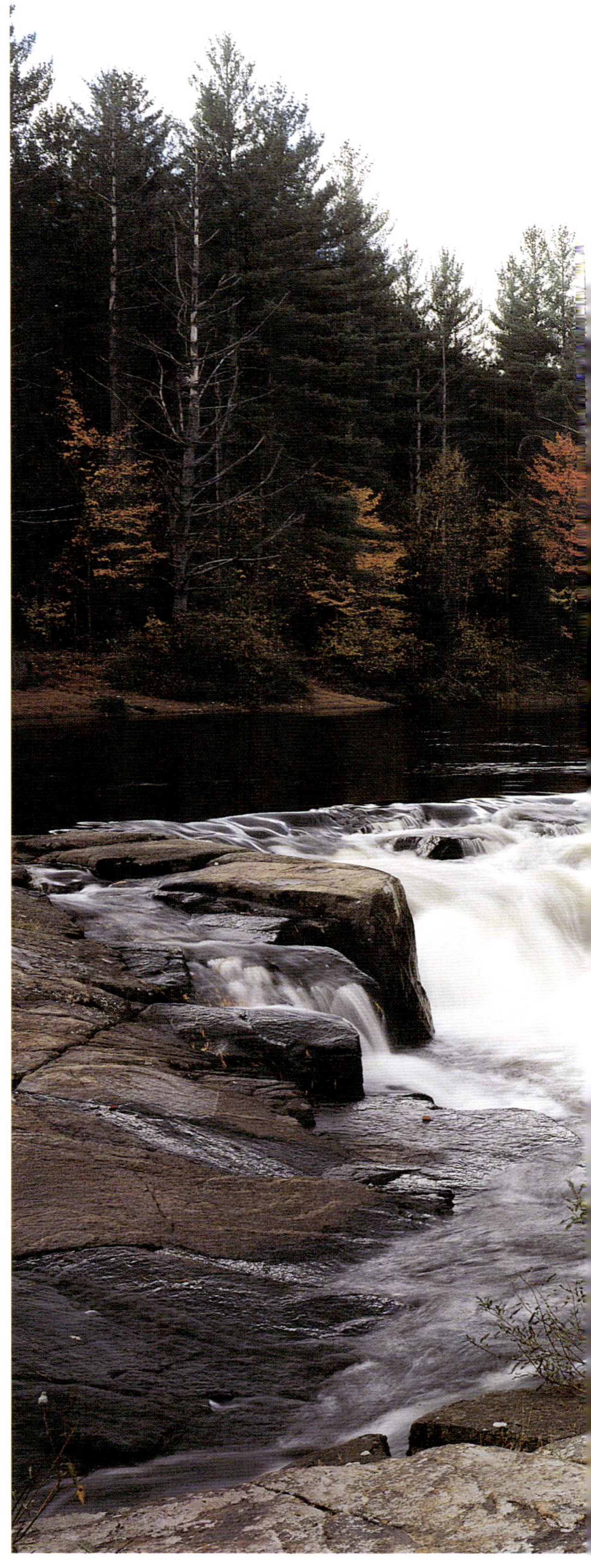

IN THE ADIRONDACKS, knocking two mountains together has the rather surprising result of creating one valley. Of course, cause and effect didn't happen nearly as quickly as the words "knocking" and "creating" might imply.

Beginning some one billion years ago, and over the course of several million subsequent years, another continent was shoved against the continental edge of what we now consider North America. Mountains rubbed against mountains. The result was similar to what happens when you smack one rock against another: both chip and shatter at the point of contact.

So where the mountains met, their rocks were crushed. Over tens of millions of years, a chain of unending cycles of freeze and thaw, torrential downpours, a few glaciers and hundreds of relentless streams all worked together to loosen the crushed rock and sweep it bit by bit out to sea.

In time, the process formed many of the valleys in the Adirondacks.

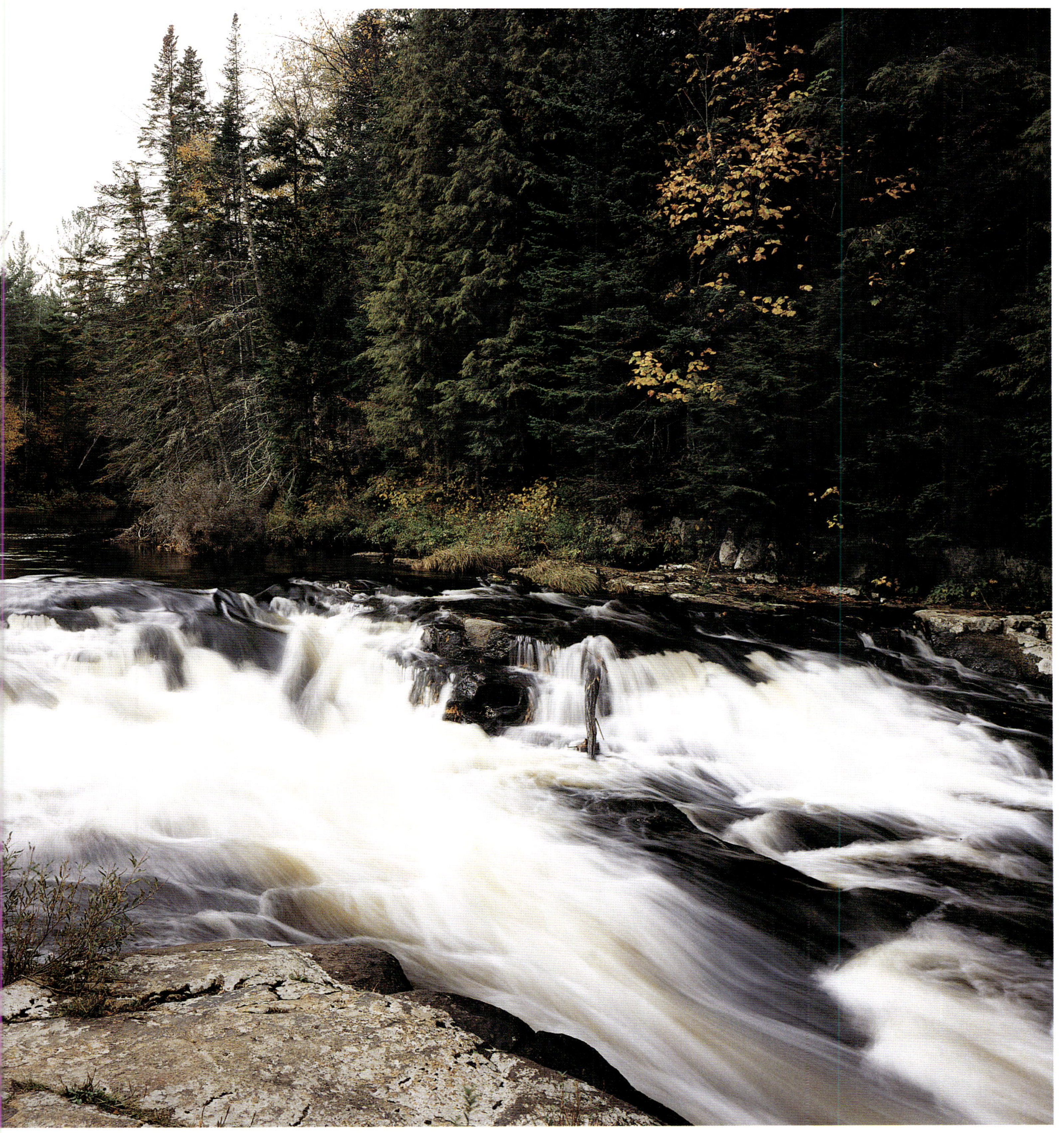

POTHOLERS

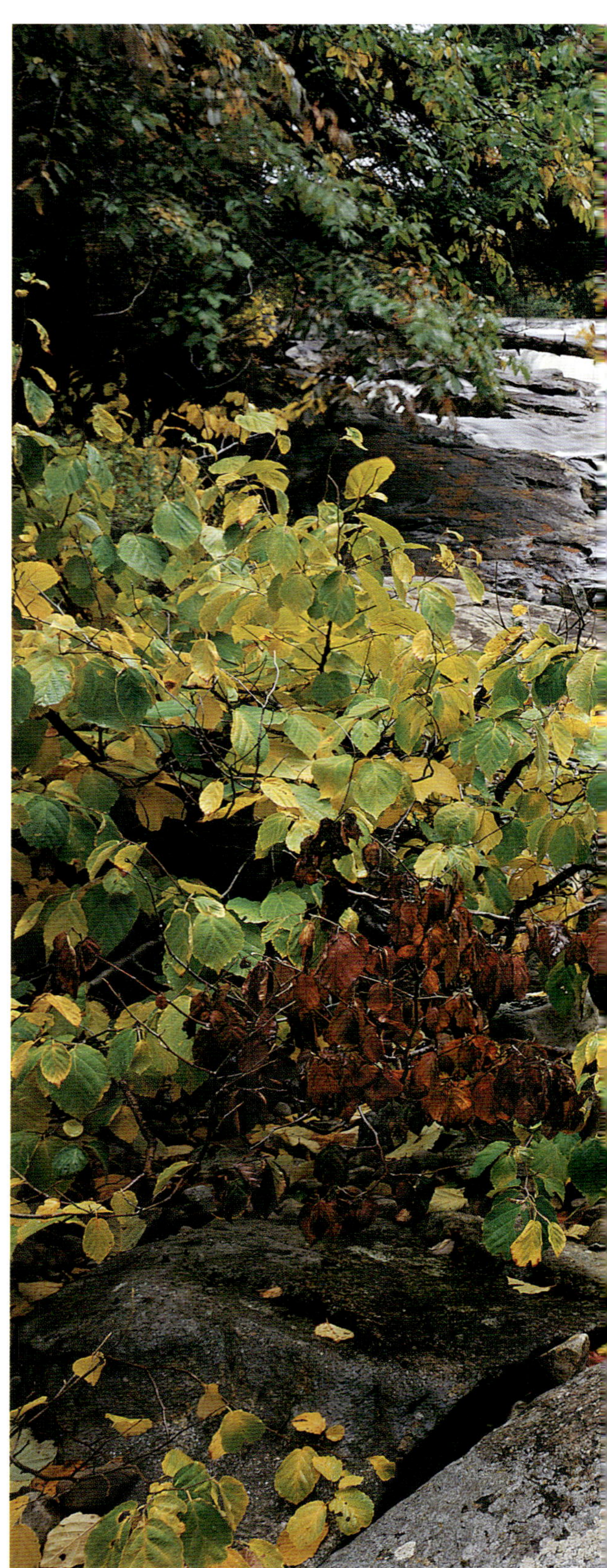

IN NATURE as in human life, forces that persevere ultimately achieve their goals. And no force perseveres more than erosion.

Often erosion seems minuscule, even inconsequential. Witness the Himalayas. They are being eroded. But for now, erosion of the Himalayas is no more effective than trying to keep up with a sprouting adolescent by letting out the seams of his clothes.

But eventually mountains quit rising. And then erosion begins to take effect. Water reacts chemically with rock, slowly dissolving it. Water trickles into rocky crevices, freezes, expands, and chips off a piece of rock. Wind or water sweeps it down a hillside. Heavy snowmelts and heavy downpours form streams, which gnaw away at the landscape.

To the normal human eye in human time, erosion may be unnoticeable. But erosion is geology's version of compound interest. Given time, it can have enormous results. Just as time and compound interest can turn a pauper's few dollars per week into a few million over decades so can erosion over a few tens of millions of years turn peaks into plains. And it always does.

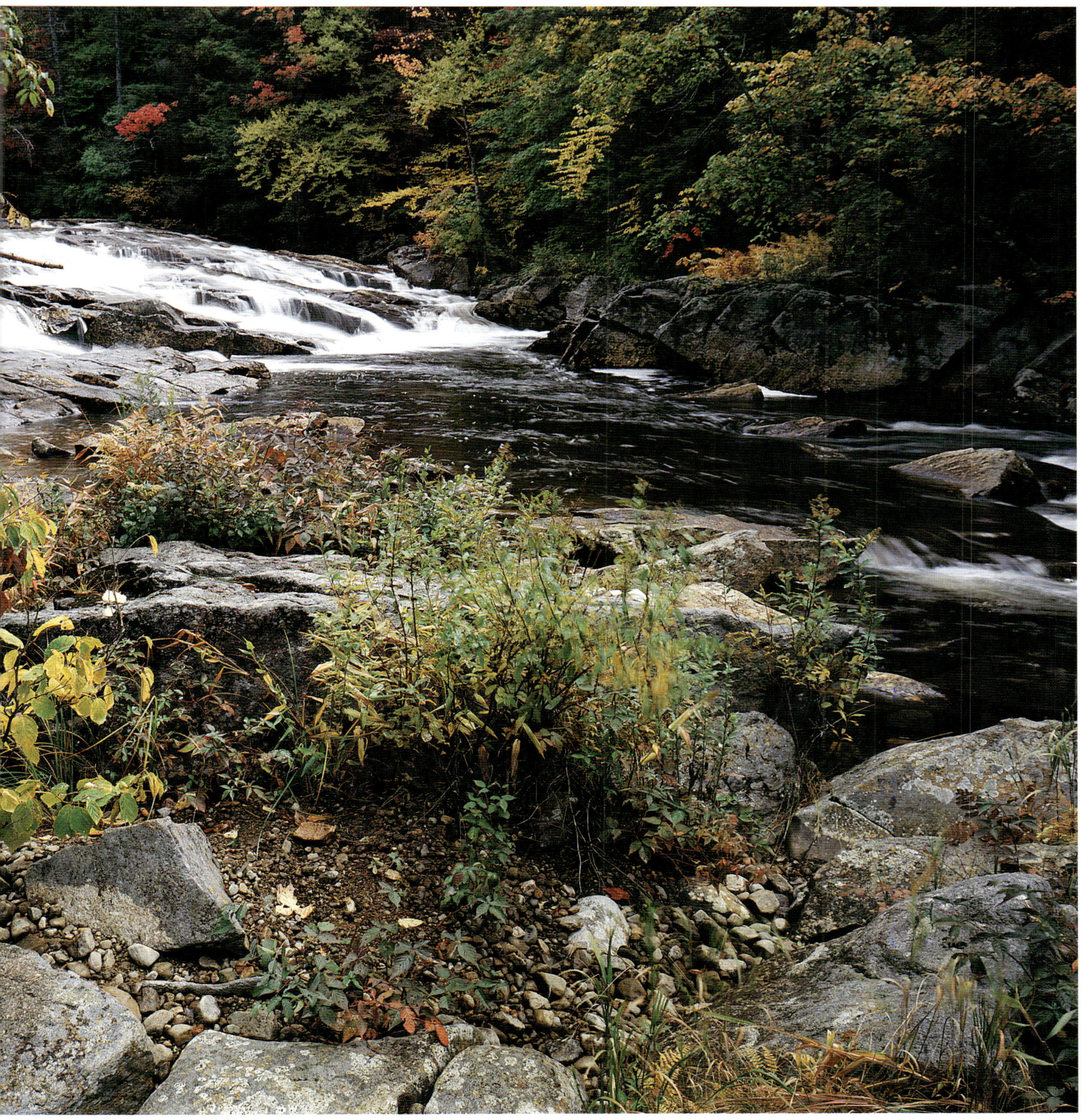

RAINBOW FALLS

LOWER AUSABLE LAKE

AT RAINBOW FALLS, a light went on—twice. On a hike of about five miles, the first two miles were down the private road owned by the Adirondack Mountain Reserve. The next mile took us to Beaver Meadow Falls and the final stretch, to Rainbow. Where the light went on—twice.

As we photographed Rainbow Falls, a boisterous but well-behaved group of college kids arrived. Dressed to the nines in the latest and what looked to be the most expensive hiking gear. A light came on: envy. As we left, two middle-aged women and two toddlers, none dressed for hiking, made their way toward us. Another light: resentment. Crossing Ausable Creek, we were not surprised to see a parking lot—for the privately owned boathouses on Lower Ausable Lake. Soon the women and kids came back, hopped into a Land Rover and sped off.

As we trudged back to our car, resentment of those who seemed to have it better and easier ate away at us. Yet here we were, larking around on a five-day trip, photographing waterfalls, a pursuit that could readily be perceived as frivolous, adventurous, or carefree. Nature works on both land and people.

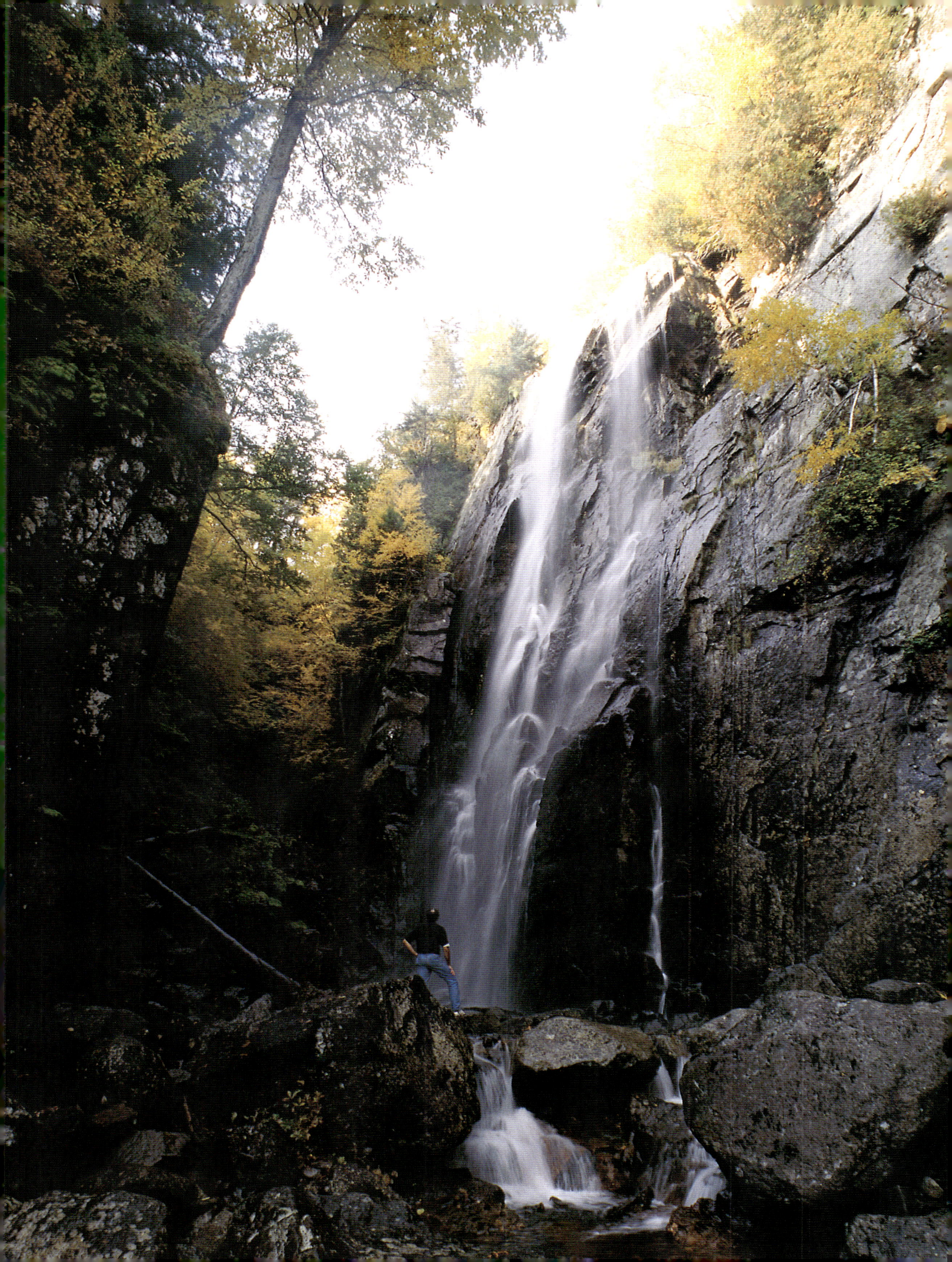

SACANDAGA LOWER FALLS

PHOTOGRAPHS are habitual liars. The photo opposite proves it. But every photo in this book grins with deception. You need to know this because, should you visit a few of these falls, they will feel different. The word "feel" was chosen with purpose. You see a photograph in a book, but in life you feel a place. You experience it.

Consider this waterfall. Before you can set eyes on the real thing, you will have already hiked three miles in hot (cold), sunny (rainy, snowy, misty) weather along the flooding (frozen, shriveled-up) Sacandaga River whose banks shimmer with autumn leaves (rattle with winter branches, burst with spring flowers). Your feet are cold, your throat thirsty, your thighs aching. A thorn-slashed forehead burns with sweat. By the time you reach the falls, your feelings will be different from those you'll find looking at a picture book while sitting in a chair snacking on pretzels.

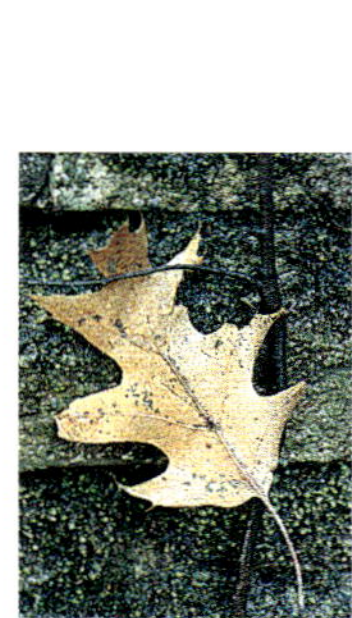

The very act of taking a photo is a manipulation. The photographer chooses the time of year, the time of day, the lighting, the angle, the lens, what to include, what to exclude. The result? Wide-angle lenses shrink waterfalls. Low camera angles puff them up, high angles let their air out. Front angles flatten, side angles inflate. Sunlight invigorates, cloudy light flatters, and so on.

Rest assured. The experience of a waterfall inevitably outweighs any shortcomings of a photograph. This photo understates the experience. The waterfall roared, dwarfing the one in the photo and shooting out a cooling mist. Huge boulders blocked the way, forcing a difficult climb to reach the brink. Cliffs under a dome of blue sky (all cropped from the photo) towered above. If you are in this place, you'll feel a sense of wilderness seldom present in a photograph.

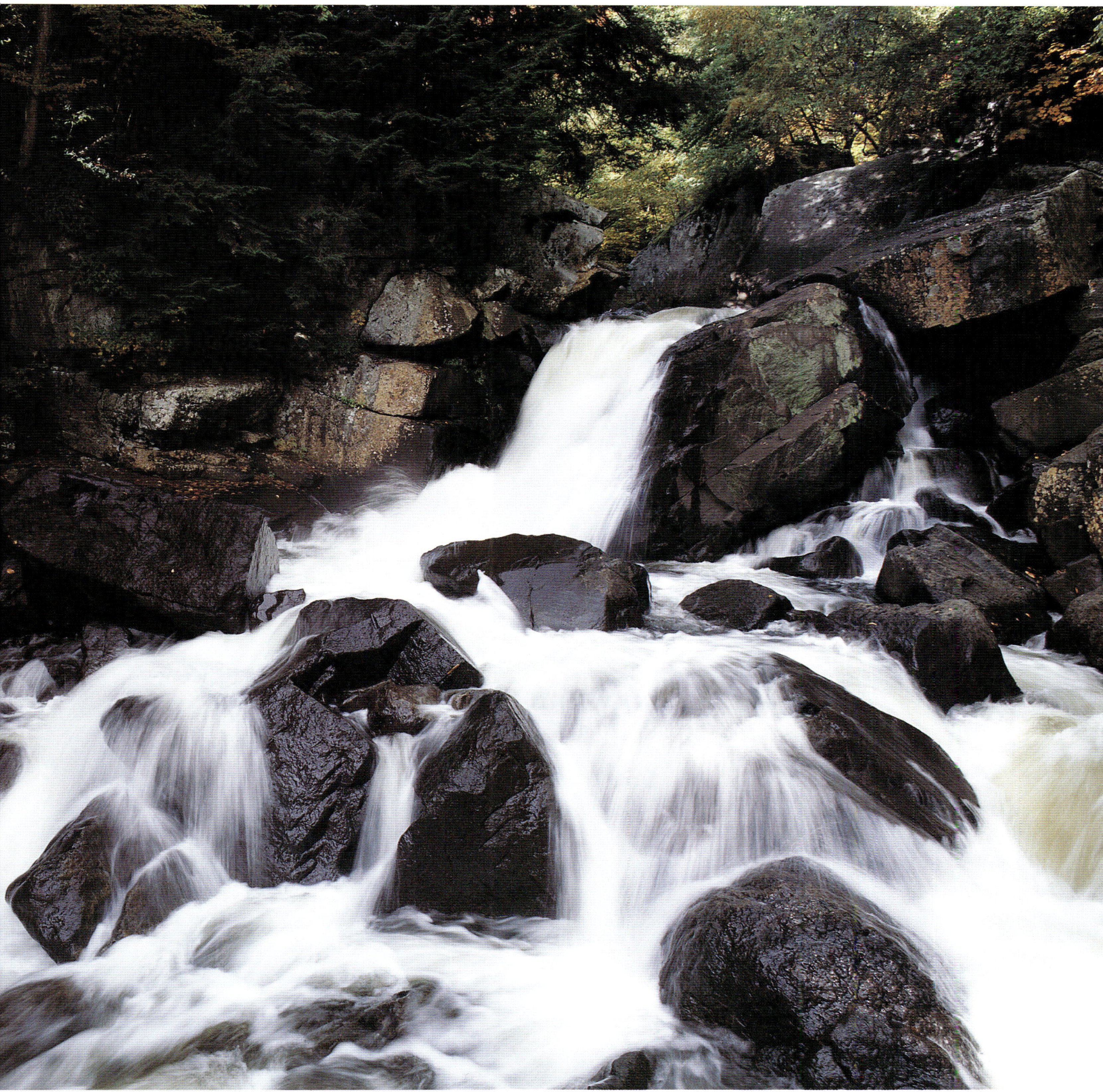

SACANDAGA UPPER FALLS

OVER THE PAST century and a half, the way we see the land has changed with how we view it. For most of history, our views of land were based on its potential as a resource for rulers and entrepreneurs, not as a pleasure to the eye or recreation for the bored. They depended on the written word in reports from hired help. Sometimes the help included artists whose paintings or sketches complemented the reports.

In the nineteenth century, reports from the American West reached the capital with proclamations of a fantastic land filled with geysers spurting hundreds of feet into the air, hot springs boiling like cauldrons, and canyons splitting the earth. Some thought these descriptions extravagant, neither stirring nor believable.

But the new invention, photography, changed their minds. In 1871, William Henry Jackson hauled his 8 × 10 view camera along on an expedition to the area. In 1872, his photos were presented to Congress and within months, a bill was passed making Yellowstone the first preserve in a system of national parks now acclaimed throughout the world.

A century later, we saw new views. These came from outer space and showed the Earth hung like a blue marble spotlighted in a darkened room. No longer did our home planet loom enormous with unlimited capacity. From the perspective of space, it seemed fragile. Small. And lonely.

It needed protection, which prodded an environmental movement.

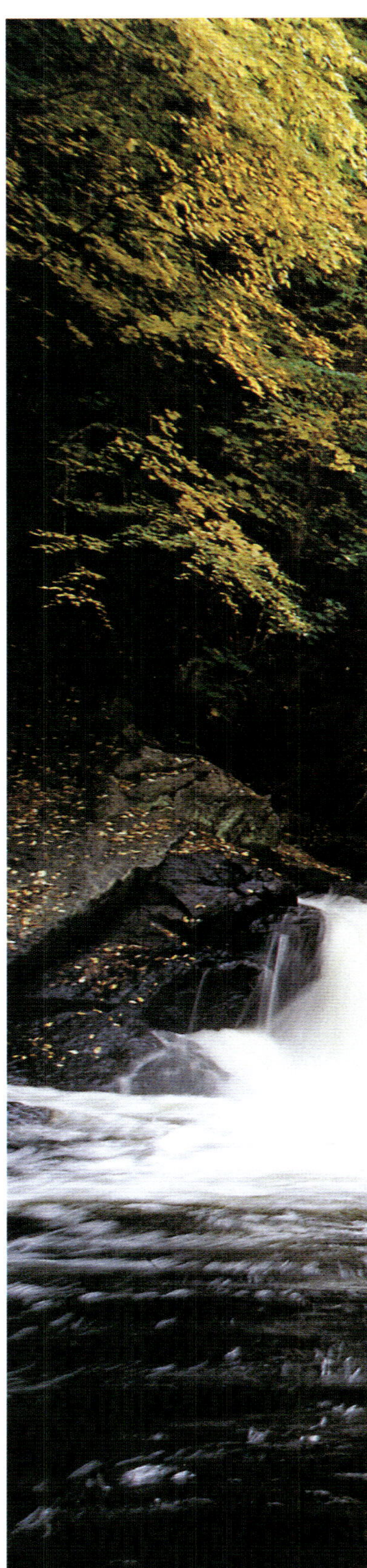

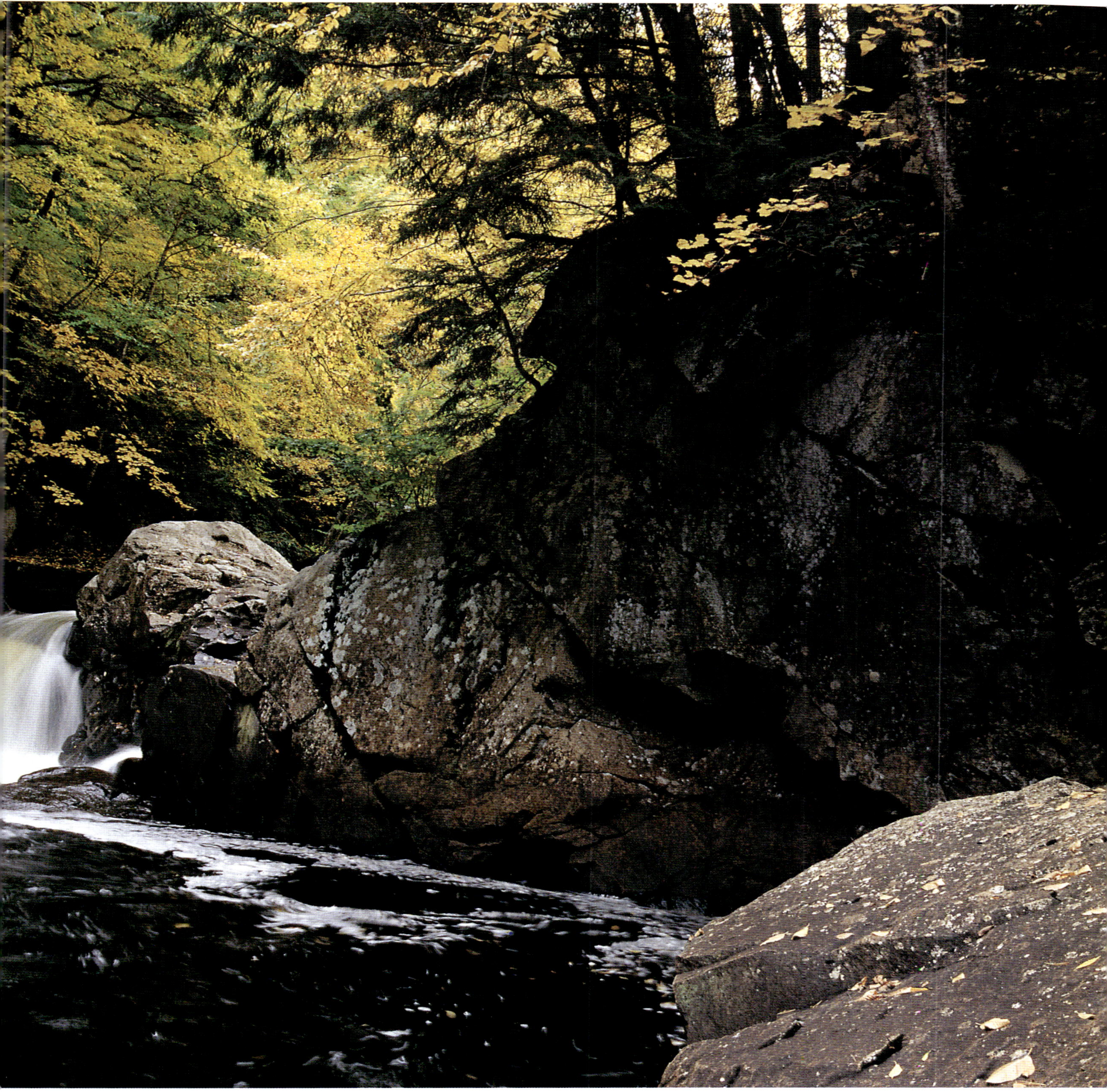

ST. REGIS FALLS

THE REASON this boulder is in the stream is because of gravity. Gravity is a wondrous force. We take it completely for granted. Never give it a thought. Yet it keeps our feet on the ground, our hats on our heads, our food on our plates. All in all, gravity is a practical thing. It brings rain to earth and keeps water in streambeds.

Let us praise gravity. It is totally reliable, always there. It is tireless, always exerting influence, always pulling, and powerful, holding our planet together. But it's modest, always behind the scenes, always accepting its role.

What's most amazing about gravity? How fast it works. Slip on a rock and you're on the ground before you know what hit you. What's most amazing about gravity? That its force is constant. Fall a few feet and you'll survive. Fall a hundred and maybe not—you'll hit with many times the force.

Gravity's pull on falling water digs out deep plunge pools underneath, sometimes nearly as deep as the waterfall is high. Gravity's pull on land, with a little help from the lubricant of heavy rain, brings down hillsides.

Gravity—invisible, incessant, and underrated.

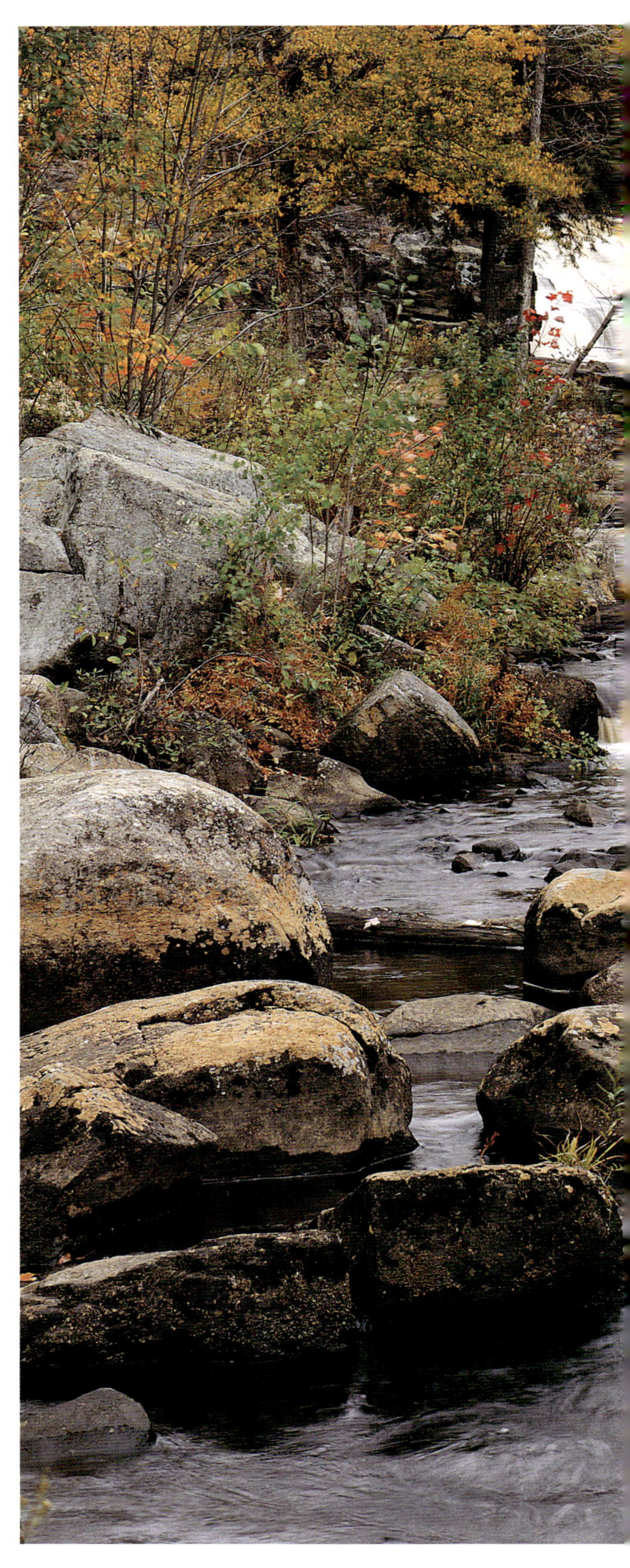

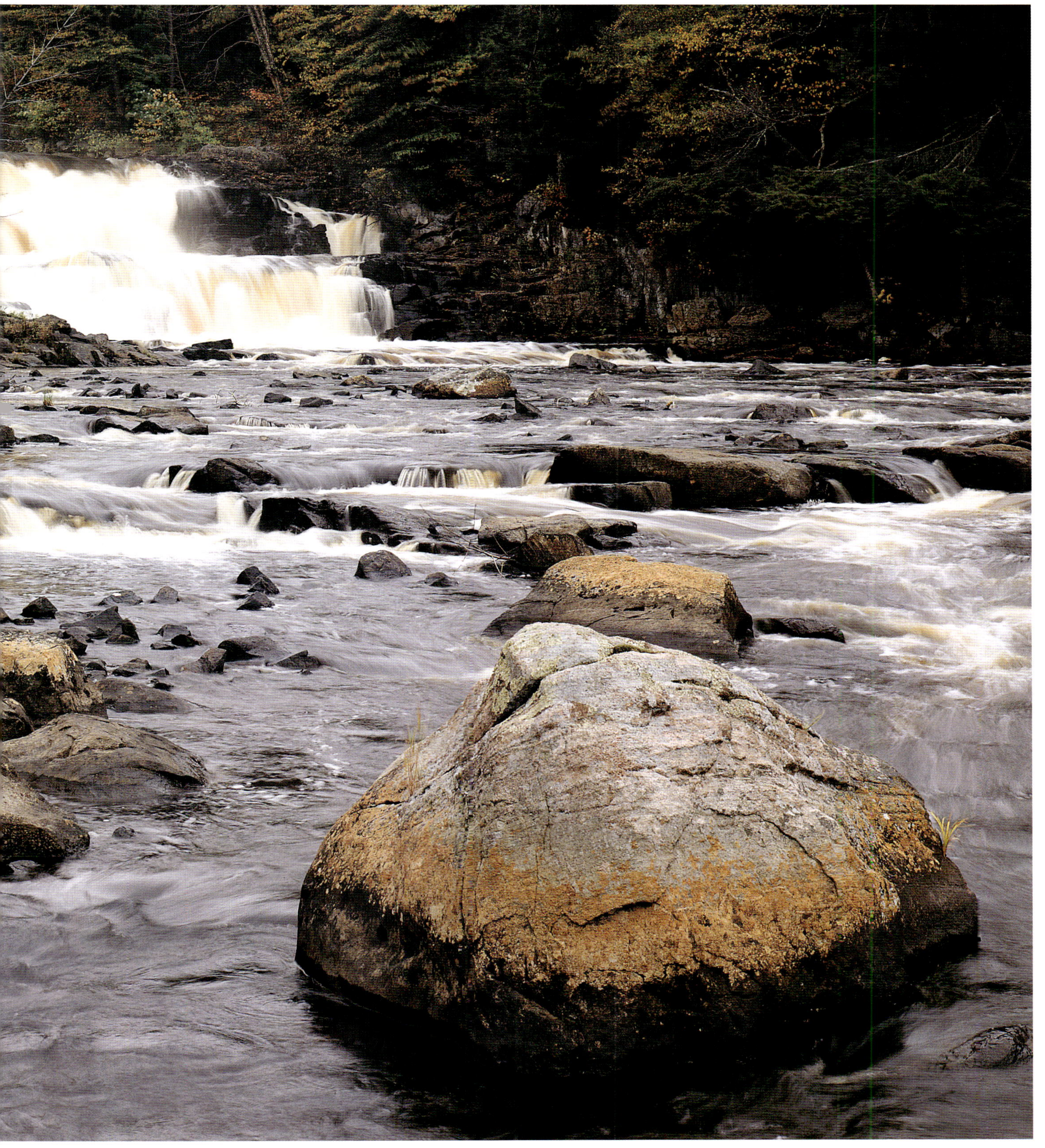

SPLIT ROCK
LOWER FALLS

NOTHING BEATS a good name. Corporations may spend hundreds of thousands of dollars to come up with a product name that seduces customers to buy. They want a name that says, You can't live without me, that says, I can do the job, I can attract that guy, I can convince the world you're a success, or I can turn you into a perfect human being while you sleep so you don't have to lift a finger. In the waterfall world, what compares to a Regal (Buick) or a Right Guard or a Caresse?

Hanging Spear Falls offers a good start. It's imaginative, original, and has panache. Although a bit obscure, it lives up to its name, seeming to form the shape of a spear. To lure a reluctant partner to join you on a hike, offer Opalescent Falls. A hint of the Far East, the seductive mystery of pearls, and a whiff of wealth.

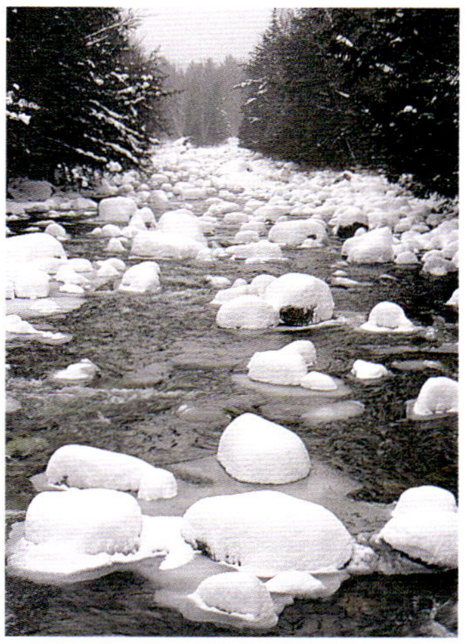

For a strong, inviting name, you can't beat Split Rock Falls. It's outdoorsy, it's enigmatic (what could split the rock?), it's rugged (fitting for male hikers and those who want to meet them), and it's accurate—the rocks are split.

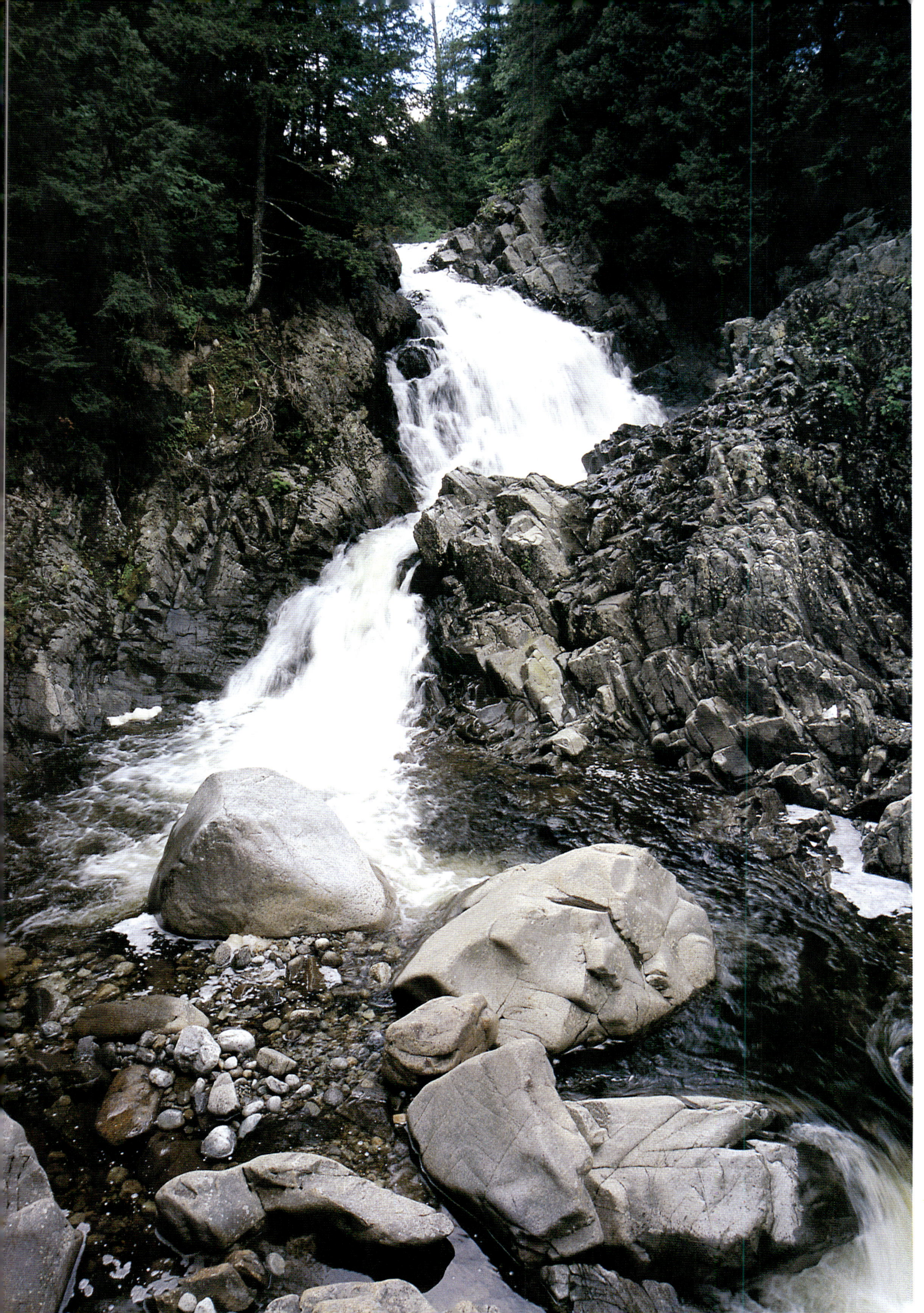

Split Rock
Upper Falls

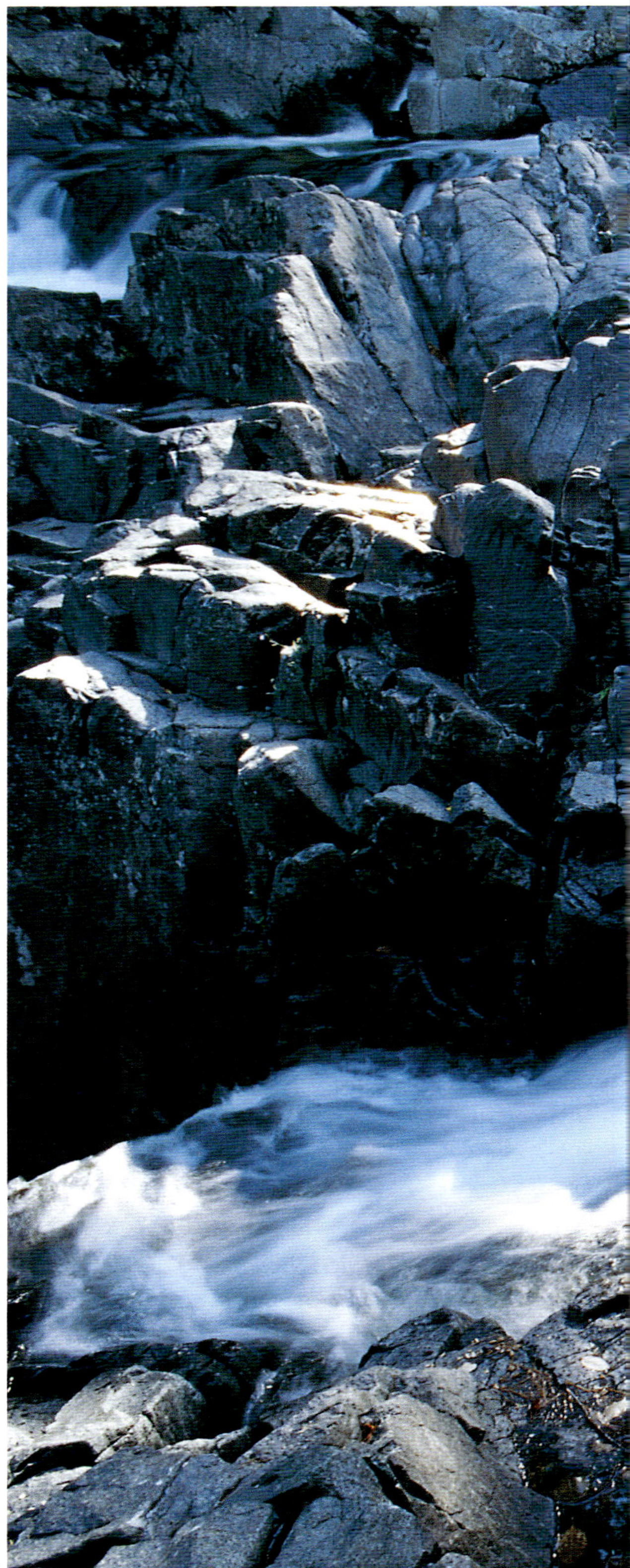

Split Rock is remarkable for two reasons: it's right next to the road, and its plunge pools are exceedingly deep for such small waterfalls.

This combination brings a summer invasion of youth who swim, sunbathe, and drink. When the stream level is down and the surface waters still, you can see through the exceedingly clear water to the bottom. Using a rock and dental floss, we measured the lower plunge pool at a depth of 25 feet. A frequent visitor told us the middle pool was closer to 30 feet deep and the upper, about 15. The depth of the third pool, at the bottom of a small cascade, reaches about eight feet. If you visit, be careful. The cliffs can be treacherous for those not used to rock climbing.

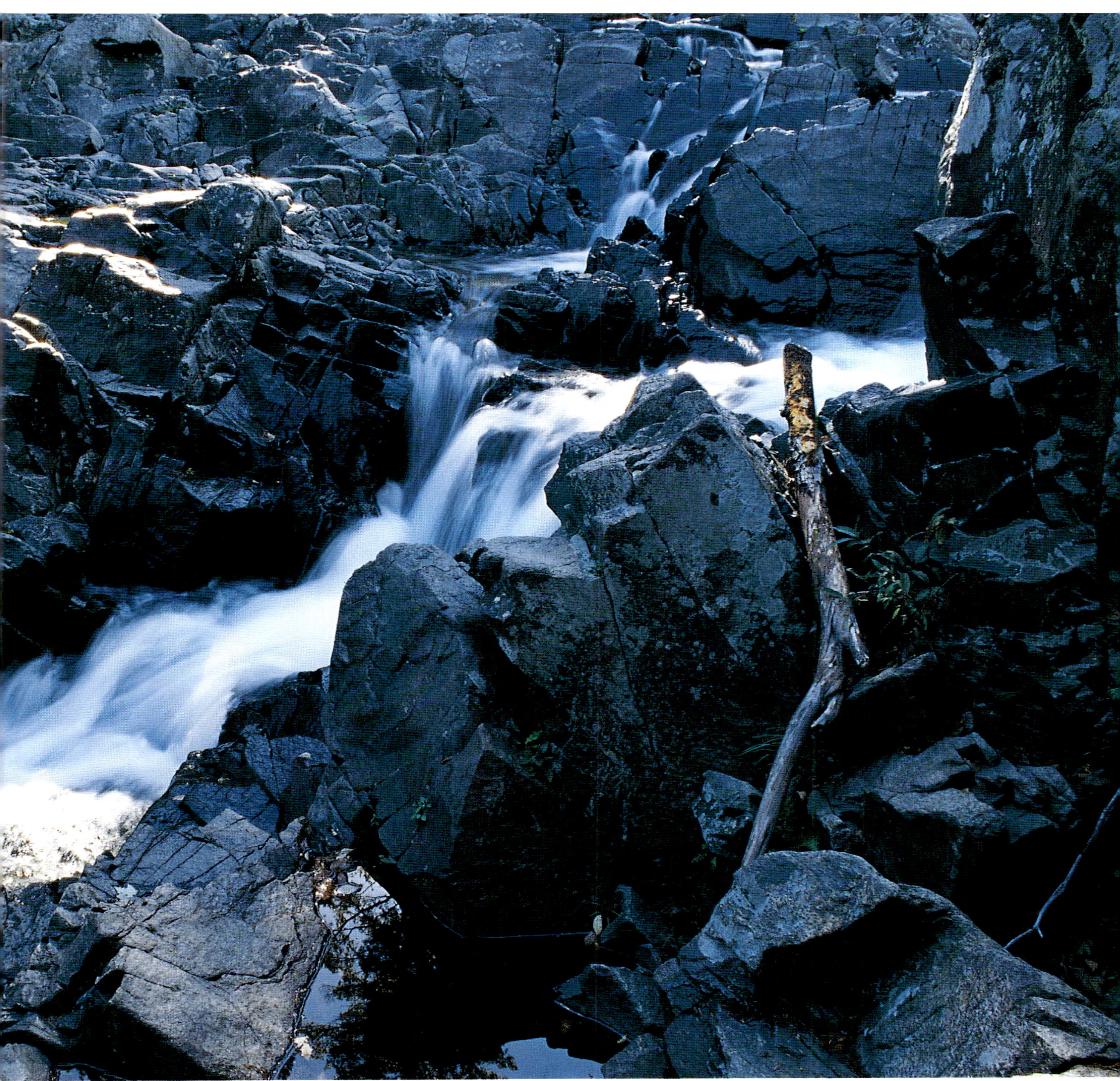

STYLES BROOK FALLS

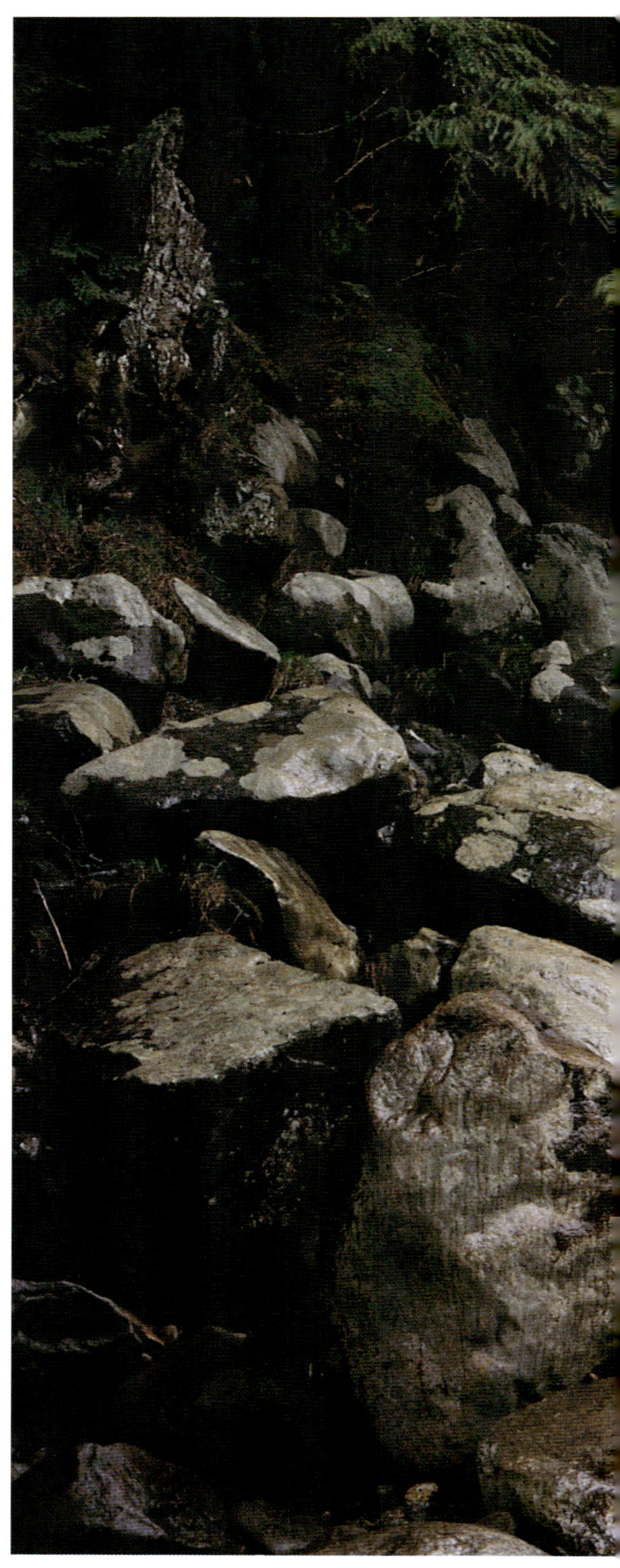

UP THE ROAD. Down the road. Back up. And back down, part of the way. Styles Brook Falls was eluding us so we pulled over and stood at the side of the road and listened. Let the music and hum of the car fade from our ears. Let the rustle of leaves die and the raucous caws of passing crows fade. Let our ears grow pure with quiet.

Like a cat wearing a bell, a waterfall always calls out its location if you're near enough to hear it. And now we could. Just the slightest rumble, more a murmur of static. Clearly the noise of active water in the distance, down the hill. Down a swale. We followed it, pausing now and then to adjust our direction. Over a rise, growing closer. Down another hill to a stream, where the murmur became a clamor, then upstream and around a bend for a short distance. Styles Brook Waterfall. A beautiful mix of rock, water, and conifer that invited us to return.

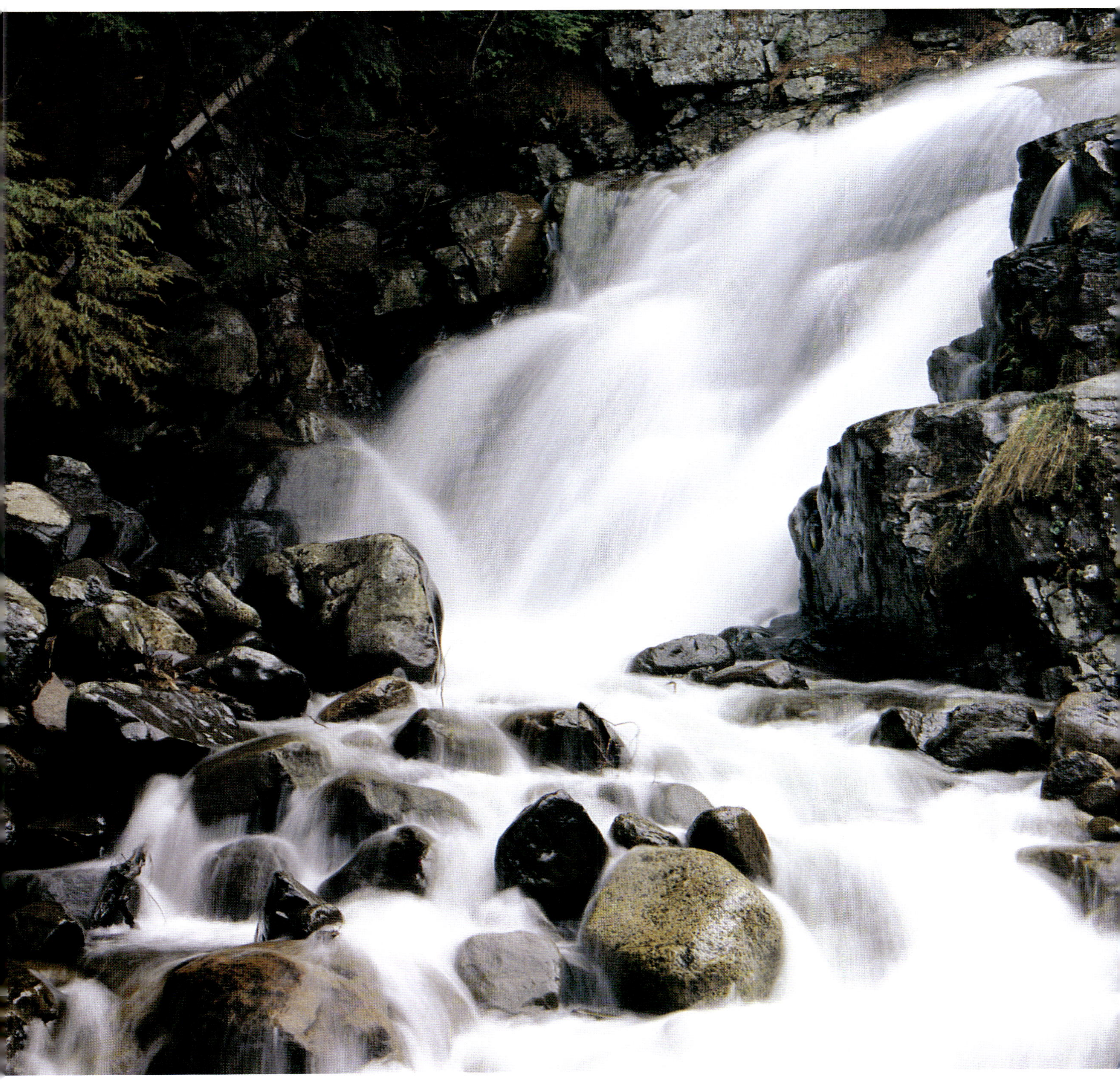

TENANT MIDDLE FALLS

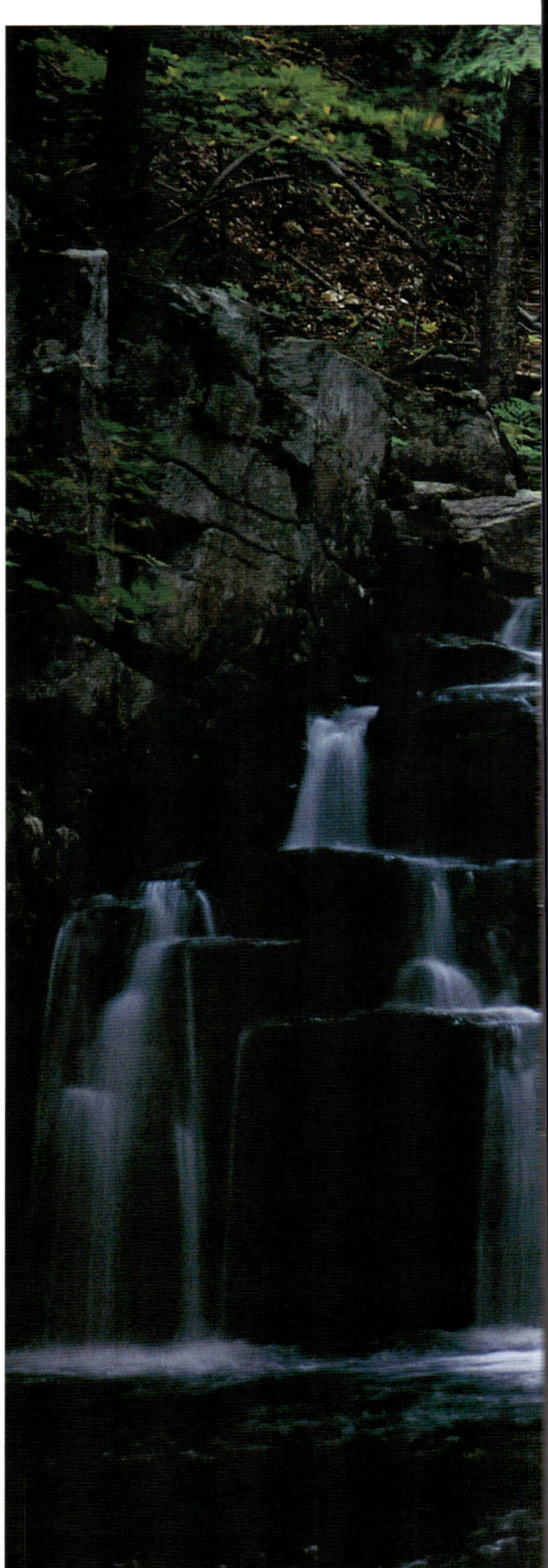

MOST OF US think of the land as having a memory, recording where it's been and what it's been through. When it rains, the land remembers where to carry the water so that it finds its way from rivulet to stream to river. And when knowledgeable geologists observe the land they can uncover the distant memories of past events.

But they also have found that the land has taken a collective knock to the head. Cold-cocked by ice, it's forgotten about three hundred million years of its life. Gone. Except for the most minute smidgens. Like a grader scraping the surface off a road, the passage of four or more glaciers in recent times has obliterated multiple layers of the Earth's surface.

In a movie, it would not be believable that a third or more of a life was forgotten. And in the realms of science too, especially in earlier times, this gap strained credibility. But all that's left from the past three hundred million years are a few crumbs.

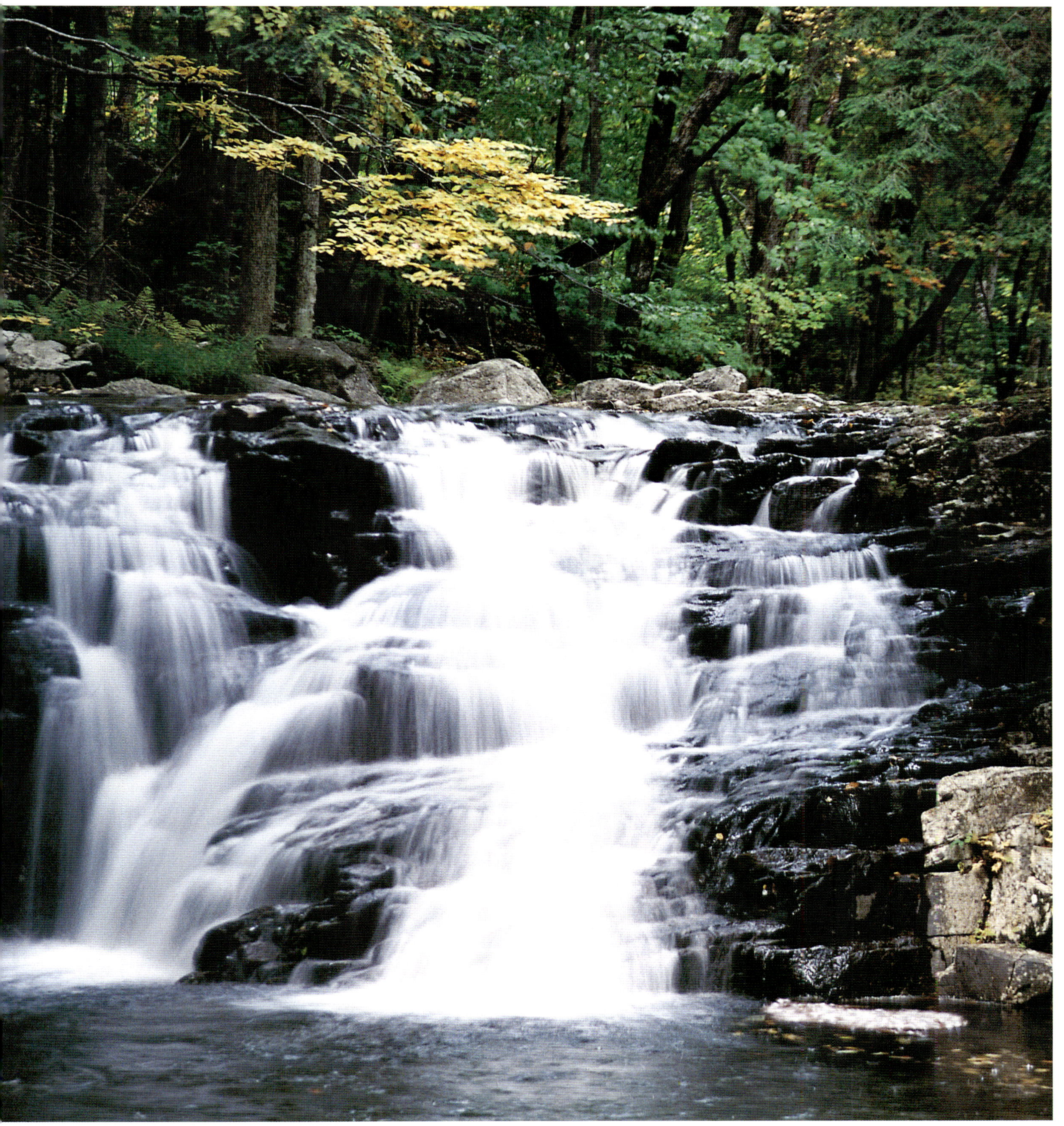

TWIN FALLS

TWENTY THOUSAND years ago, Twin Falls was buried beneath ice. The Wisconsin Glacier was at its peak. Seventy-five thousand years of cooling temperatures and accumulating snows expanded the glacier, pushing it from northern Canada all the way to Manhattan and northern Pennsylvania.

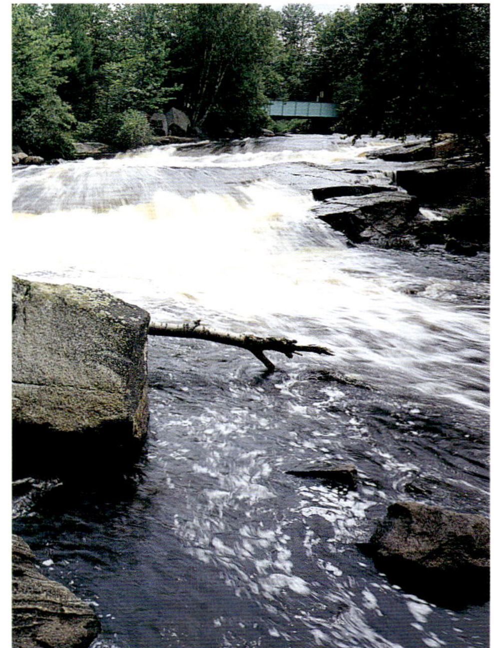

It was thousands of feet thick. It buried all the Catskill peaks and perhaps even the Adriondack peaks. Erratics, boulders picked up and later dropped by the glacier, appear 4,600 feet up on Mt. Marcy.

If the glacier didn't cover all the Adirondacks peaks, it certainly isolated them. Whiteface, Marcy, perhaps Algonquin—only a few hundred feet of the highest peaks could have poked through the glacier. A few islands in a sea of ice. And certainly not oases, or tropical islands. Though perhaps free of glacial ice, they would have been cold, snow-covered most of the year, inhospitable, inhabited by only a few tundra plants, perhaps a few small mammals.

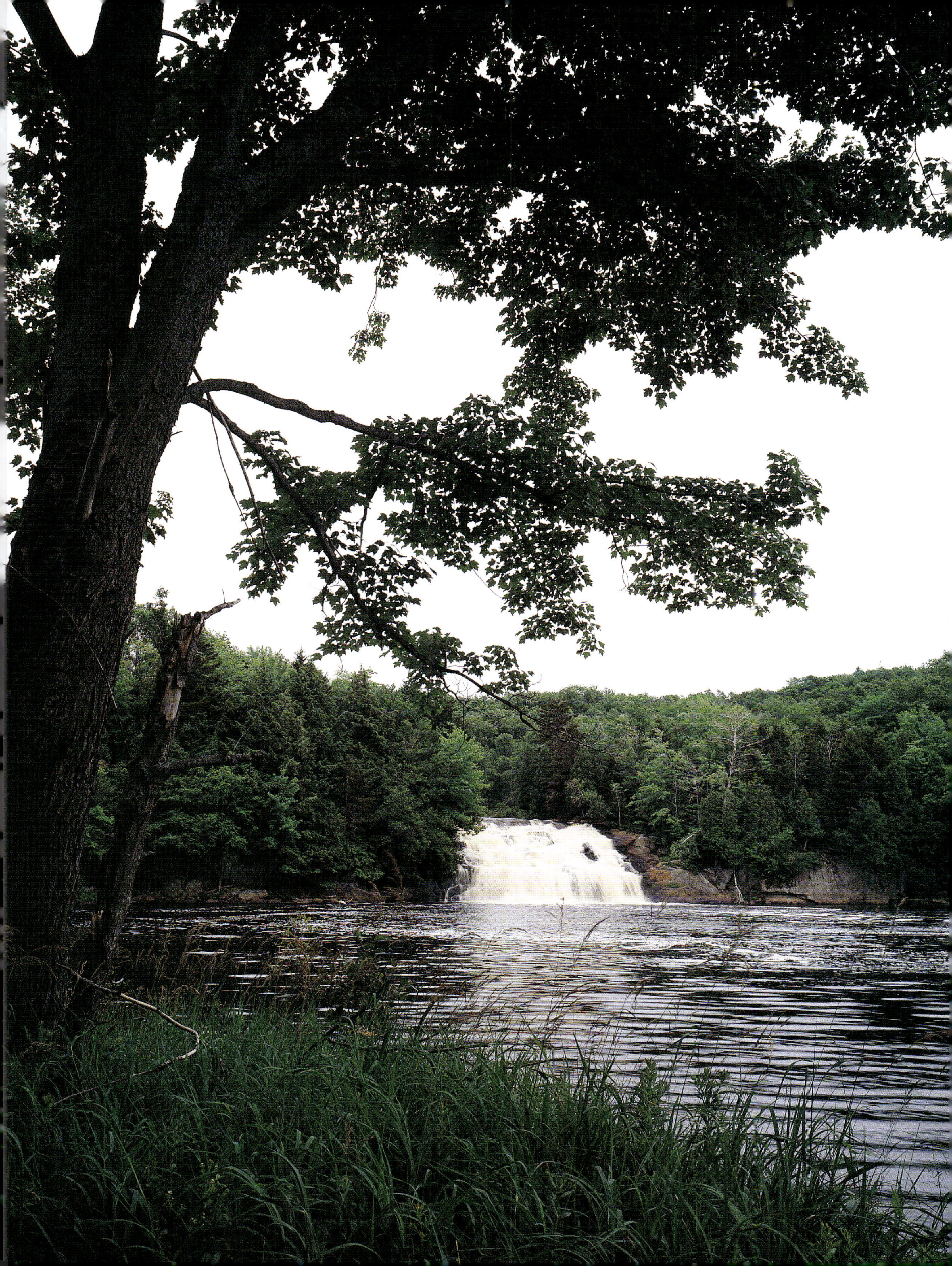

WADHAMS FALLS

A ROAD runs over it. A lake shimmers above it. A library stands beside it. A powerhouse sits below it.

Wadhams Falls combines town and waterfall. It would be a typical ten-house Adirondack town briefly lining a state highway—were it not for the waterfall. It would be a typical cascading Adirondack waterfall—were it not for the town.

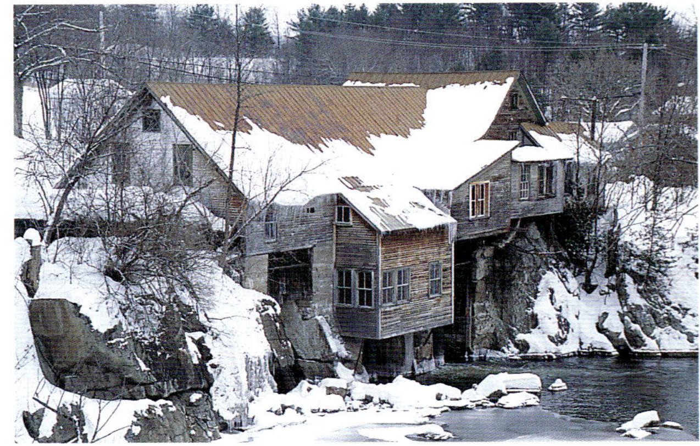

The waterfall is on the Boquet River. Its strong flow and steep drop have powered a variety of operations. The flow of water from Wadhams Falls has sliced logs, ground grain, forged metal, and most recently, shot out a stream of electrons.

In 1904, the first turbines spun by the Boquet River sent their power directly to an iron ore mine in Fort Henry. Today, neighborhood televisions spinning their soap opera yarns and reading lights flickering in the 100-year-old library both draw power from turbines spun by the same falling Boquet River.

Should you stop by the library and powerhouse at different times, don't be surprised to see the same person taking care of things. That's the way it is in a small Adirondack town.

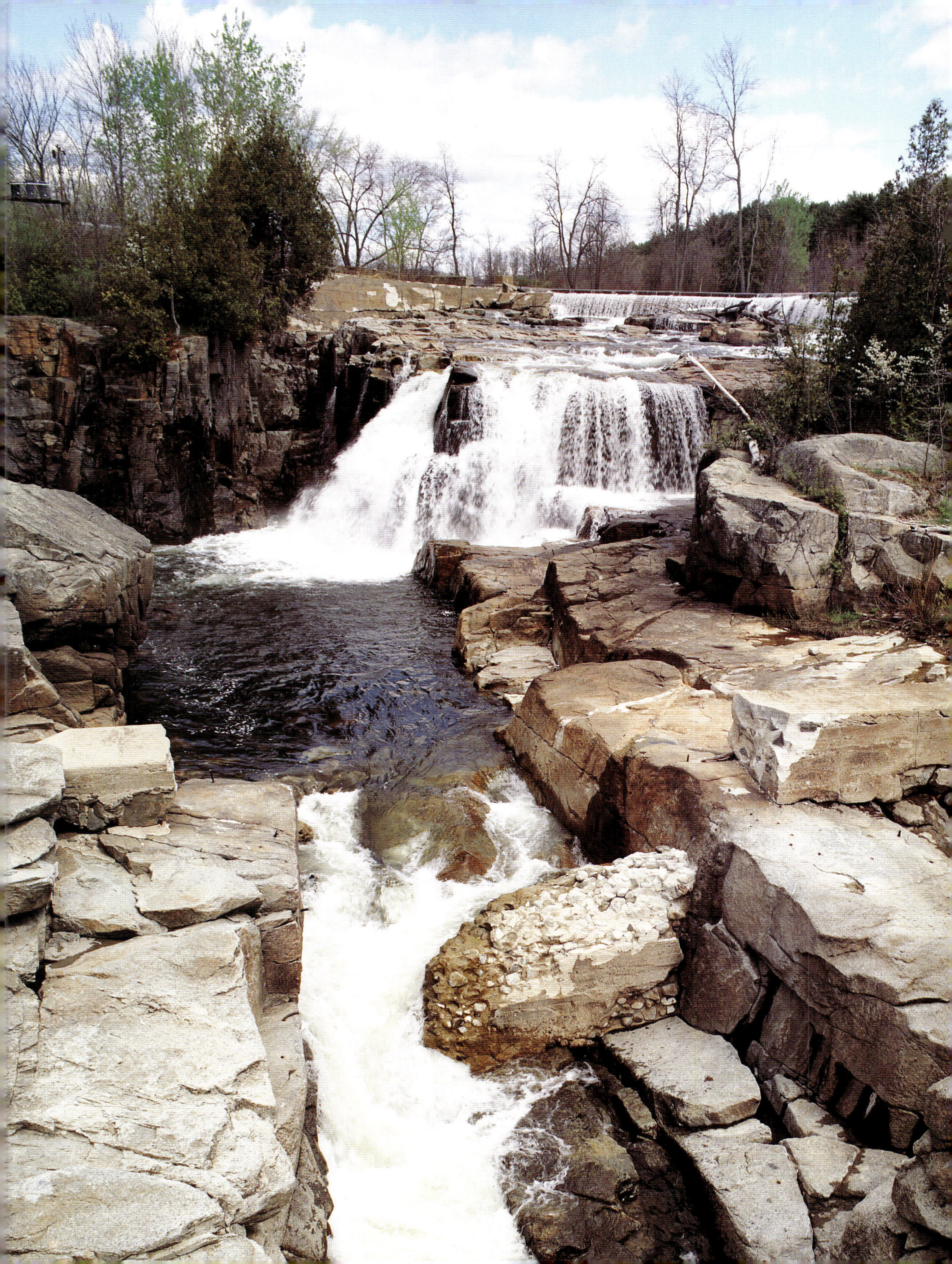

FALLS AT WILMINGTON NOTCH

ALONG ROUTE 86, between High Falls Gorge and the entrance to the Whiteface Mountain Ski Area, you will find the state-operated Wilmington Notch Campground. Immediately behind and below the campground, a massive cascade of rapids and waterfalls dominates the West Branch of the Ausable River.

Watch your step as you traverse the hillside leading to the river. The steep terrain descends through a hemlock grove, which has produced a thick and—particularly in wet weather—slippery carpet of needles.

The vantage point offering the most picturesque view of the cascade is a high, rocky cliff to which several weathered conifers cling. Again, be extremely careful where you step—the vertical drop is straight down, and there are no guardrails.

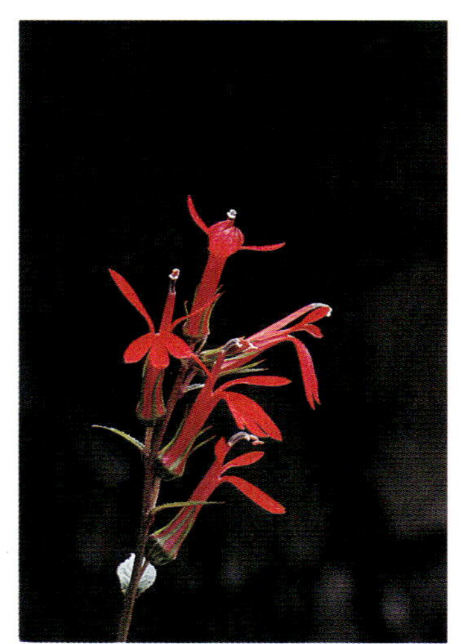

The falls have no name. In fact, no maps—not even the campground's official brochure and mural-size trail map—make any reference to the falls. We asked the ranger on duty at the campground headquarters if the waterfalls had a name.

"Nope," he replied, "it's got no name."

It appears as though the establishment wants to downplay the existence of the falls, perhaps because of its treacherous location and lack of easy access. The rumor that the fishing at the base of the falls is excellent may also have something to do with it. Thus we show you here one of the Ausable's—and the Adirondack Forest Preserve's—best-kept secrets: the falls at Wilmington Notch.

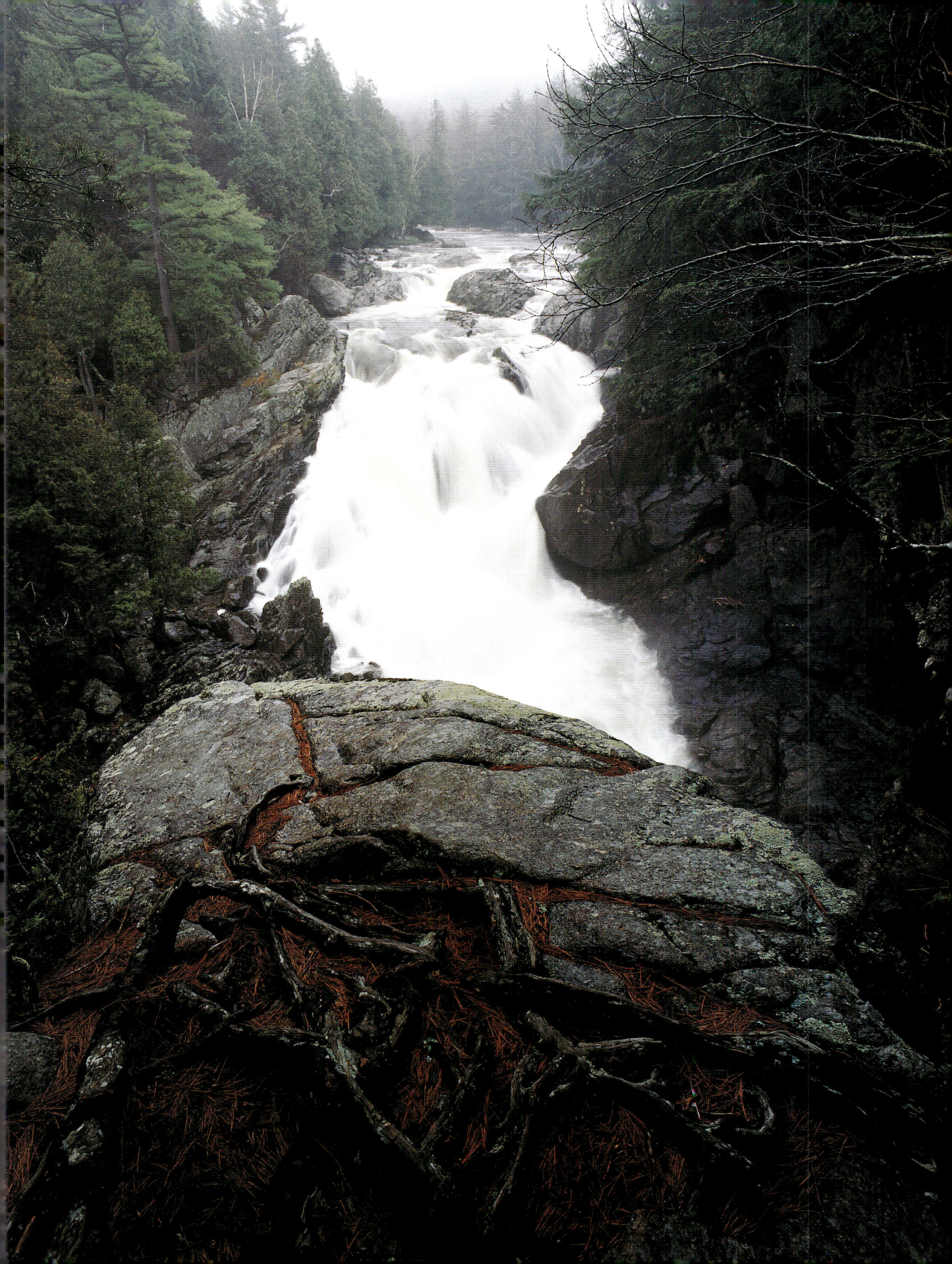

WATERFALLS OF THE CATSKILLS

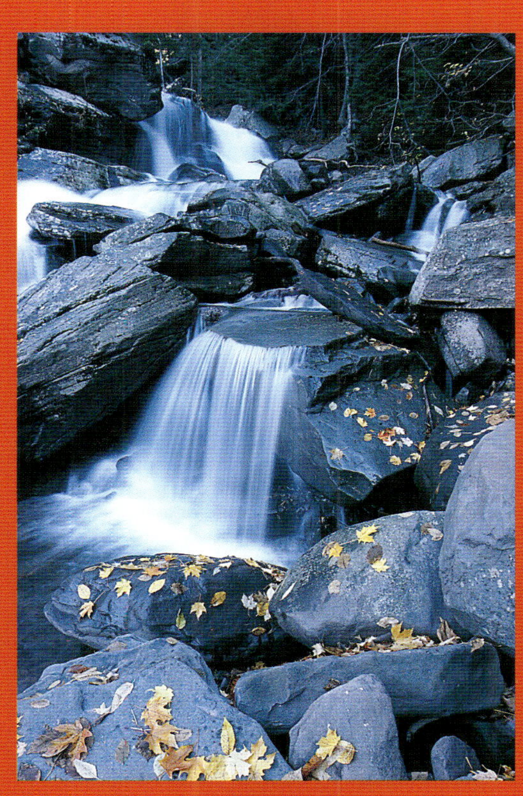

ANONYMOUS
NEAR BUTTERMILK FALLS

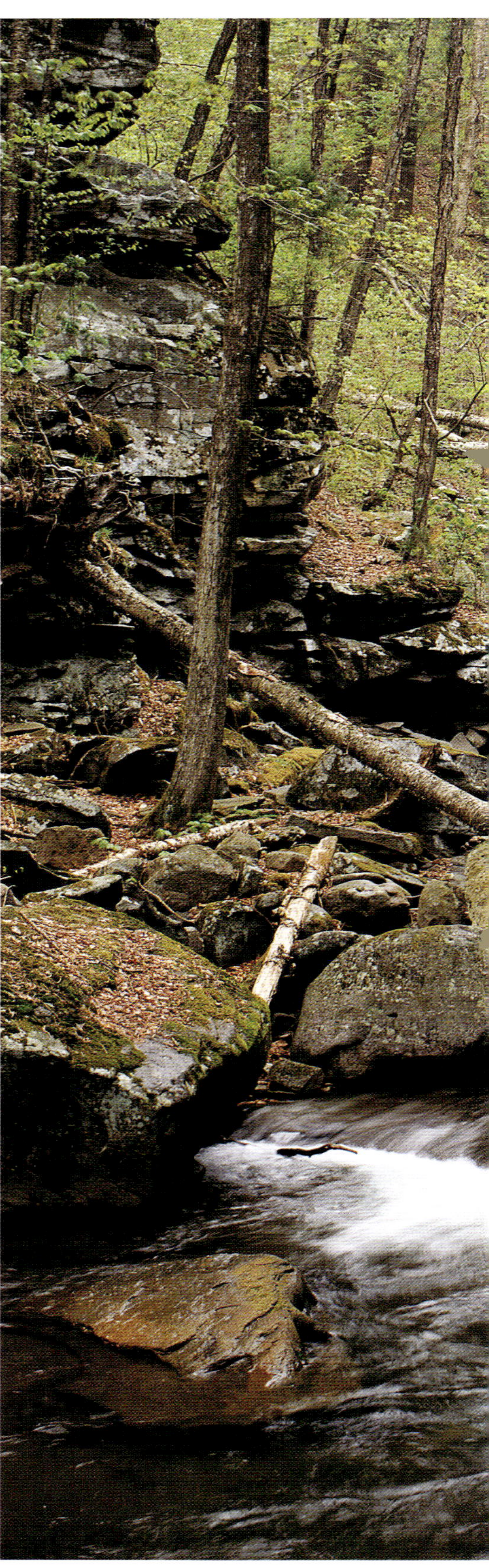

WATER IS AMAZING. Piped into our homes, often from great distance, it's something we take for granted. But who among us can't remember reading in grade school of early settlers who hauled water daily from a creek? They didn't contemplate water, they simply needed it for survival. They went to great lengths to get it, to settle near it. How many of us have ever been in the position where we were desperately struggling to reach water for survival?

Water provides survival in more ways than replenishing the human body. It is the only abundant liquid on the planet's surface. That it also exists as a vapor and as a solid, in the temperature range where we survive, makes it more unusual.

The molecular structure of water allows it to dissolve a large variety of substances readily. Without that feature, few life forms could gain sustenance. It carries nutrients throughout our bodies, it transports nutrients through the network of a tree and in the body of a lake or ocean.

Internally cohesive, it can form drops that greatly stretch and elongate before breaking, or form a skin on the surface of a stream or pond across which water striders stroll as easily as we cross a parking lot. And unlike any other substance, when it freezes into a solid, it becomes lighter. Thus ice floats, streams never freeze solid, and the life within survives.

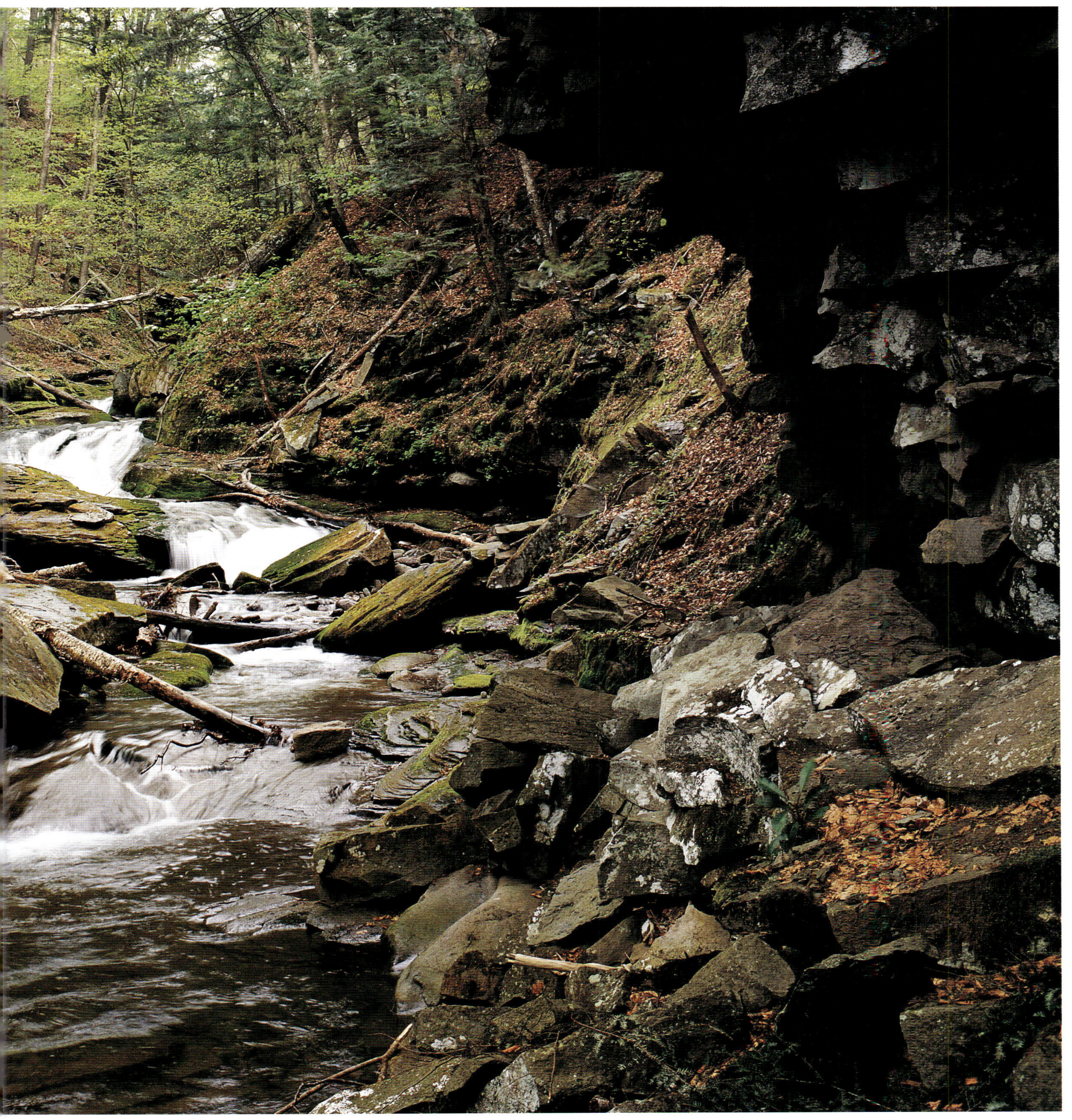

ARTIST'S GROTTO

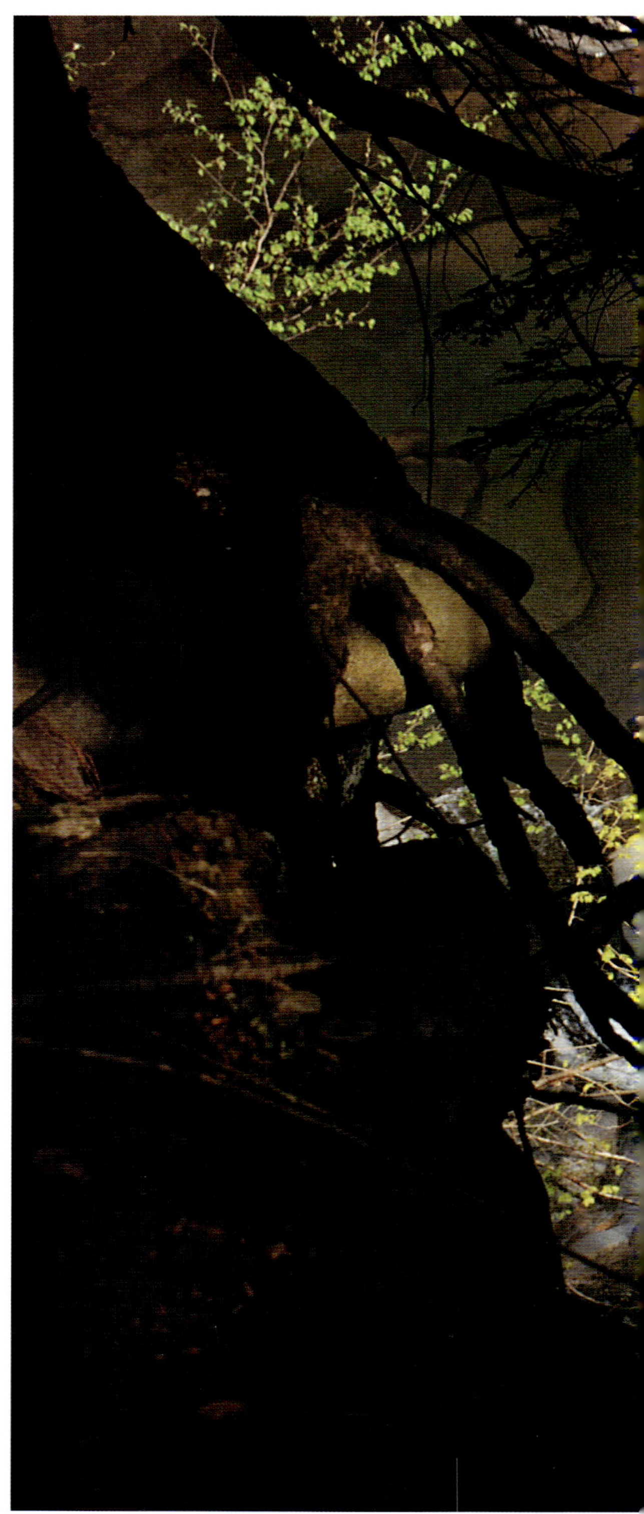

WATER IS LAZY. This is true of waterfalls in particular. They always seek the path of least resistance. They have no choice. It's their nature. Indeed, waterfalls arise when resistance drops. Most waterfalls occur only when hard rock adjoins weaker rock.

In the Adirondacks, the weaker rock has two origins. It may have been a softer material forced into the harder rock when, many miles under the surface, both were soft and plastic. Or it may have been crushed during the collision of land masses.

In the Catskills, the weaker and harder rock most often originated during sedimentation in ancient seas. If the sediment was mud or silt, soft brittle shale formed. If the sediment was sand, sandstone was born. If the sediment consisted of millions of tiny sea creatures, limestone solidified. Both sandstone and limestone are considerably stronger than shale.

Wherever rock exposes a weakness, water finds it. Be it rock crushed by continental collisions or sediments accumulating during regional erosion, water drills into it. Chews it up. Tears it out. Sweeps it away. And leaves behind a waterfall.

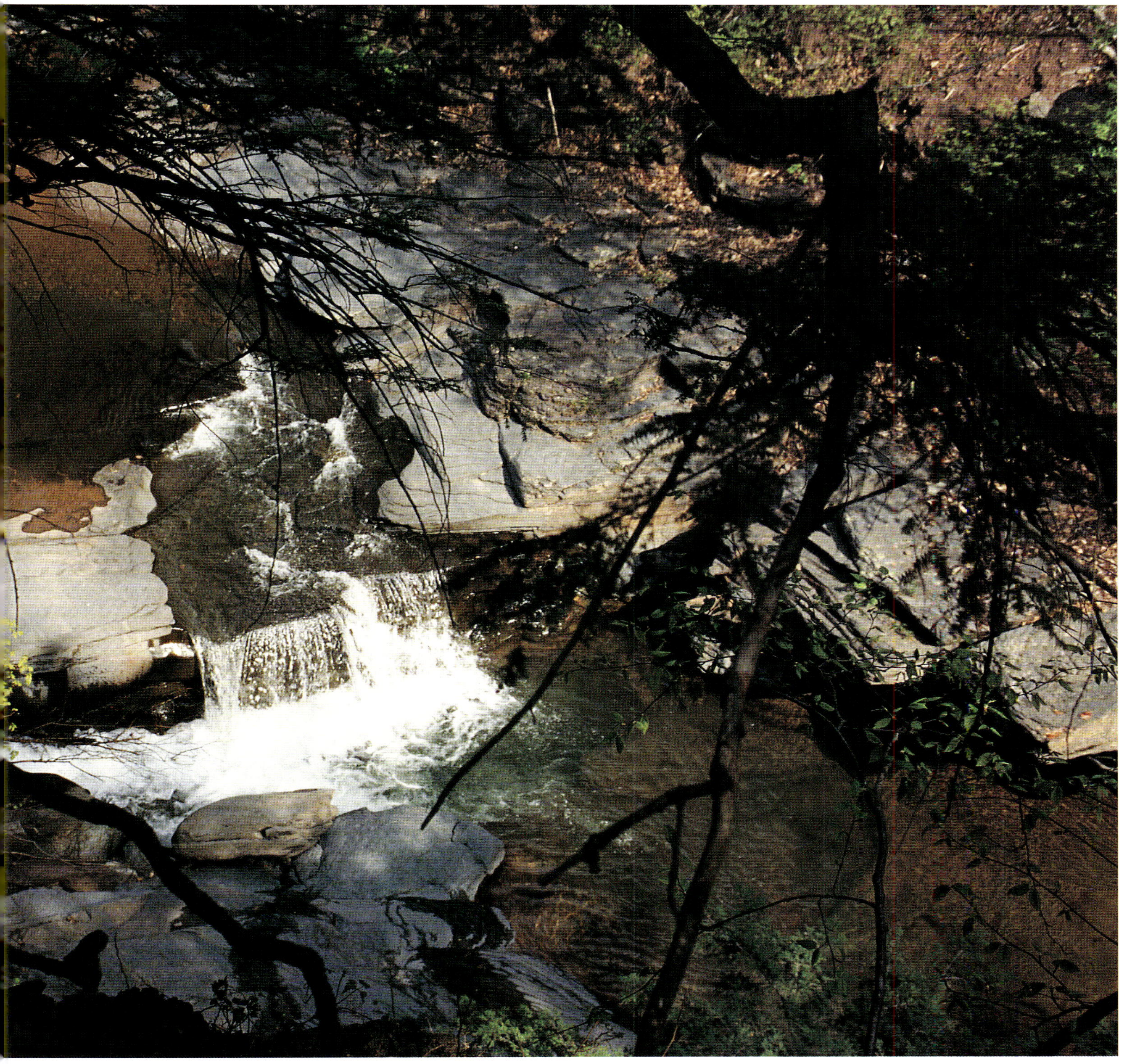

ASHLEY FALLS

SOME WATERFALLS are simple. Take Ashley Falls. A stream of water shoots out from a ledge and leaps into a pool below. Not much more than a natural spigot; in a waterfall's vocabulary, the equivalent of "See Spot run."

Others are a bit more complex. They leap, land, splash, veer right, then left, duck behind a rock, and then fan out and down.

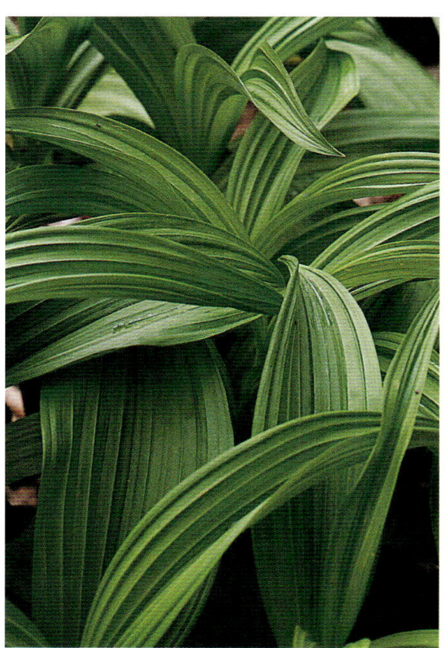

A few, such as Ashley's neighbor, Bastion Falls, are a veritable dance revue of water movements. One moment, all its streams of water are aligned and kicking their legs in a unified move, then stamping simultaneously to ground so strongly you can almost feel the vibrations in your bones.

But just a few feet downstream, the water divides into a variety of movements. One streamlet arcs into the air, while another branch snakes through an obstacle course of rocks, and yet another fans out like a rippled sheet over a shallow slope of rock, while a fourth feeds into the eye of a pool.

Waterfalls with waterfalls within entertain. Simple streaming waterfalls mesmerize.

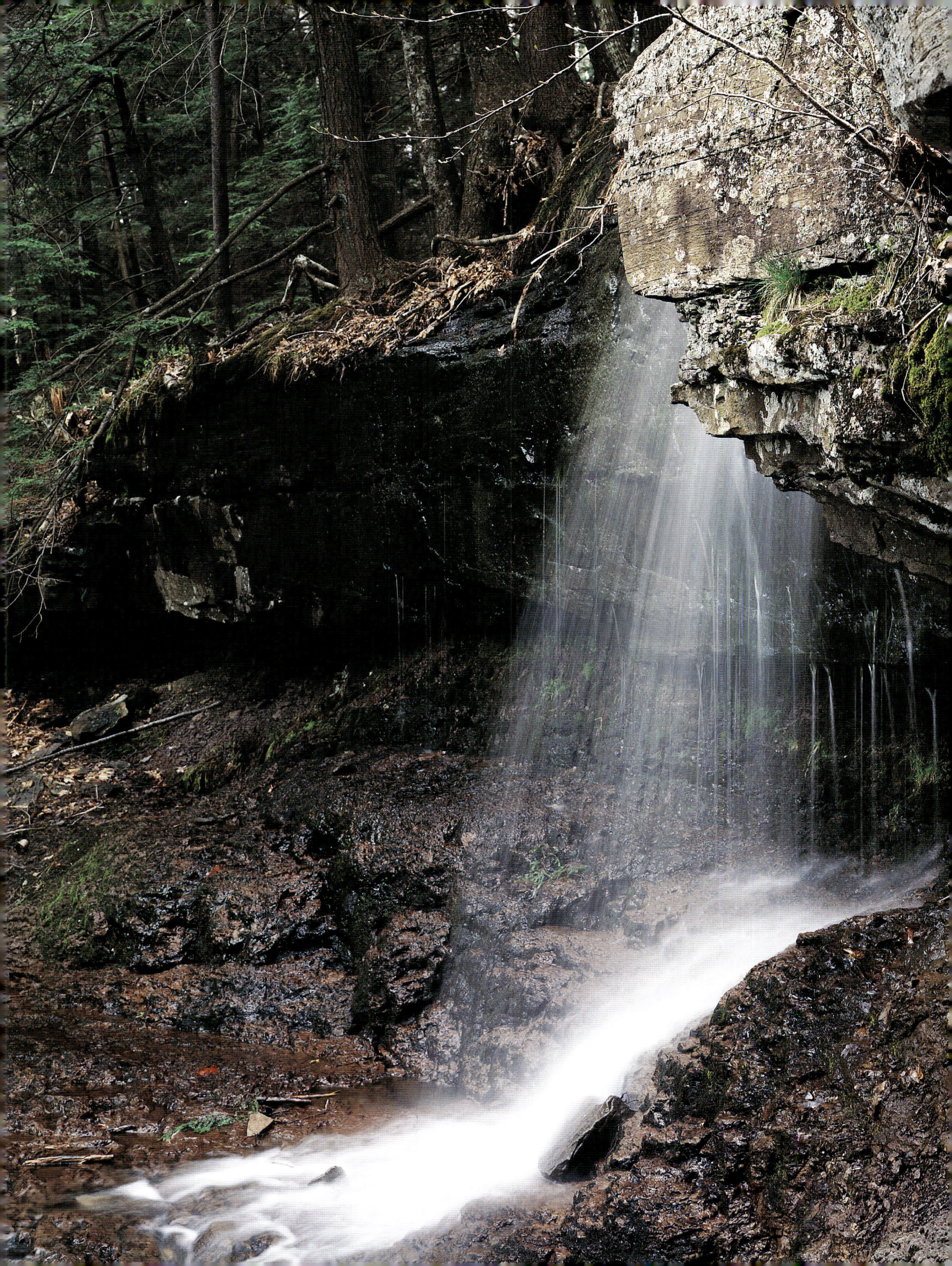

AWOSTING FALLS

FACTS—trivial, meaningless, or essential—follow.

For the past 200 million years, North America has drifted northwestward an average of two inches a year.

Glaciers nearly a mile thick covered all (or nearly all) of the Adirondacks and Catskills. Their formation stole enough water from the oceans to lower them by 300 feet. The weight of the glaciers depressed the land beneath them 27 feet for every hundred yards of ice.

When the glaciers melted, the land, relieved of that burden, rebounded to its original altitude over thousands of years (in parts of Canada, it's still rising).

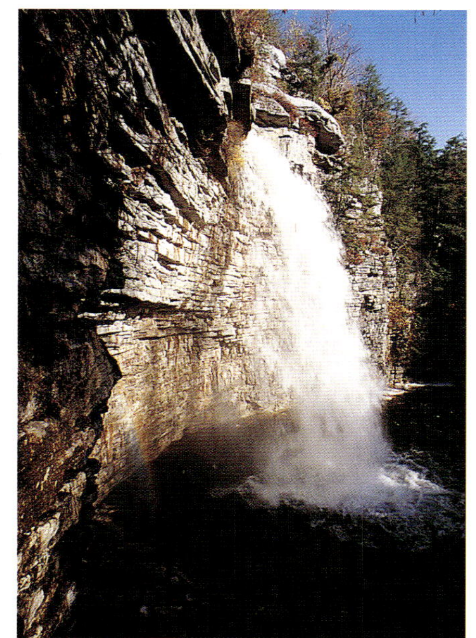

Four hundred million years ago, the earth rotated faster. Days were 22 hours long and years had 400 days, even though there were no calendars (nor any animals, trees, or people). We are currently in the warm interlude of an ice age—forecast: cold weather on its way for the next 75,000 years. Periodically, the North and South Poles flip-flop. We're due for a flip-flop any day. It might even happen while you're reading this book. Check your compasses.

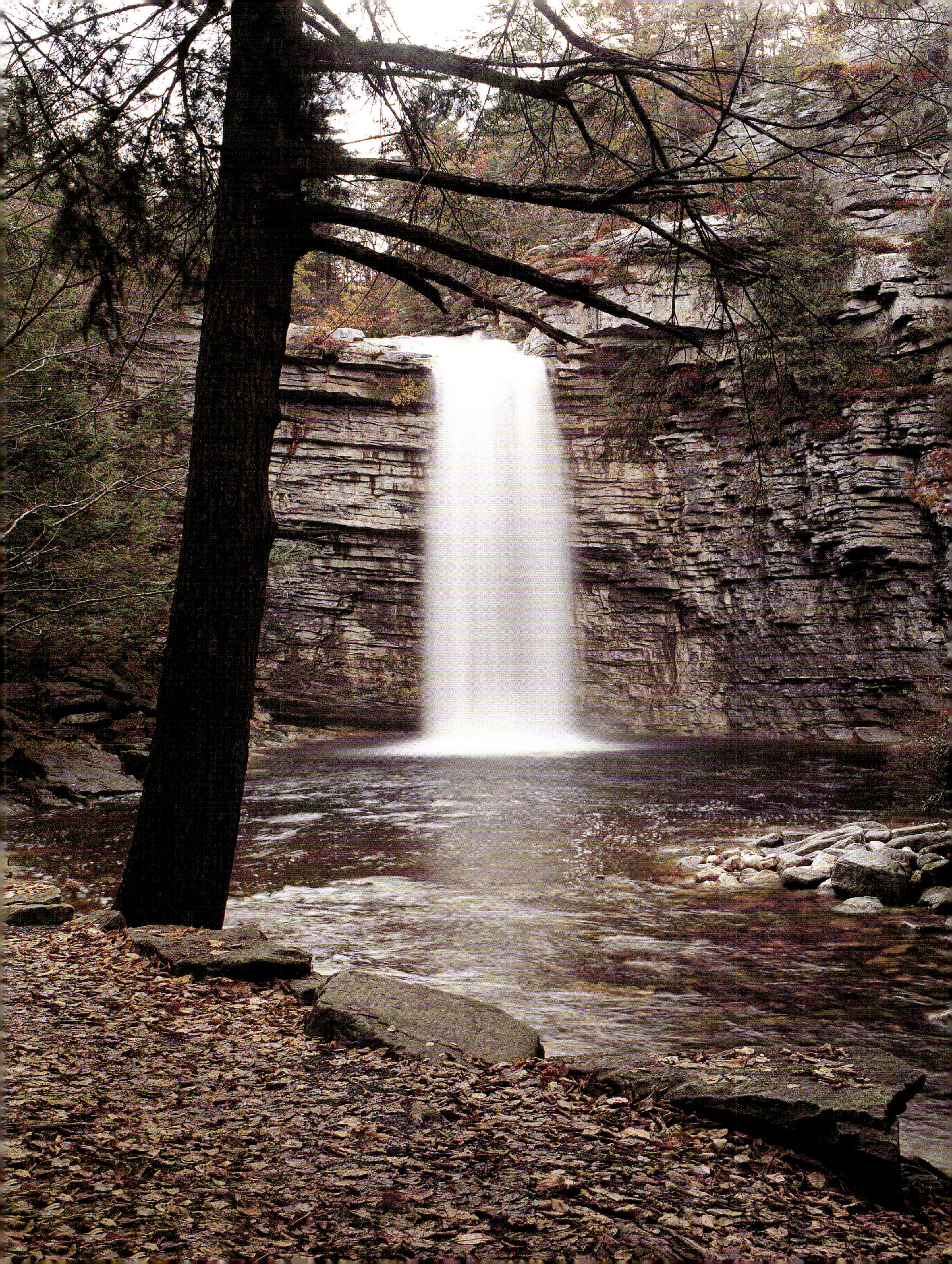

BACKYARD WATERFALL

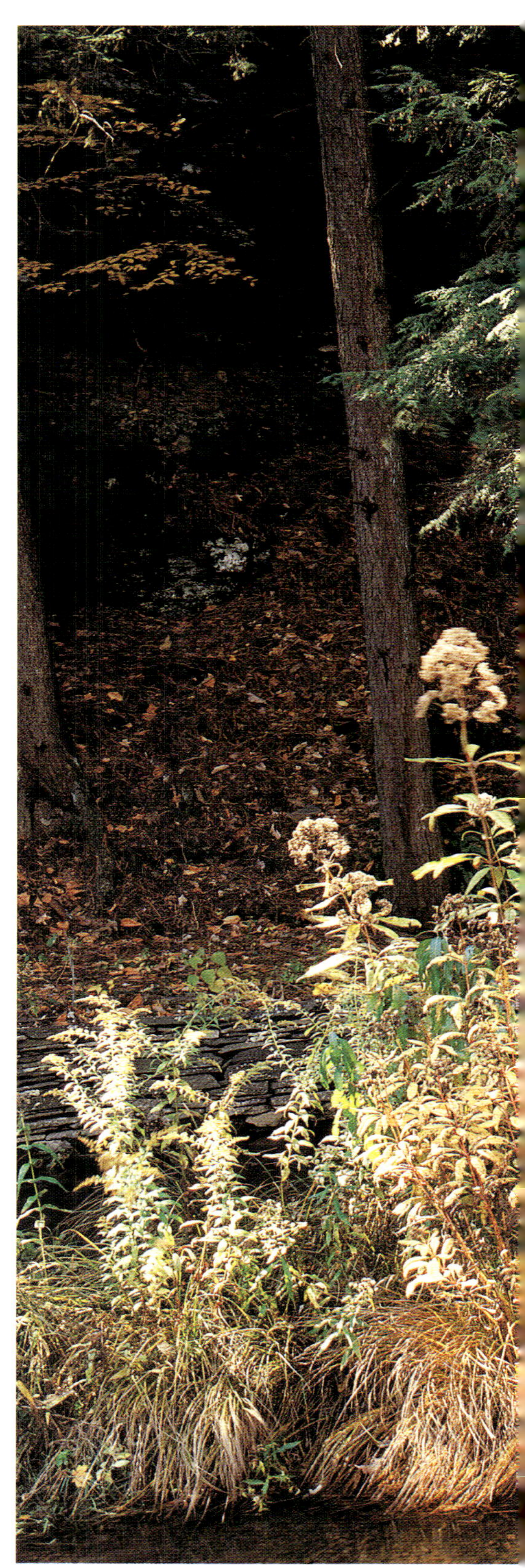

WHAT'S IT like to have a waterfall in your backyard? To part the curtain at sunrise, and watch the bedrock running its comb through the stream? To settle your head upon the pillow, snap out the light, and listen to the water stroking and murmuring on rock throughout the night?

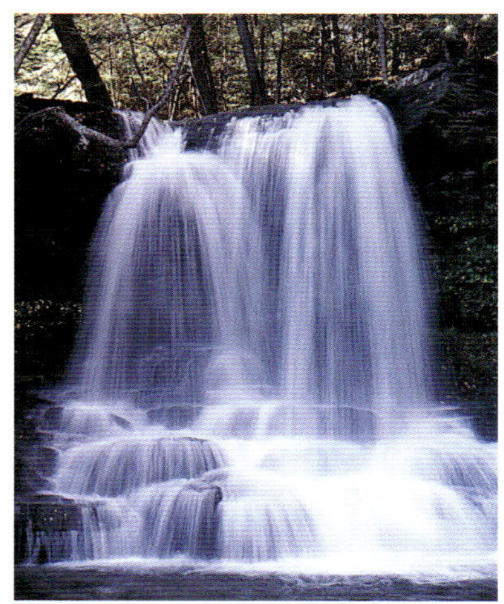

For three seasons, the motion and sound never stop. Do you tire of the incessant hiss, close the window and wrap the pillow around your head? Do you weary of the constant brushing of water against stone and pull the curtains closed?

Can the beauty we seek for a moment weigh on those who possess it for a lifetime?

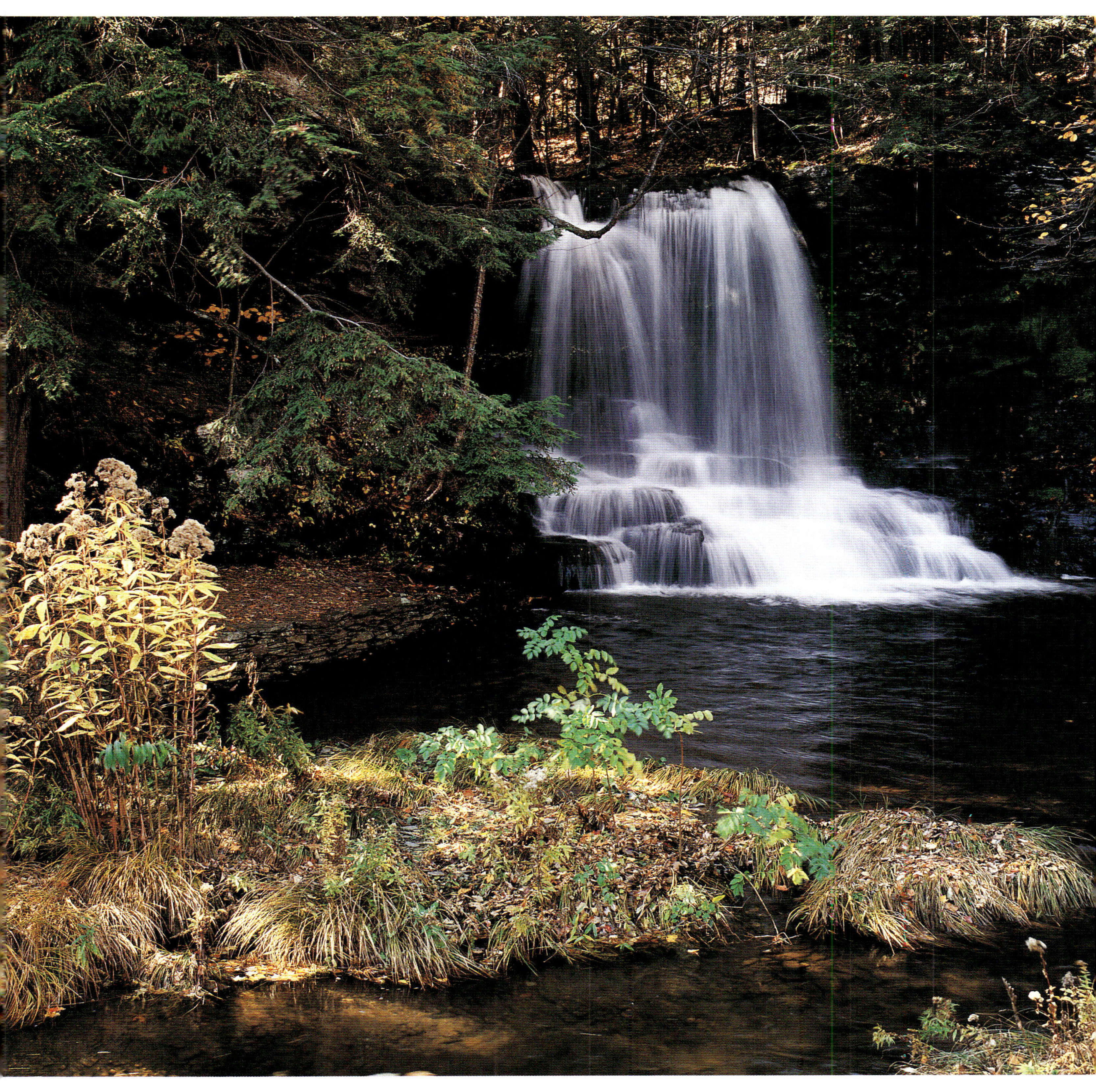

BASTION FALLS

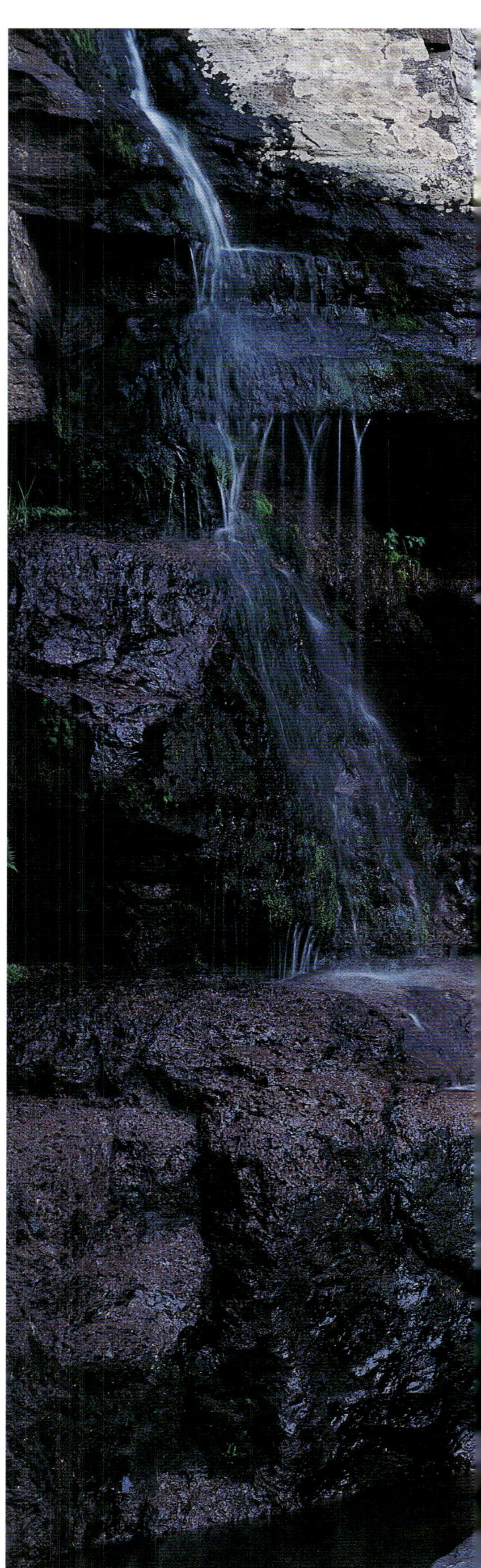

WHAT IS THE spiritual attraction of a waterfall? Time and again in our photographic travels, we come across people absorbing a waterfall's aura.

Could it be physiological? A chemical reaction in a person initiated by the moving water? After all, only a few years back scientists showed that vigorous exercise releases endorphins, a natural opiate that stimulates the brain.

It's been suggested that falling water creates an abundance of ions that makes us feel happy—the same sort that malls release into their environments to keep shoppers feeling happy and ready to buy.

But it's more than a chemical reaction. It's a feeling of change and movement, of freedom, of breaking loose from the physical and social constraints that have bound us for all our lives. A leaping waterfall liberates us, unzips our skin so, in spirit, out we tumble to frolic in the splashing water.

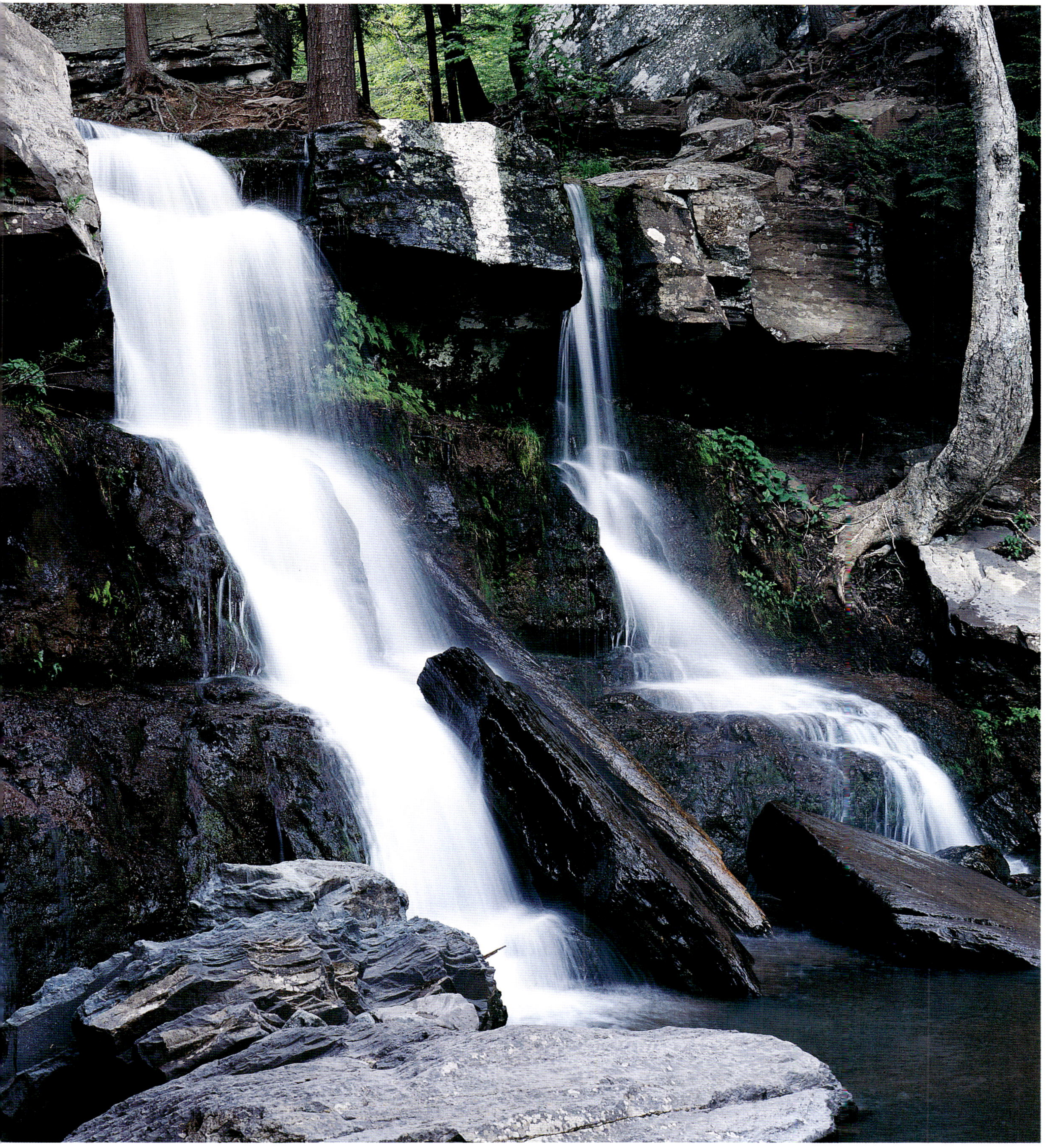

BUTTERMILK FALLS

THE WATERFALL before you is a paradox. All waterfalls share the same paradox. They move constantly without ever moving. Just look. The waterfall is here, in a fixed location.

The water always falls here for here is where the water falls. Too much time among the waterfalls and away from people? Maybe. But look. Miles upstream, the water slides over rocks, making its approach. Takes its good old time before it reaches the waterfall, spills over the brink, splashes into the pool, swirls around a bit, then slips downstream to glide eventually into the ocean. From there, who knows if it will ever find its way again to this exact spot where rock turns vertical and water falls over it, never to be seen again.

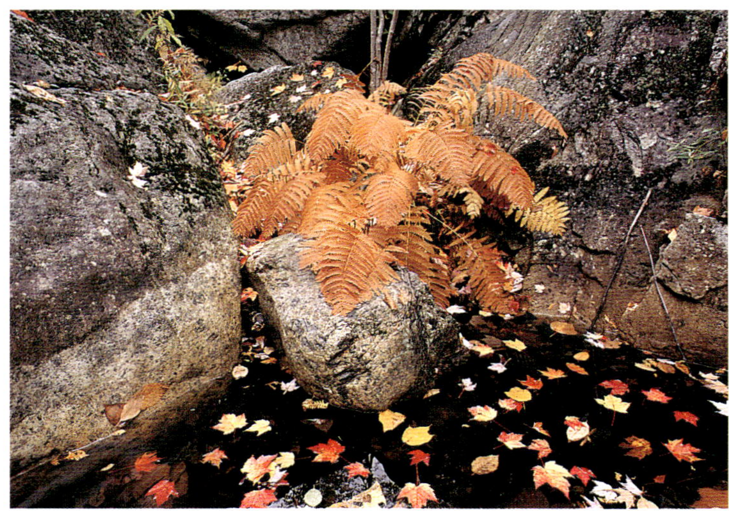

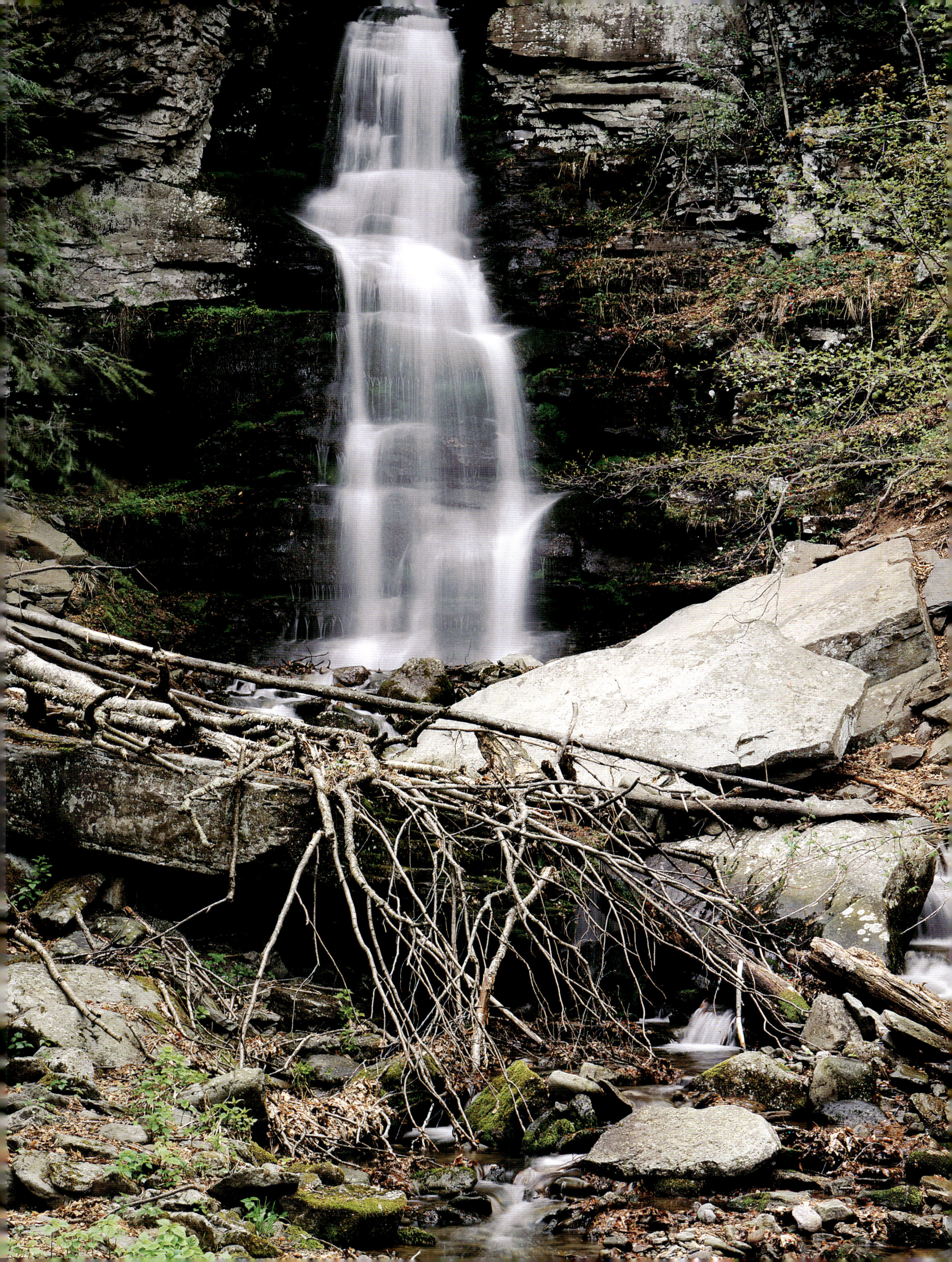

DOG'S HOLE

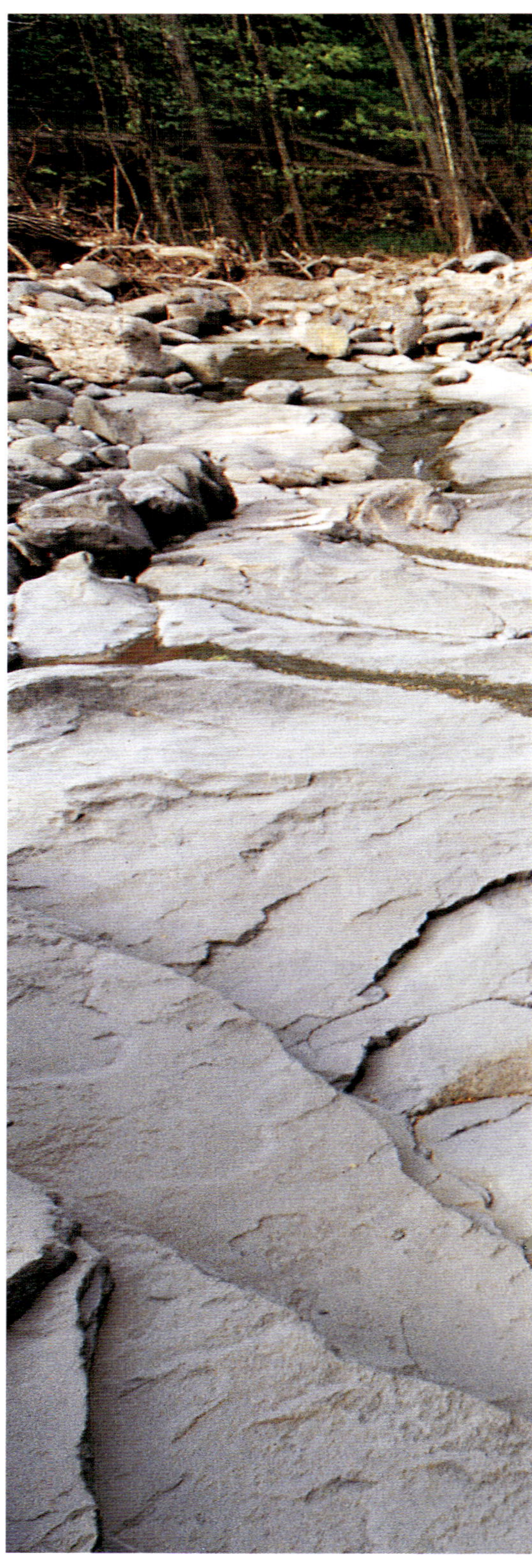

IN THE modern world, doing things faster has become a mantra. Products like desktop computers are improved so that their performance doubles every eighteen months while their prices halve. Packages fly across the country for next-day delivery. Microwave ovens reduce cooking from hours to minutes; e-mail zips around the world before airmail even leaves the ground.

Rocks, however, continue the old ways. Their cycles remain unchanged. No managerial edict, no customer demand will shorten the time it takes to make (or break) a rock. A rock is a simple object. No electronic circuits or synthetic genes. It lacks the features and benefits required by a marketplace. It is born of natural forces. Always, it finds its way deep into the earth, where heat and pressure mold it. Always, it works back to the surface, where heat, cold, water, ice, and chemicals fragment it. Always, it reveals our origin and existence.

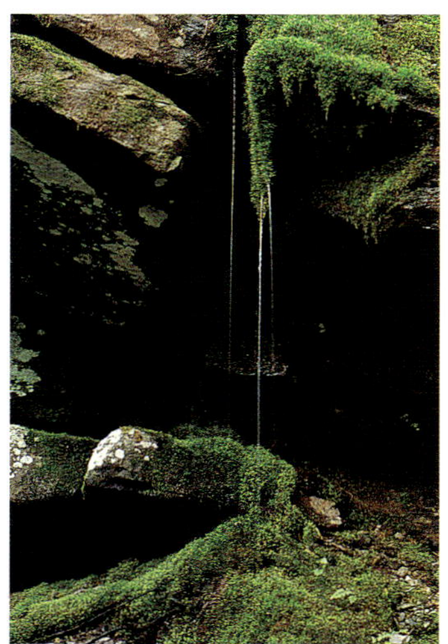

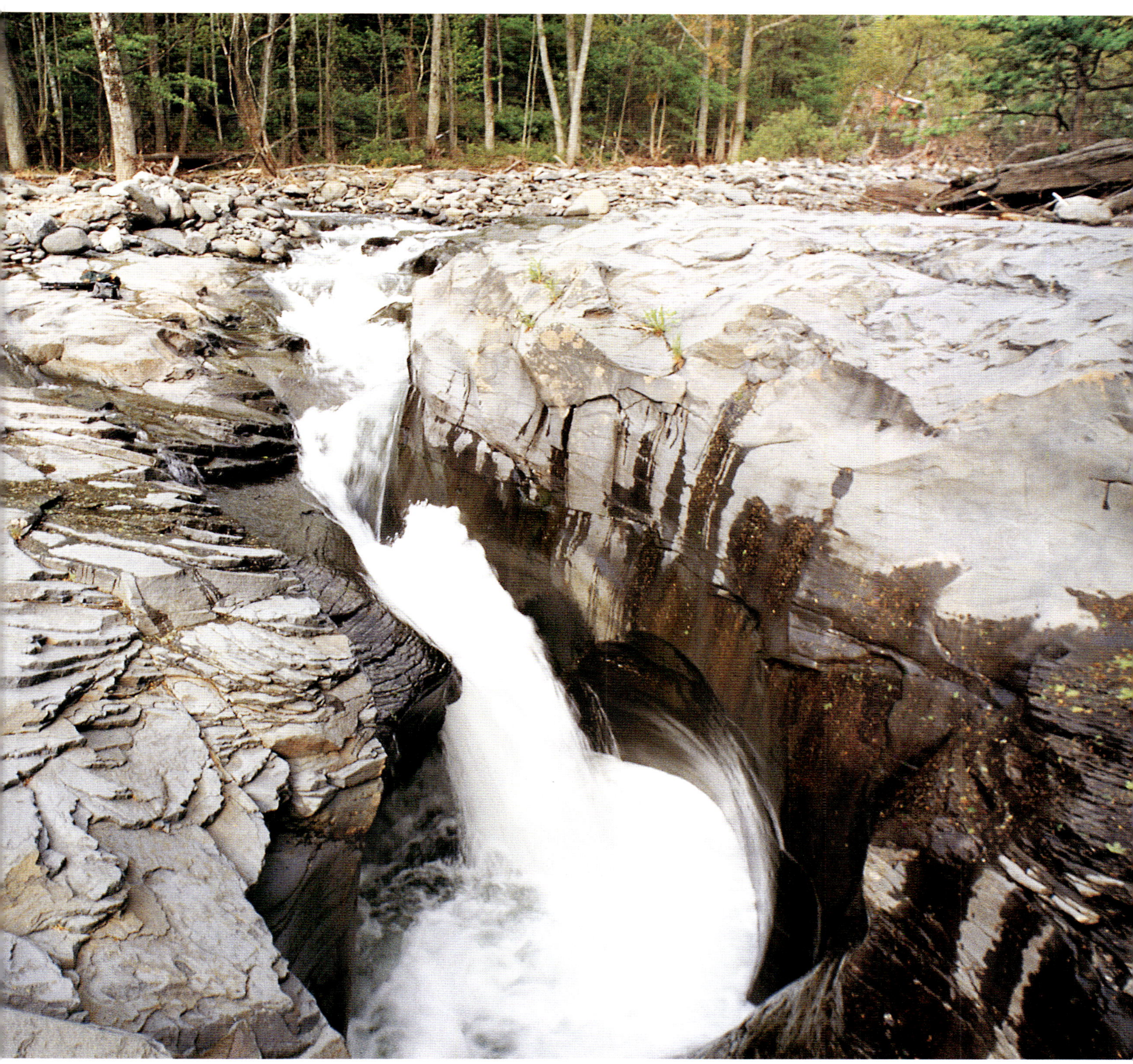

FAWN'S LEAP

NOWHERE is it more obvious than at a waterfall that the mountains are being torn down. See for yourself. Debris from the mountain clogs the stream.

The stream is dismantling the mountain. Streams break it apart pebble by pebble, boulder by boulder. Indeed, geologically speaking, the Catskills are not mountains. Not even hills.

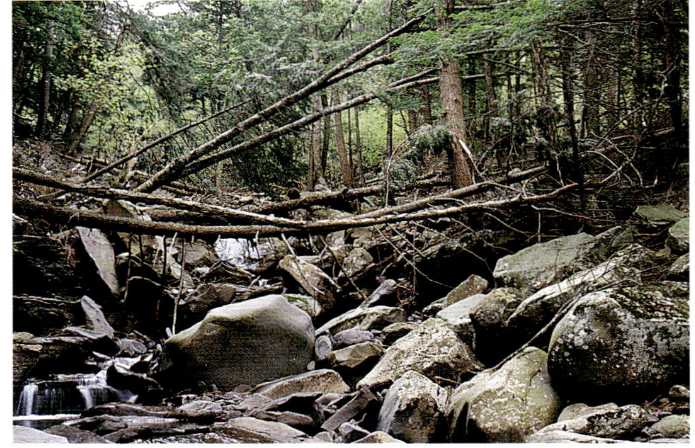

You might say the Catskills are valleys. Better yet, they are a plateau that, eons ago, felt warm gentle streams trickling across its back. But the climate changed and several glaciers plowed through those streams. The glaciers melted into huge lakes from which erupted flooding streams that ripped deep into the plateau. When the melting and flooding subsided, the ordinary streams, like those of today, formed and continued scraping deeper into the earth. Valleys and narrow ravines called cloves resulted.

Where there are valleys and cloves, there are mountains, mountains which, even while they are losing altitude to erosion, are growing higher because their valleys are deepening. Thus the Catskill Mountains might more appropriately be thought of as the Catskill Valleys.

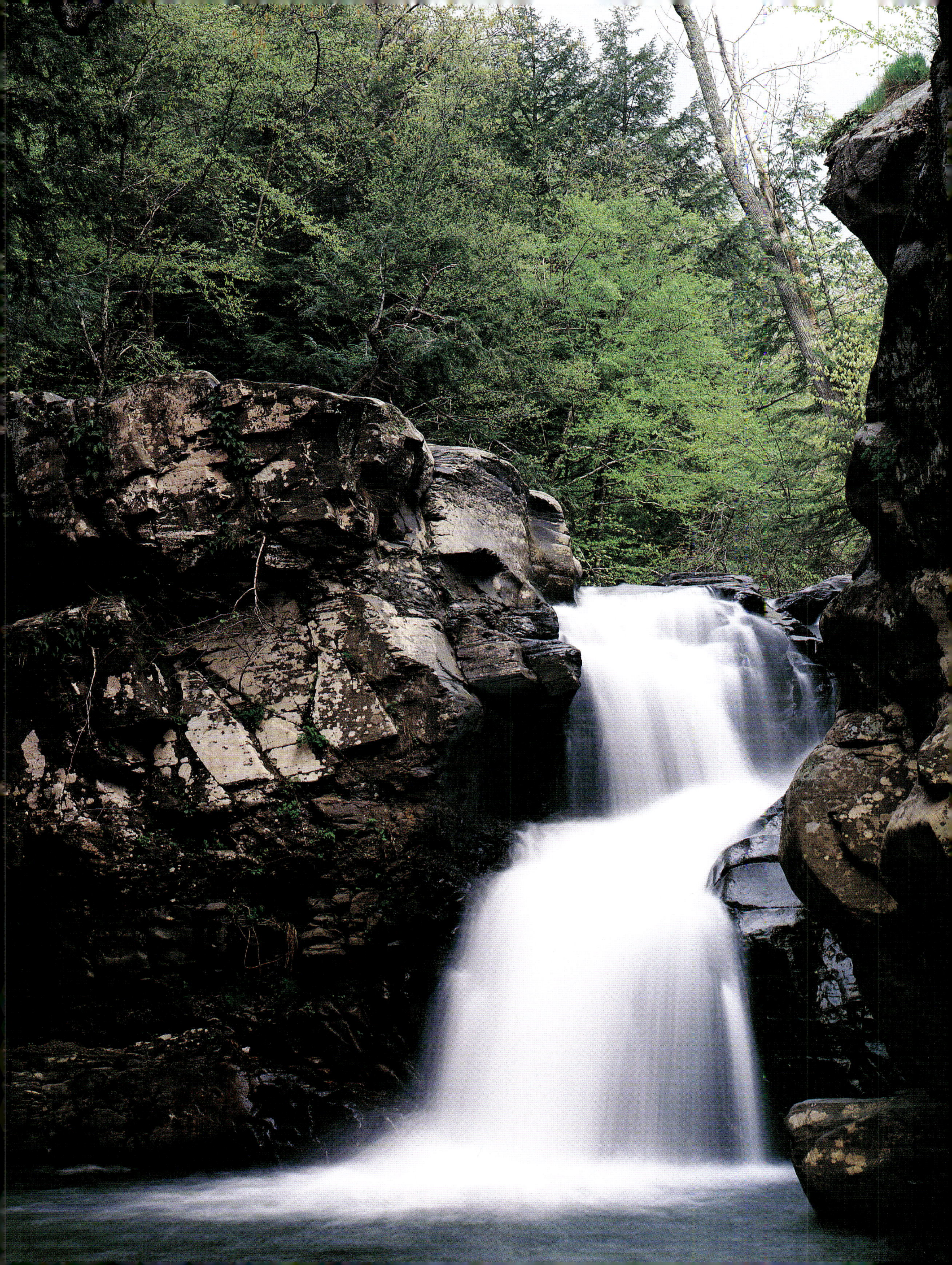

FERNDALE FALLS

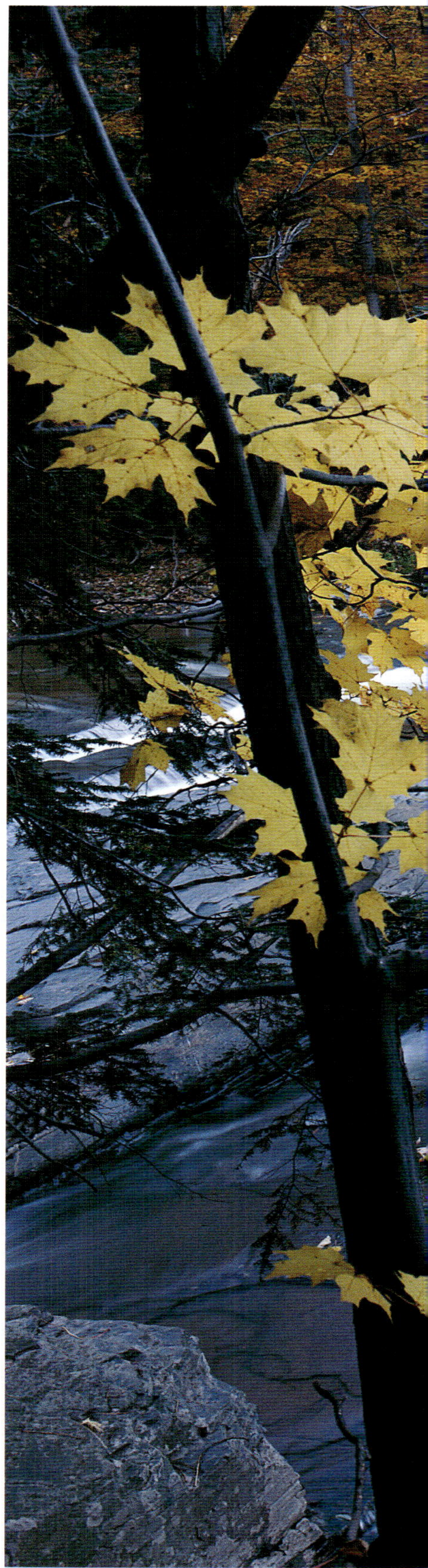

ALL IT TAKES is a spring melt or a few inches of summer rain. Then they're everywhere—the seasonal streams, the temporary waterfalls. They appear and disappear within hours, leaving behind only a ditch of damp rocks.

From a distance, they're all but invisible. From nearby, they're not impressive, hardly more than a roll of paper towels that has unraveled and rolled downhill. But their role is important. They are the beginnings of a watershed.

They are the first source of water collection on the mountain. Their own micro-watershed may be less than a square mile, but like branches of a tree, they connect into ever bigger brooks, then into streams, and then into rivers. By the time the summer rain that fell on a Catskill mountain drains into the Hudson or the Susquehanna rivers, the original streamlet will have dried up. But the water is still there.

Beneath the dried-up stream, below the soils, inside the mountain, lies the bulk of our fresh water. Although ponds, streams, rivers, and lakes offer tangible evidence of large amounts of fresh water, by far the largest amount, some 97 percent, intangible and invisible, lies below our feet as groundwater.

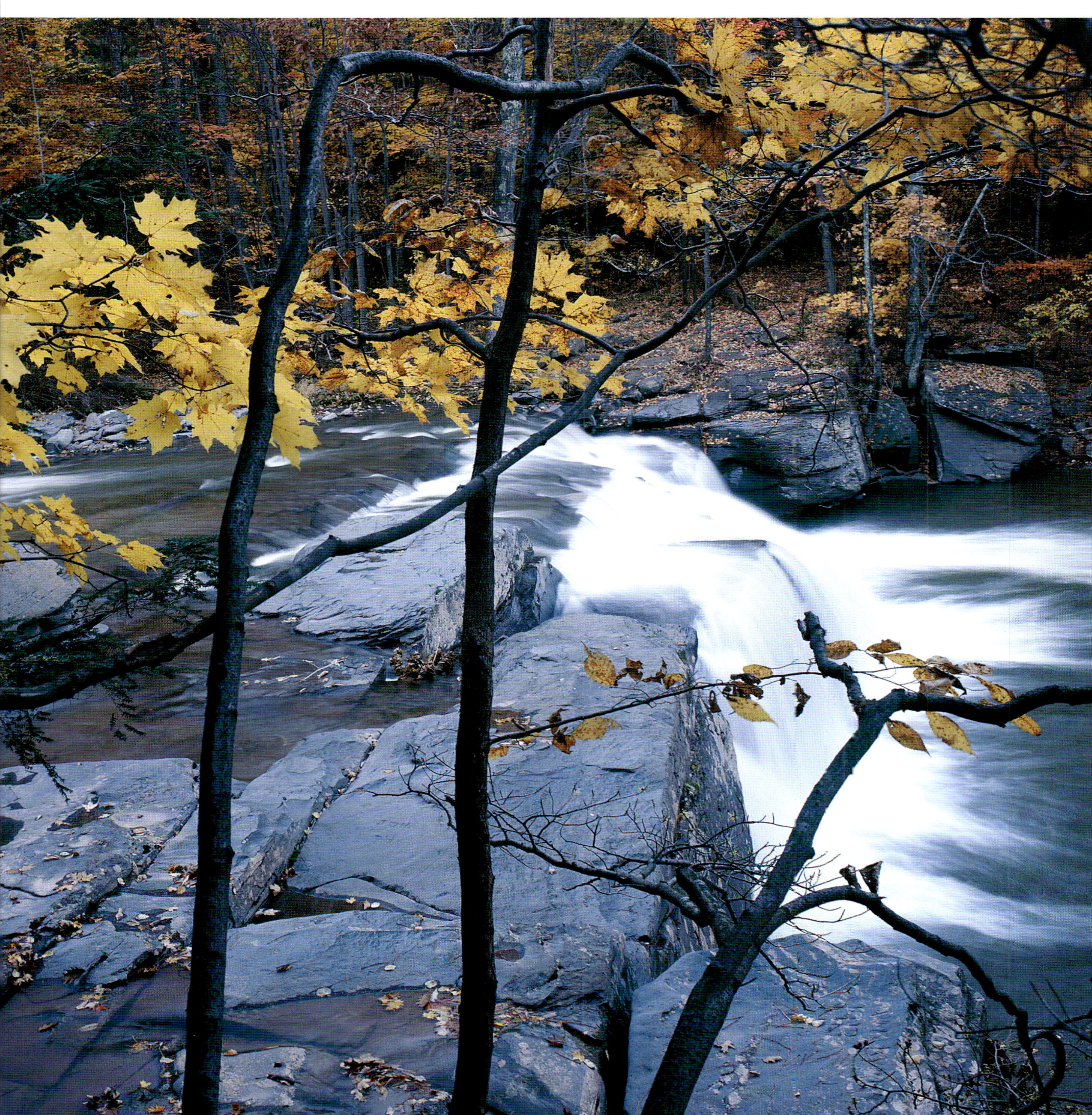

FROST VALLEY CASCADE

THE LOVELIEST waterfall you will ever see is probably not in this book or in any book. It will be a happy coincidence of season, light, viewpoint, and you.

It may cascade next to a highway as this one did. It may dry up in summer. It may appeal to you because of a certain twist in its course or because it slips off an overhanging rock which allows room underneath to stick your head and view the world through the distortions of falling water. It may be the music the falling water creates as it strikes up vibrations in an unstable stone. The water may shimmer a particular way, or reflect a certain delicate color, or drop and fan out in an appealing geometry.

It won't be the biggest waterfall. It won't be the prettiest waterfall. But for you, if you keep your eyes open, it will be the most attractive waterfall. It will be your waterfall.

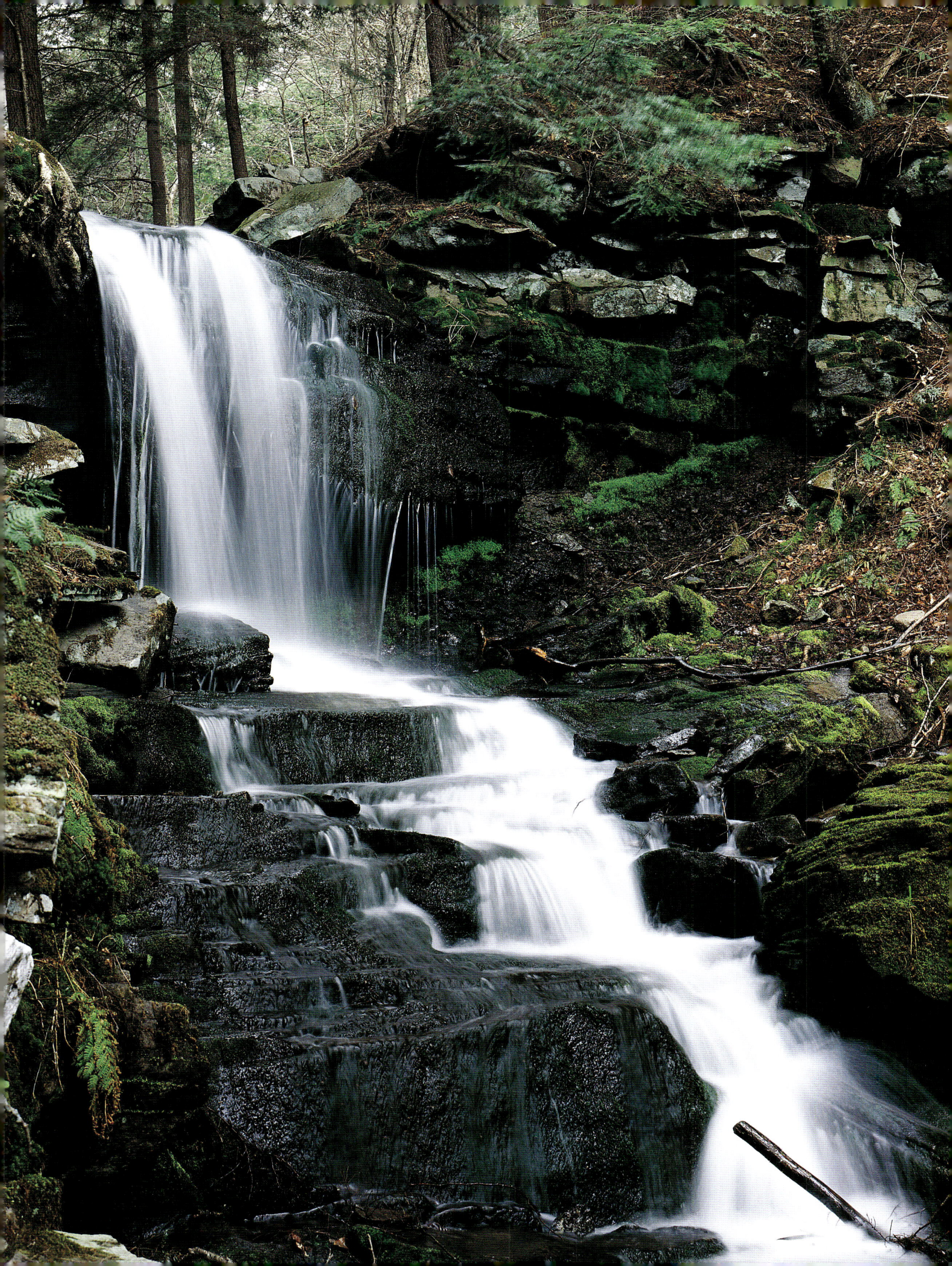

GLEN FALLS

YOU FIND waterfalls in the wilderness. You find waterfalls in cities, in villages, and in state parks. You find them in private preserves and on private property. You find them in local parks.

You find waterfalls next to the road. You find them next to the path (five miles from any roads). You may not find waterfalls if no one has cut a path to them (although they're still there). You find them next to power plants. You find them next to houses and in campgrounds. You find them beside hotels, restaurants, and bed-and-breakfast inns.

You find waterfalls in tourist attractions and by hidden roadside pullovers. You find waterfalls in calendars, tourist brochures, and advertisements.

Waterfalls have a way of making themselves known. They have drawing power—the power of beauty, the power of the dollar, whether derived from the tourist or the electron. Fishermen like waterfalls because they rejuvenate the stream (and fish) with oxygen; hikers like them because they provide a sense of destination, and are refreshing. Waterfalls have a way of getting themselves found.

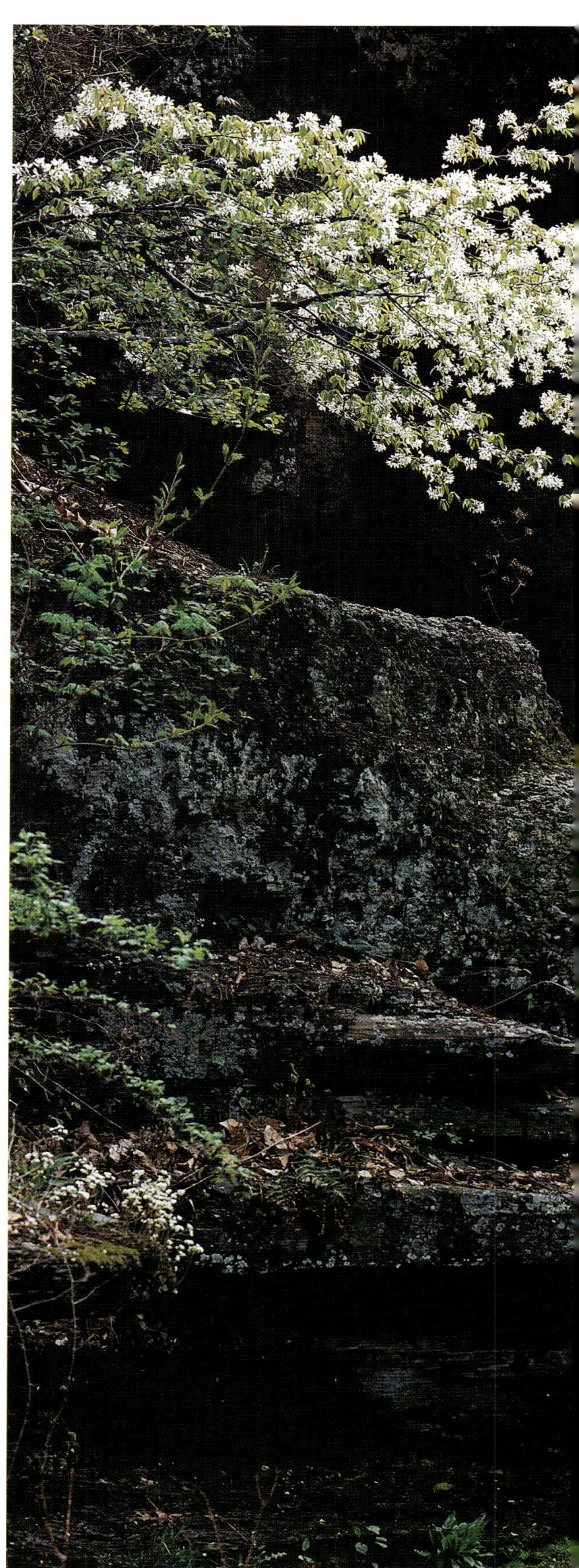

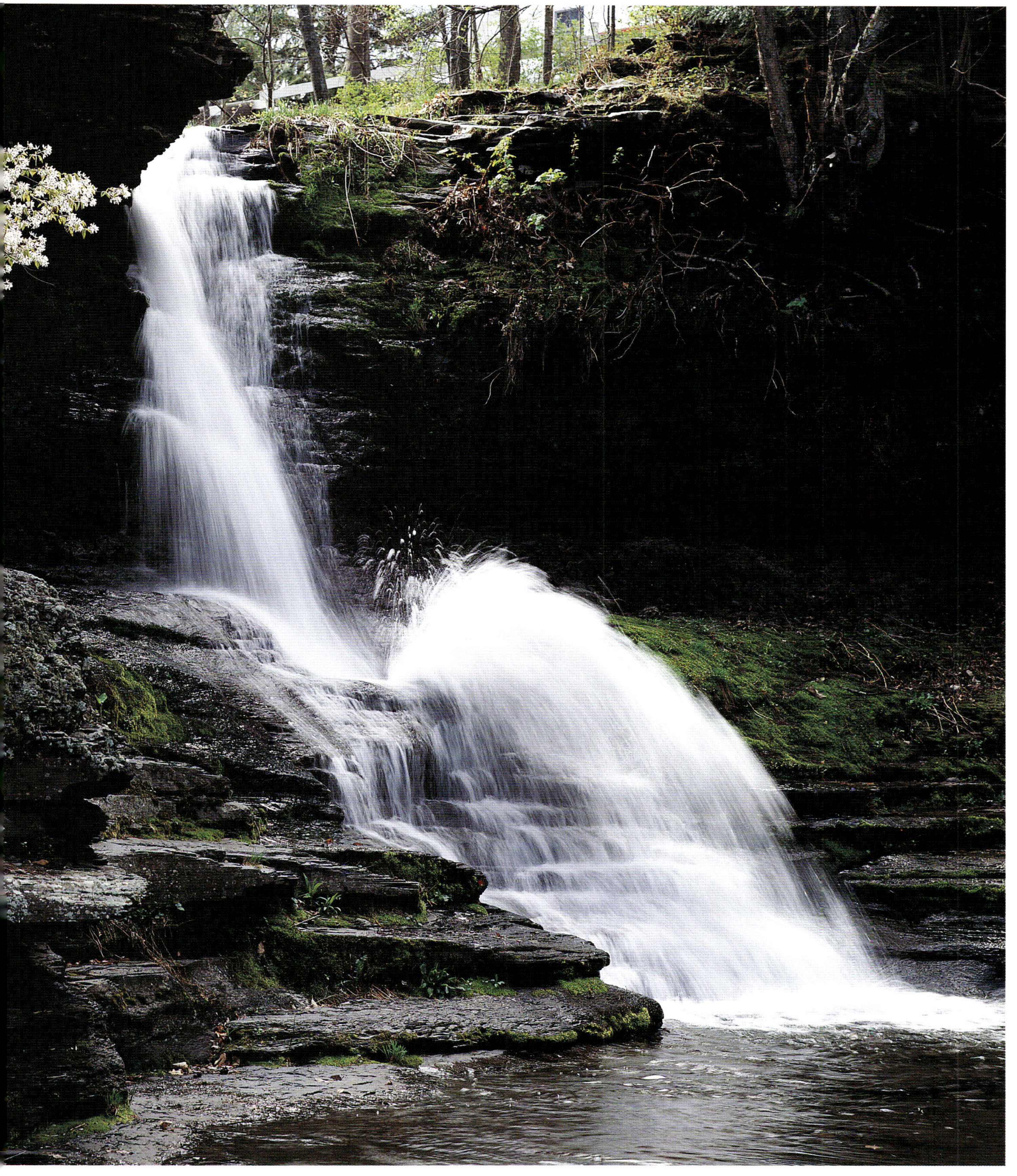

HIGH FALLS

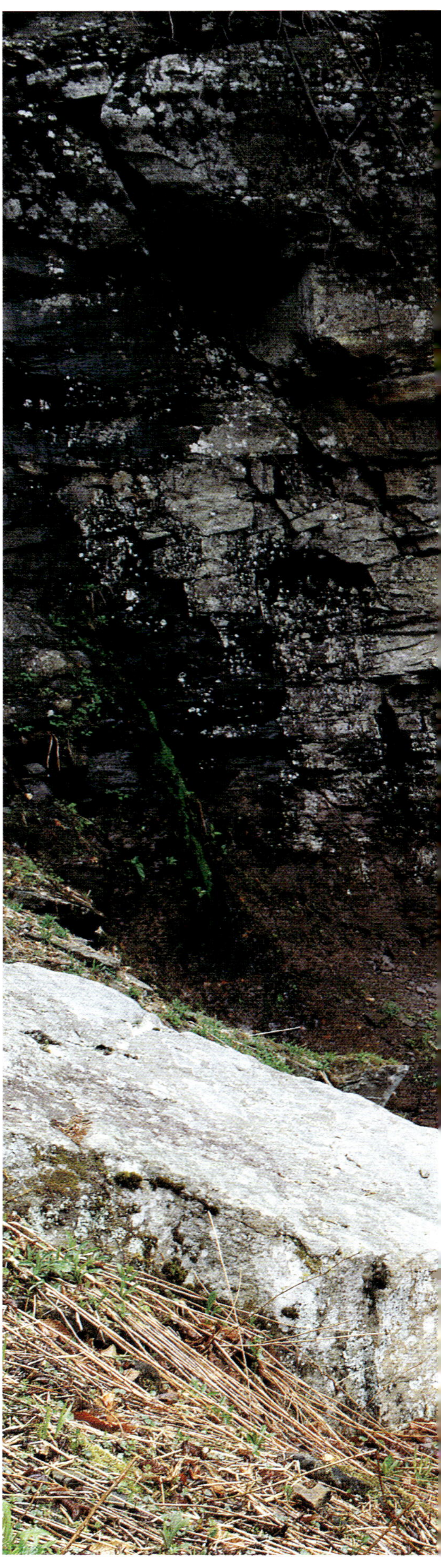

OBSERVING falling water can be a pleasant pastime. High Falls makes for excellent observation. The short hike to it leads to a viewing platform where you can sit and observe. At the top, out of your view, as the brook reaches the brink of the falls, the underlying lip of rock peels back the water's skin freeing millions of sparkling crystals to tumble through the air in a kaleidoscope of patterns.

The patterns revealed by falling water depend on the underlying platform of rock. Multi-layered falls offer the crazy bounces of a pinball. Water shoots off in one direction only to ricochet in another. Strands of water streaming down a furrowed slope intertwine and collect into a ponytail, gushing off one shelf and landing on another where they explode in a white starburst against black rock. Deflections, redirections, disruptions, diversions, gatherings, and separations occur thousands of times in the few seconds it takes for a stream to negotiate its drop.

The patterns in sheets of water falling through the air are mesmerizing. Like autumn flocks of starlings, the water shifts in ever-changing formations. For a few seconds, its profile narrows and loops like a lariat dropping over a fleeing calf's head. Then it turns to expand into a sheet flapping on a clothesline.

Eventually the tricks played by air resistance and falling water run out of cliff, and the water slips back into the sleeve of stream.

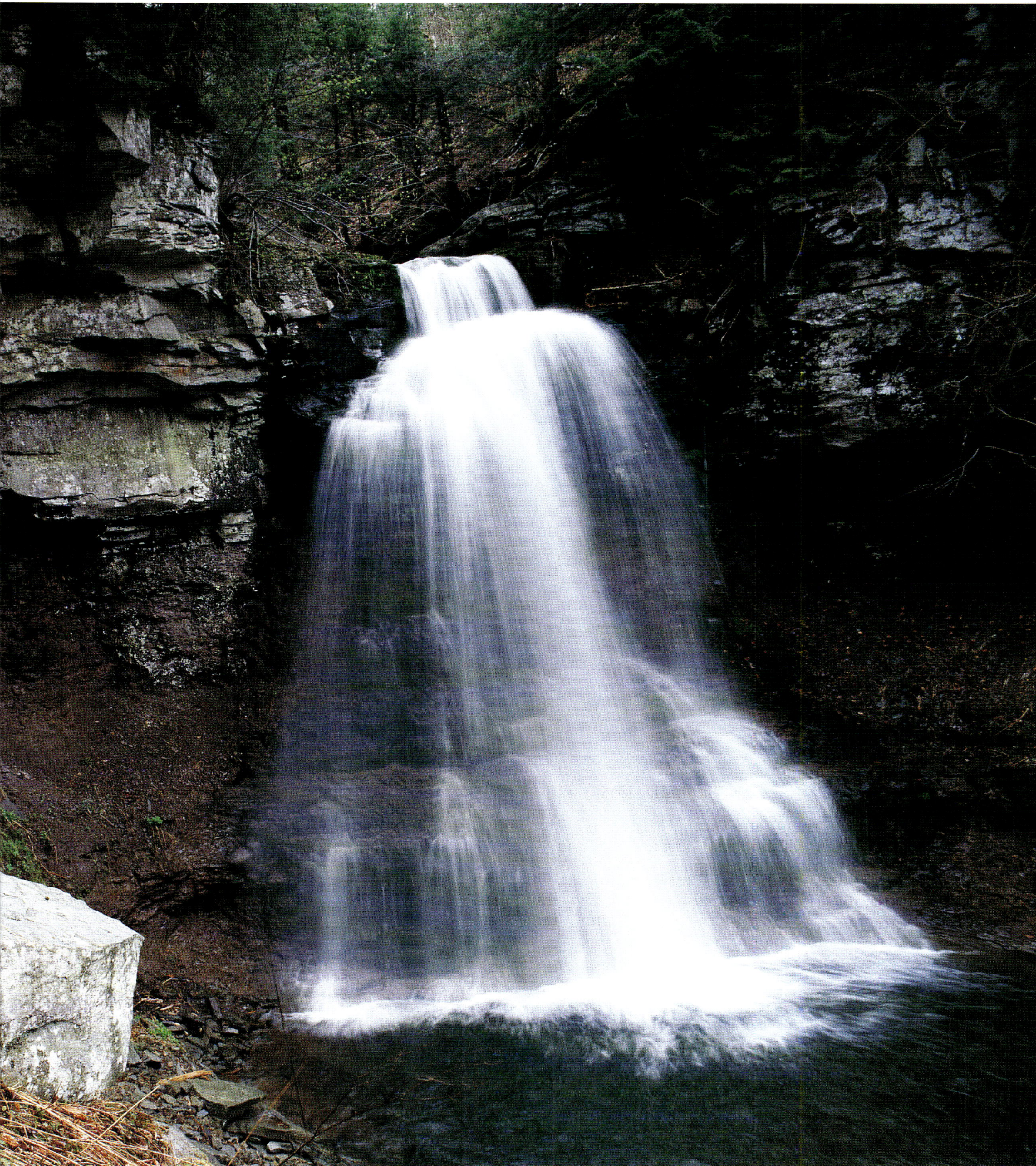

KAATERSKILL FALLS

THE NAME that most often springs to mind at the mention of the word "waterfall" is Niagara. Spectacular though it may be, Niagara Falls, ringed with paved pathways, encircled by throngs of tourists, buzzed by low-flying helicopters, and nipped at by mobbed boats, may not inspire those seeking a more personal experience.

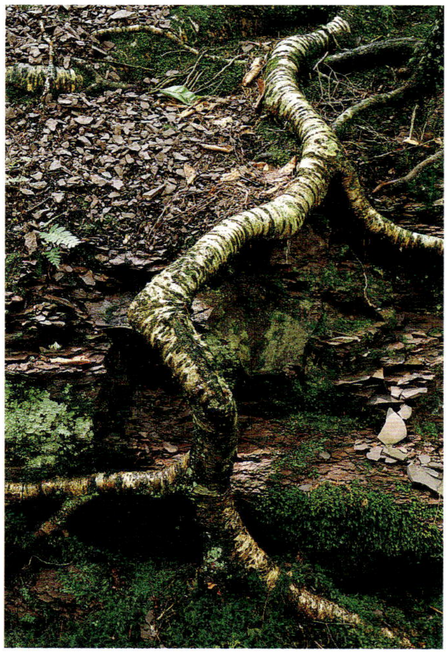

The best wilderness waterfall in New York State, perhaps in the East, the one that most evokes the essence of waterfall, is Kaaterskill Falls. A narrow ribbon of water that gleams in the sunshine and bends with the wind, drops 175 feet, as if from the sky. The lower falls drops 85 feet. It is not the tallest falls, nor the broadest, but its setting is the best.

Approaching from below, you first catch sight of it several hundred feet overhead, leaping from a cliff. The cliff forms a huge amphitheater that opens a large arc of sky in the forest canopy. The water quickly courses across a short landing, then takes a second smaller leap to spill at your feet amidst a jumble of car-size boulders and bent, broken, contorted trees wracked by winter's ice coatings.

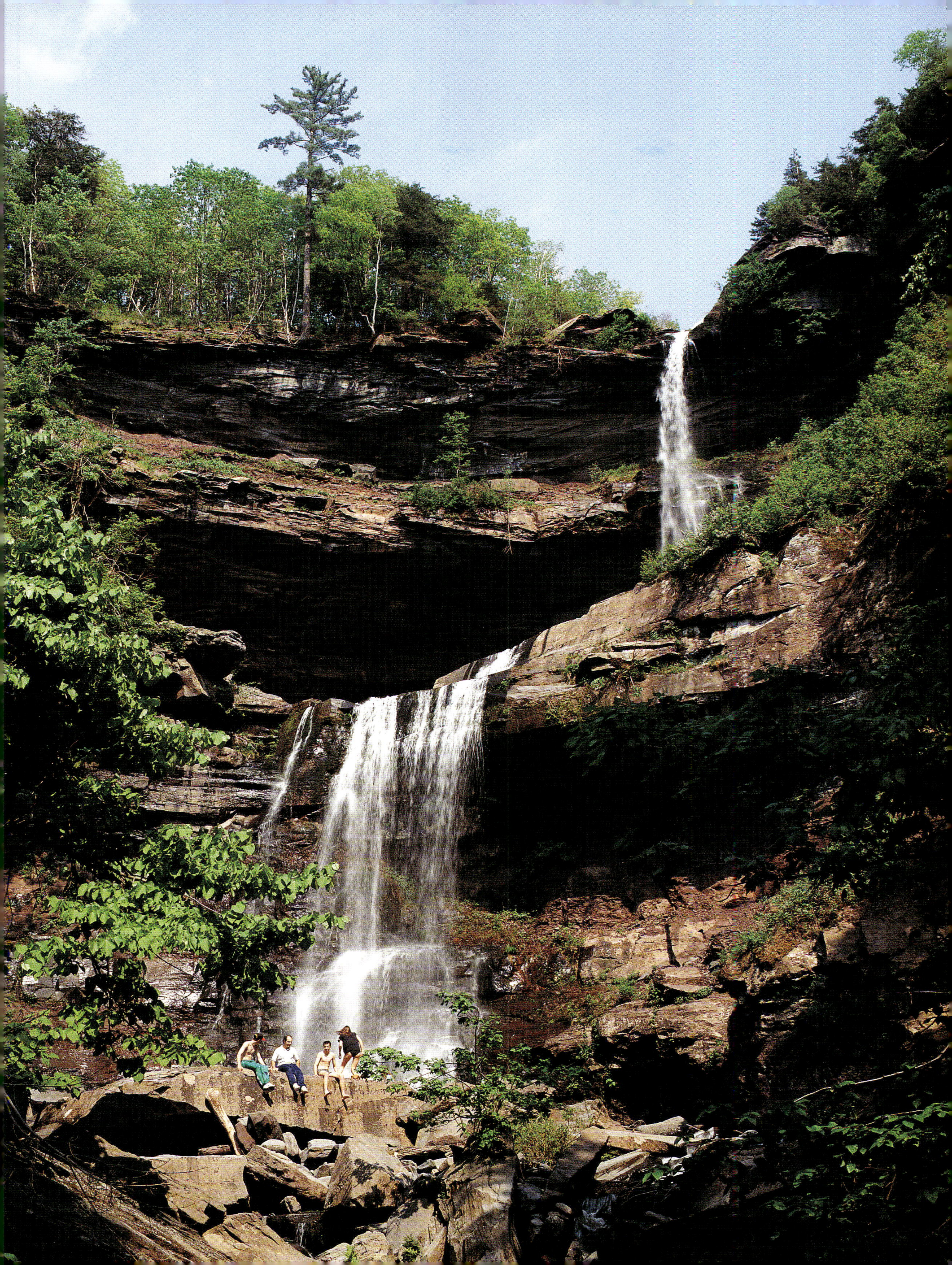

KAATERSKILL FALLS

KAATERSKILL FALLS has a past. It has been romanced by artists and entrepreneurs. Its greatest influence was during the nineteenth century when the site inspired Hudson River painters Thomas Cole and Frank Church to paint it repeatedly, romanticizing the Catskill wilderness surrounding it.

Winslow Homer and Thomas Nast, the political cartoonist, also found inspiration in the mountains. Through the character Natty Bumpo, James Fenimore Cooper describes Kaaterskill in his novel *Pioneers*. Washington Irving sank Rip van Winkle in a great sleep nearby, perhaps close enough to be mesmerized by the sound of the falling water.

The proximity of the Catskill wilderness, with Kaaterskill Falls as a focal point, to the Hudson River and New York City attracted entrepreneurs. Some of them decimated natural resources, taking out entire hemlock stands just to use their bark in tanneries that processed hides from around the world. Others brought in people.

Starting in the 1820s, these developers built the grandest tourist hotels yet seen in America: the Mountain House, the Kaaterskill Hotel and, atop Kaaterskill Falls itself, the modest Laurel House. For a time, the falls were turned on and off like a kitchen faucet—on when a fee was paid, off when it wasn't. Even now, atop the falls, carved into the bedrock are dates and lovers' names going back well over a hundred years.

As trees became scarce and automobiles plentiful, the chic of Kaaterskill faded. The state purchased key properties, destroyed the decaying hotels, and returned the land to a nearly natural condition.

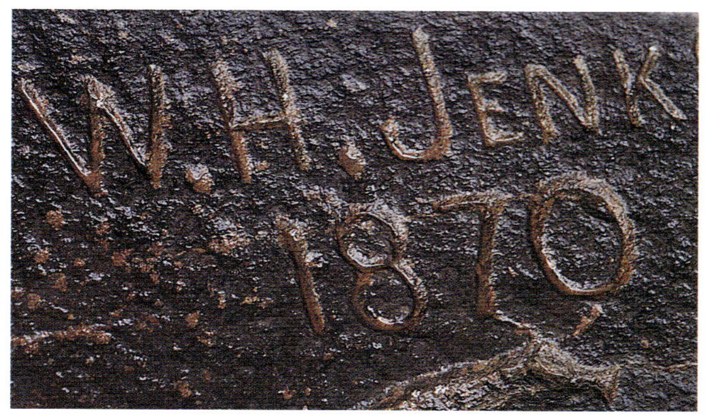

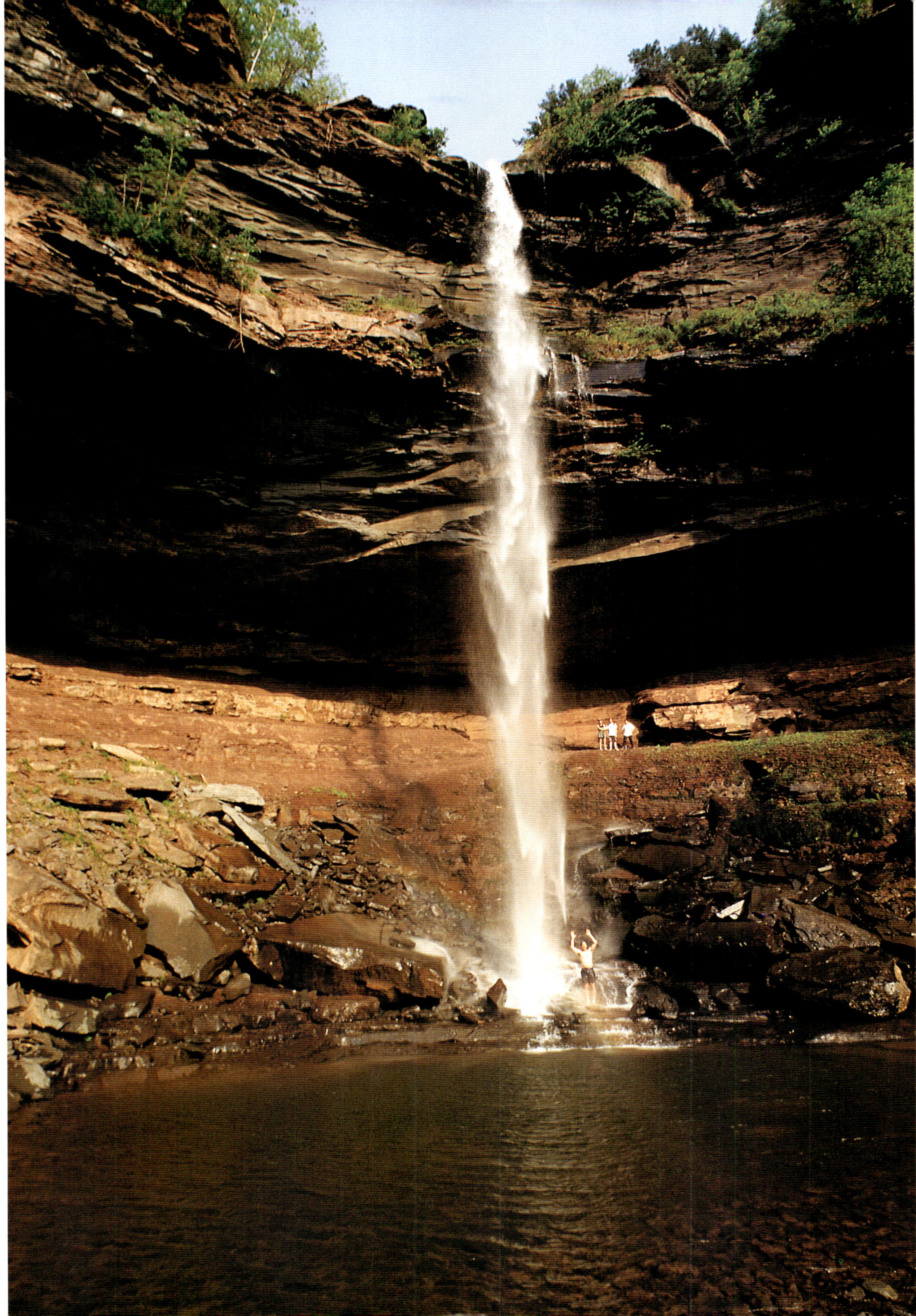

MANOR KILL FALLS

WITHOUT water, there are no waterfalls. Without water, there is no life. Our affinity for water is instinctual. Our dependence on it means survival.

Is it coincidence that the surface of our planet shows nearly three-fourths water and that, by percentage, our bodies contain only a few tablespoons less? Seen from outer space, our planet shimmers blue, the blue of water reflecting sky.

Though abundant and readily available in our lives, water offers unusual properties that make it the essence of life. Two atoms of hydrogen bond to one atom of oxygen in the shape of an isosceles triangle to make a molecule of water. As molecules go, water is small, reactive yet stable. So small, it often squeezes into tiny spaces, like sand at the beach. So reactive that, once near other molecules, it often joins them or modifies them. So stable, a significant amount of heat is necessary to vaporize it, and a similarly significant amount of cold to freeze it.

Our lives depend upon water, our bodies are built to manage it.

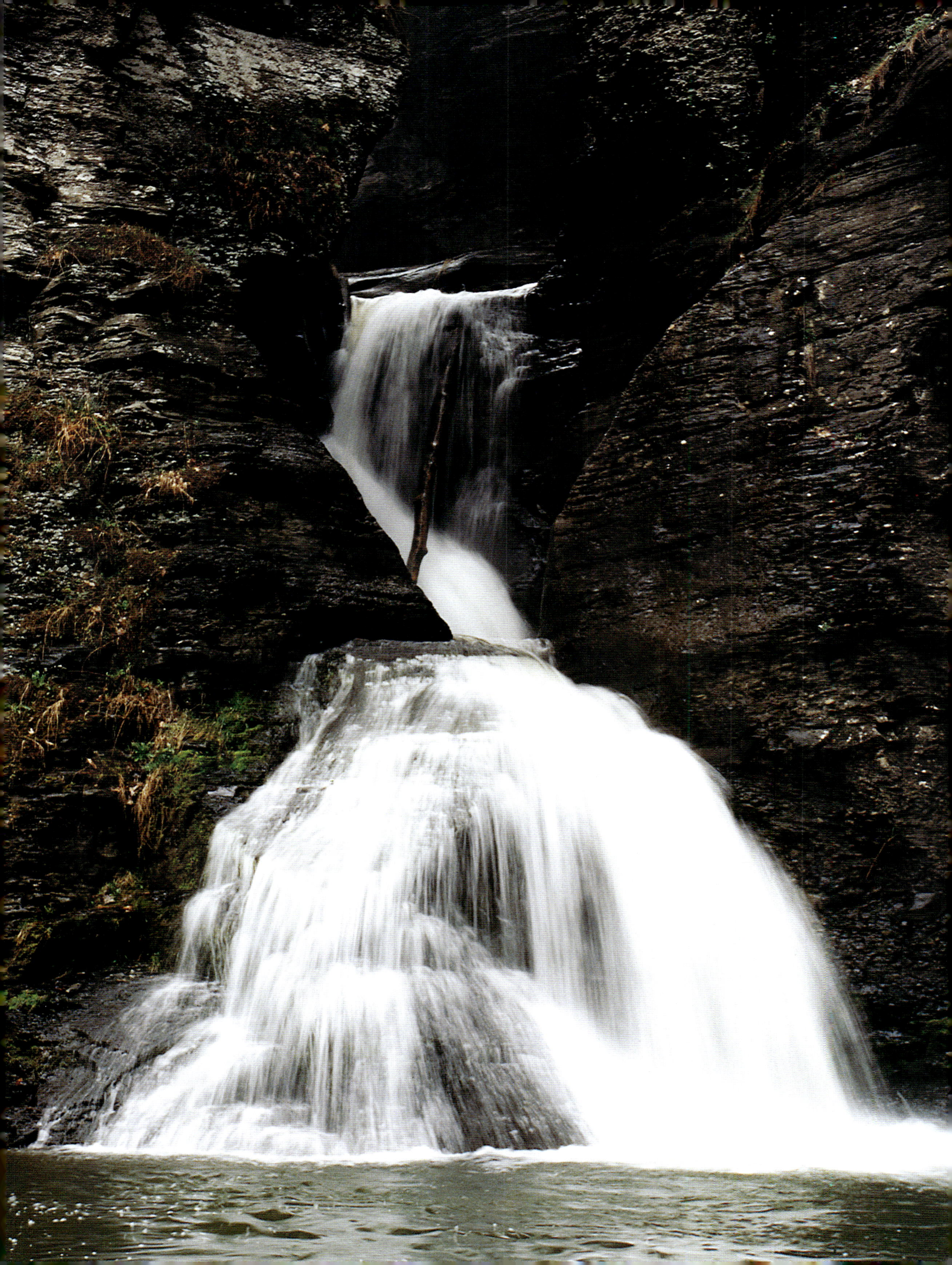

PLATTEKILL RD. TRIBUTARY

OVERNIGHT, clear skies pricked by starlight yield to rumpled sheets of gray. Dawn. A cold front. By midmorning the first drops of rain hit the ground. By noon, a steady drizzle. In the forest, the rain coats leaves with a sheen of moisture. The world shines. Some drops slip through the barrier of leaves and branches and strike the ground directly in a miniature explosion that sends dirt particles flying.

At first, the dry dirt readily absorbs the water. As the rain increases and the water soaks deeper into the soil, plant rootlets thinner than your hair greedily suck up the water.

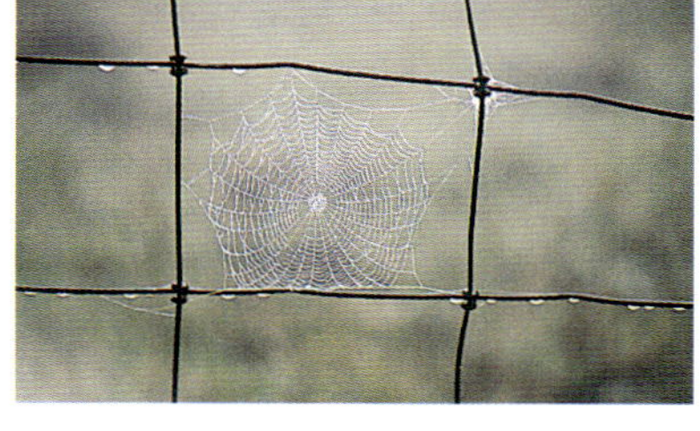

But the rain grows stronger. Water on leaves, branches, and rocks coalesces into rivulets. Gravity pulls them down to earth where they converge into streamlets still small enough for ants to ford. The streamlets converge again and again, ever rolling downhill to gather in ruts and runnels that lead to seasonal stream beds that feed into permanent creeklets that flow into creeks and rivers to regenerate waterfalls and our spirits.

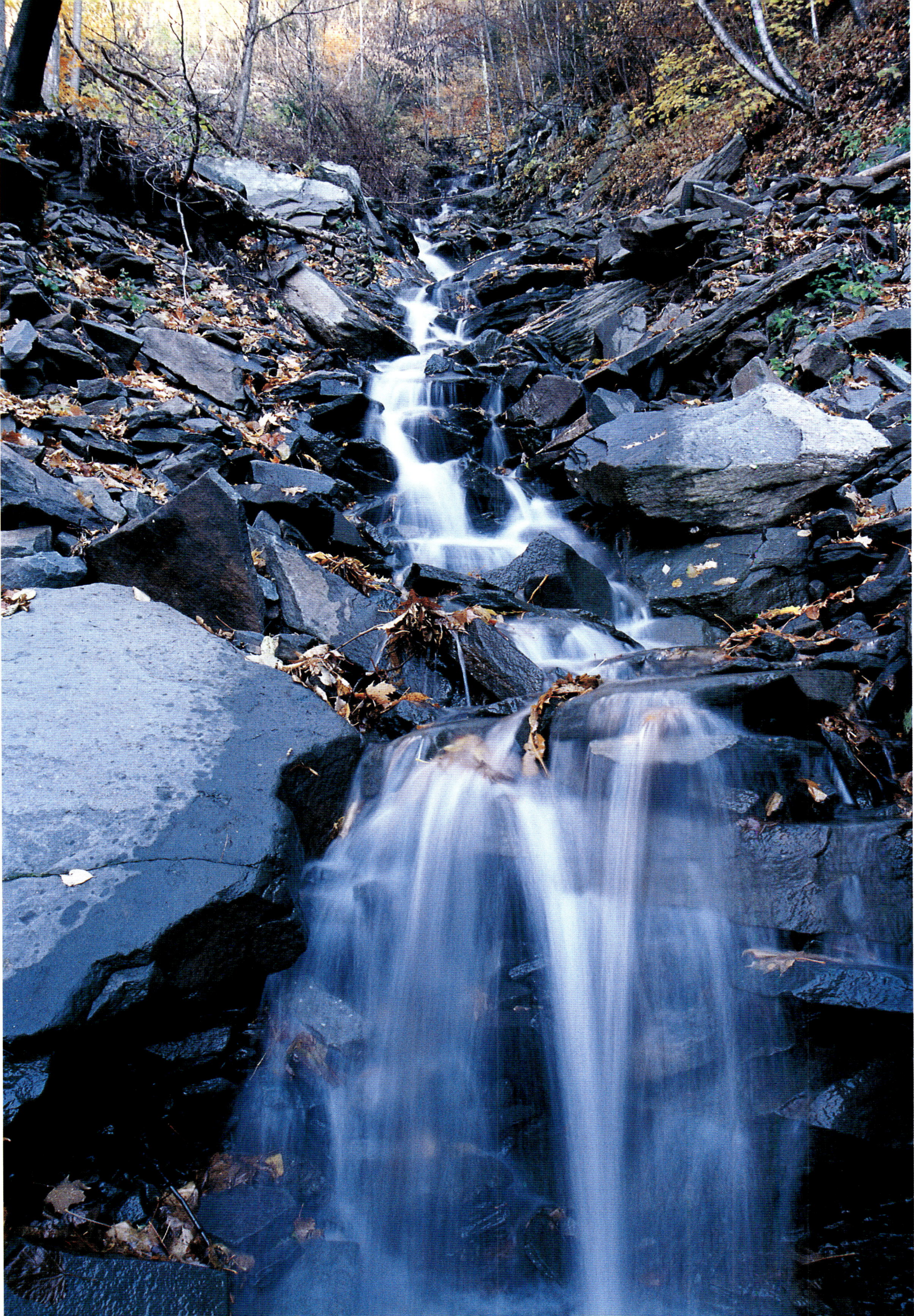

SAWMILL FALLS

HOW DO you photograph a waterfall? How can you capture the scent of pine, the numbing cold of spring water, the rushed whispers of entwining streams, the moist breath exhaled by moving water, the ankle-twisting rock jumbles? How can a photograph a few inches high and wide represent the overwhelming sensory experience of "waterfall"?

It can't. After photographing a few hundred waterfalls, you learn to adapt. You concentrate on that which is visual and that which is internal. Up close, the visual is water moving over rock, sparkling drops tumbling through the air, ribbons twisting through crevices. Back up a bit and the visual includes banks of rock and ferns, flowers dangling from cliff rims, wooded hills treed with cedars and maples. Incline your head upward and a swath of sky mirrors the path of the stream.

The falls' appearance depends on the light. The revelations of light manifest waterfalls in ways too myriad to describe. Your choice: take the light as you find it, wait, or return.

Conveying feelings in a photograph often exceeds one's skills. Unlike a painting, your choices of rendition are limited. You can move yourself but not elements of the scene. You can wait for the light but you can't revise it. If you make a photograph you like, you have succeeded.

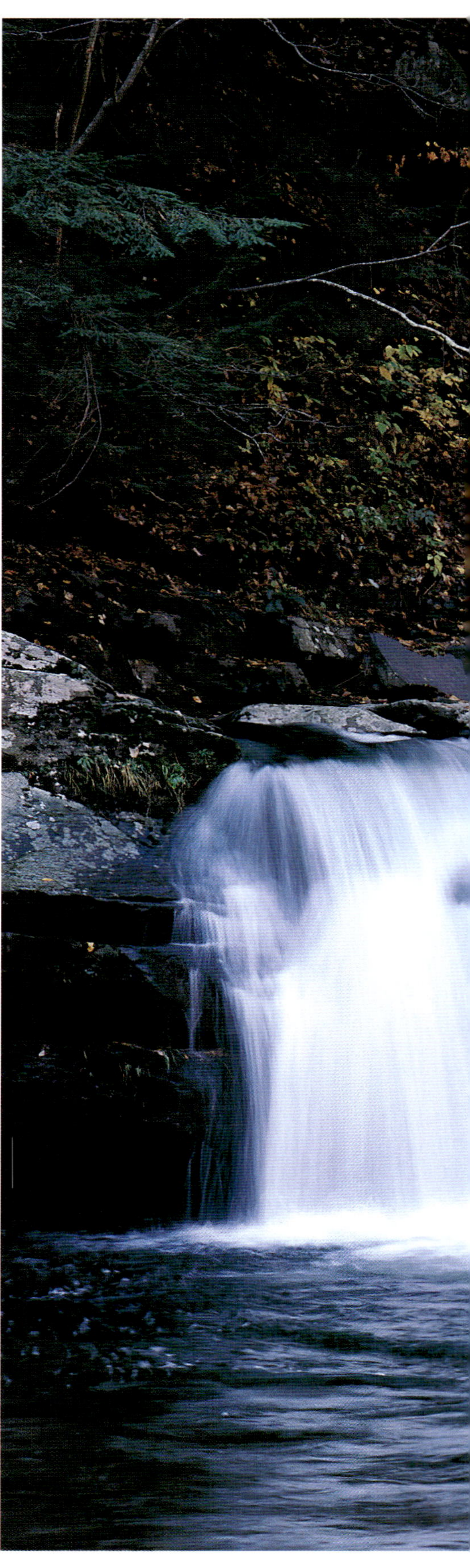

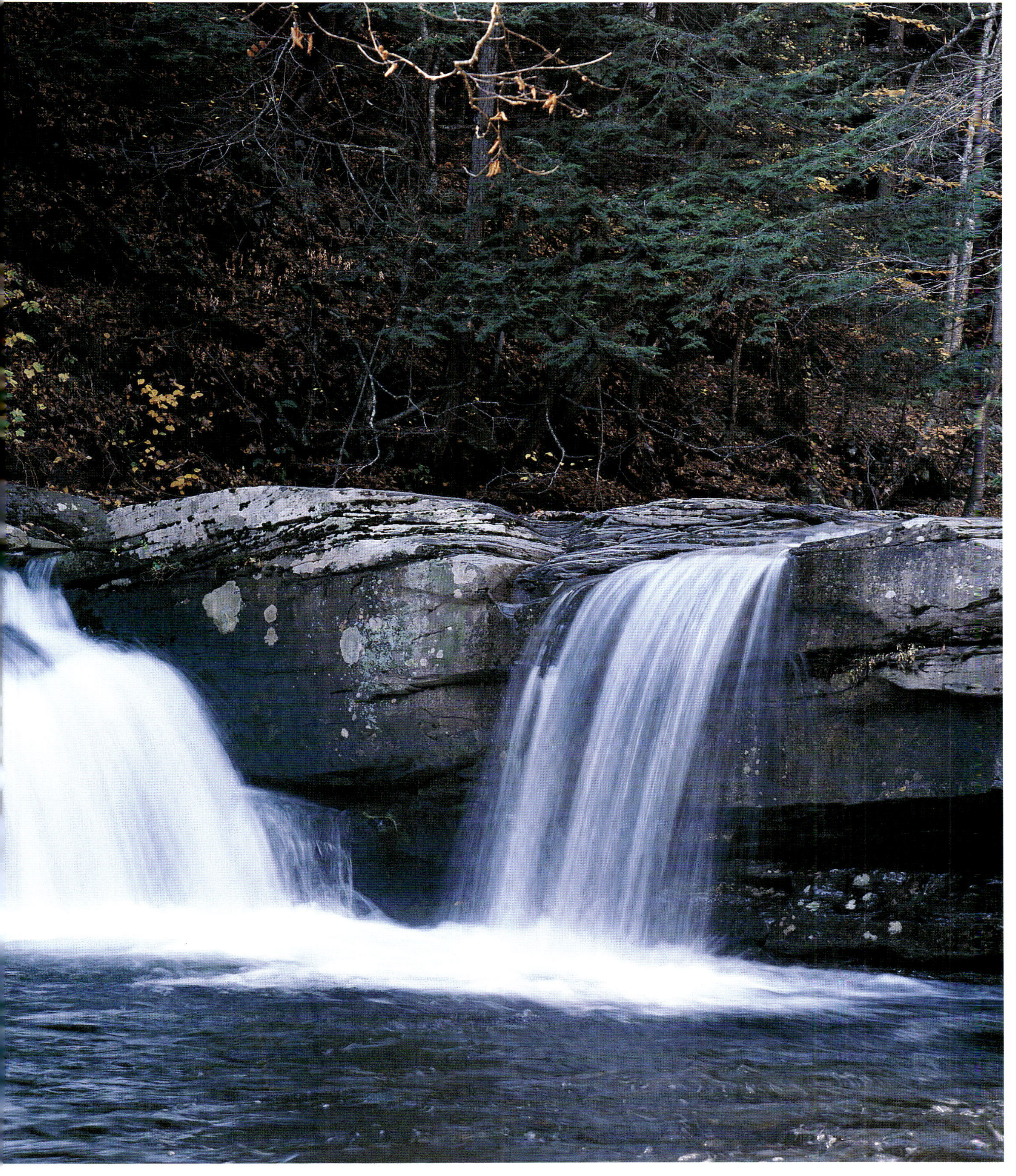

SHINGLEKILL FALLS

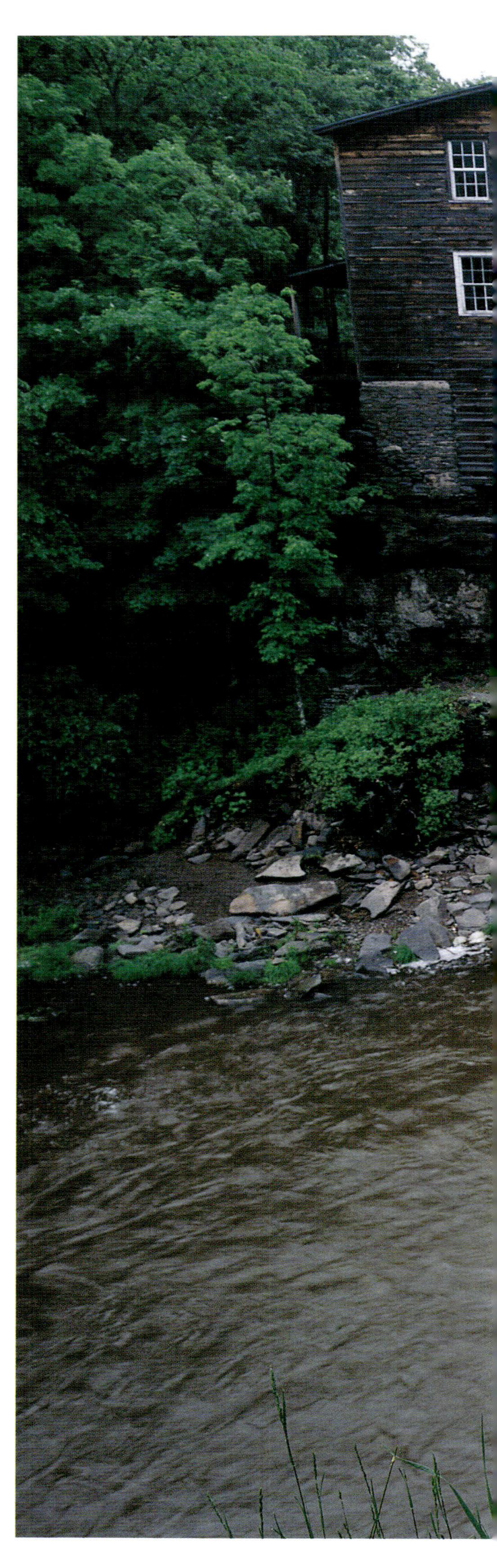

FOR SEVERAL reasons, many waterfalls plunge right next to roads. Or perhaps it would be more accurate to say, many roads run beside plunging waterfalls.

One of those reasons is that waterfalls and their streams often carve wide pathways through mountains that make it convenient for highway builders to adapt, in an example of "following the path of least resistance." This applies to both the water and the road-builders.

Another reason for roads leading to waterfalls is that those who came before us sought the falls for their power, their energy, their ability to turn a large saw, a millstone, or a turbine profitably.

The road to Shinglekill Falls first brought settlers to a grist mill built in 1788. Now, on one side of the falls, it brings us to an antique store built around the disassembled grist mill and, on the other, to a bed and breakfast (Tumblin' Falls House) whose verandah overlooks the falls.

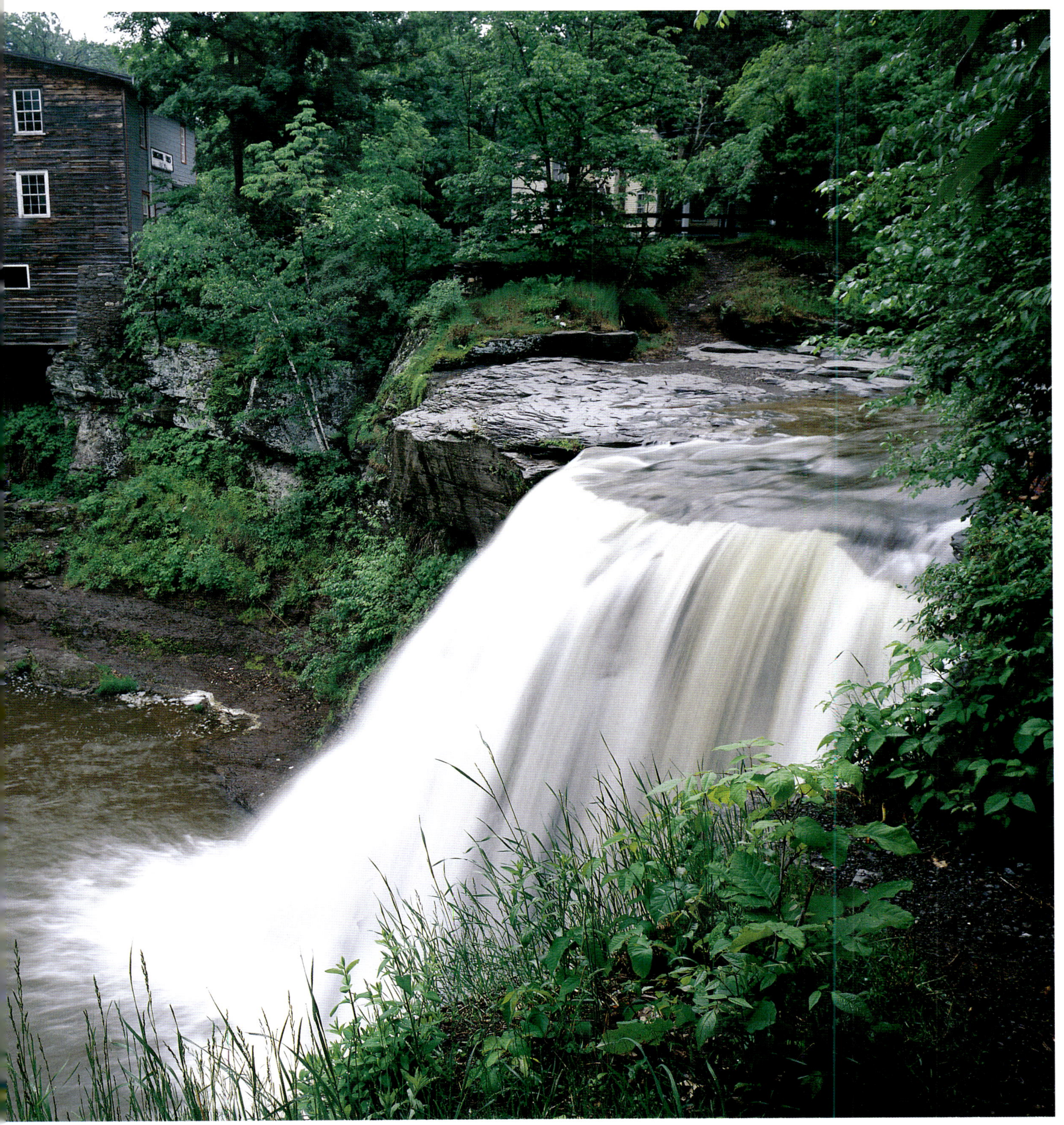

TOMSCO FALLS

TOMSCO FALLS is home to two natural wonders: a waterfall and its owner. David Rashkin, octogenarian and retired pharmacist, and his wife, Sylvia, have turned their backyard waterfall into a full-time pastime.

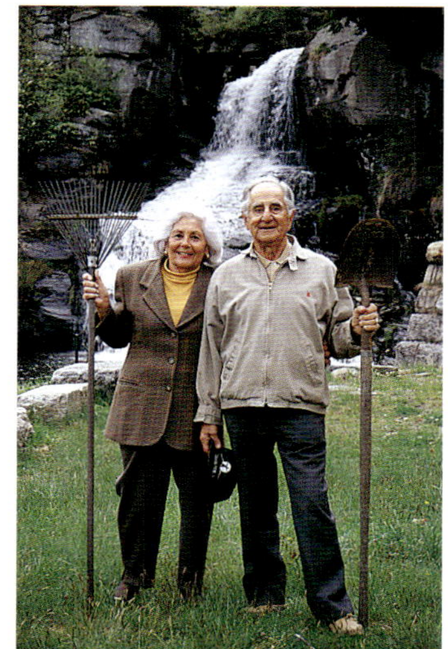

As fast as the water rushes downhill, Rashkin charges uphill showing us around the place. He dashes through a tour of the grounds, telling us in minutes what would normally take an hour to tell paying visitors (a couple of bucks to cover the insurance).

We hear the folklore of the native plants, their healing powers, derivations of their names. He leapfrogs downhill. We hear about the celebrities who've visited—Geraldo taped part of a show here; Miss New York State came to be flattered by the surroundings in her photographs; Trident, to show their chewing gum was waterfall-fresh.

He charges back uphill, picking up wayward branches and telling us the state will buy his falls and make it a park as soon as they get enough money. He veers right and shows us the dam he built; he poses for us on his bridge and leads us to the best viewpoint for photographing the falls.

He takes us into his dining room and shows us the wall-size mirror angled toward the picture window so it reflects the falls to his eye as he eats his meals.

By the way, "TOMSCO" is an acronym in honor of the Six Nations of the Iroquois: Tuscarora, Oneida, Mohawk, Seneca, Cayuga, and Onondaga.

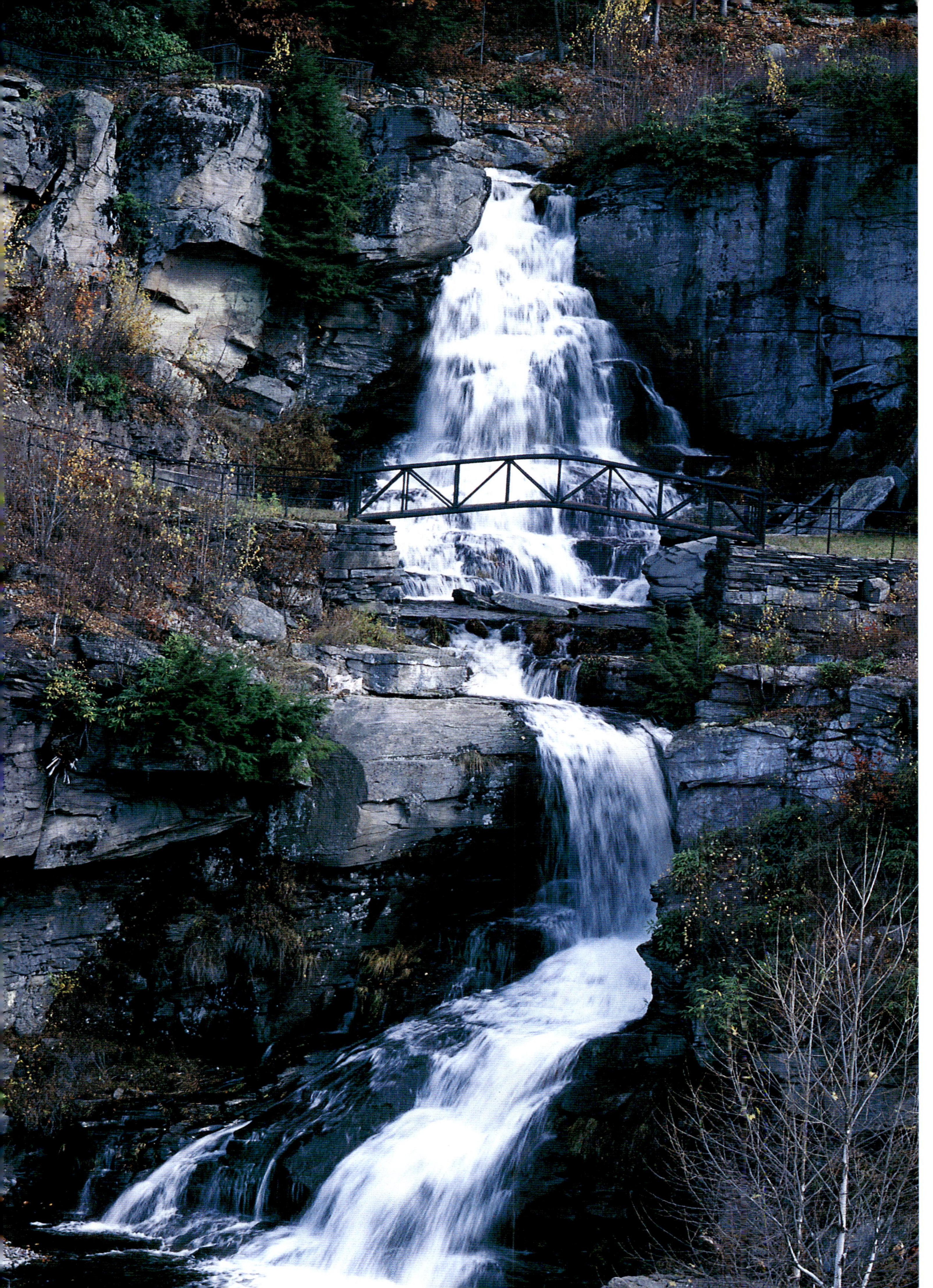

VERNOOY FALLS

THE IDYLLIC exterior of a waterfall belies a hidden secret kept close by most waterfalls. They are self-destructive. The leaping and cavorting, the sun-splashed dazzle and gay burbling of a waterfall charm the eye of all but the most dedicated waterfall behaviorist.

But that joyful exterior hides a personality bent on destruction. First of the surrounding land, ultimately of itself. Destruction is the very nature of a waterfall.

The evidence? You have only to look downstream from a waterfall to see the path of destruction left in its travels. The trail of rocks and debris in and along the streambed, the gouged-out banks, limbs ripped and dangling by a load of winter's ice, trees undercut and tilting precariously, soon to succumb to gravity.

Inch by inch, year by year, a waterfall claws its way upstream, uphill towards the highest reaches of the stream. For thousands, even tens of thousands of years, if left undisturbed, it edges its way upward to the streamhead where it can climb no higher. When that happens it can only tear away the step directly beneath it. When that step is worn away, the waterfall is no more.

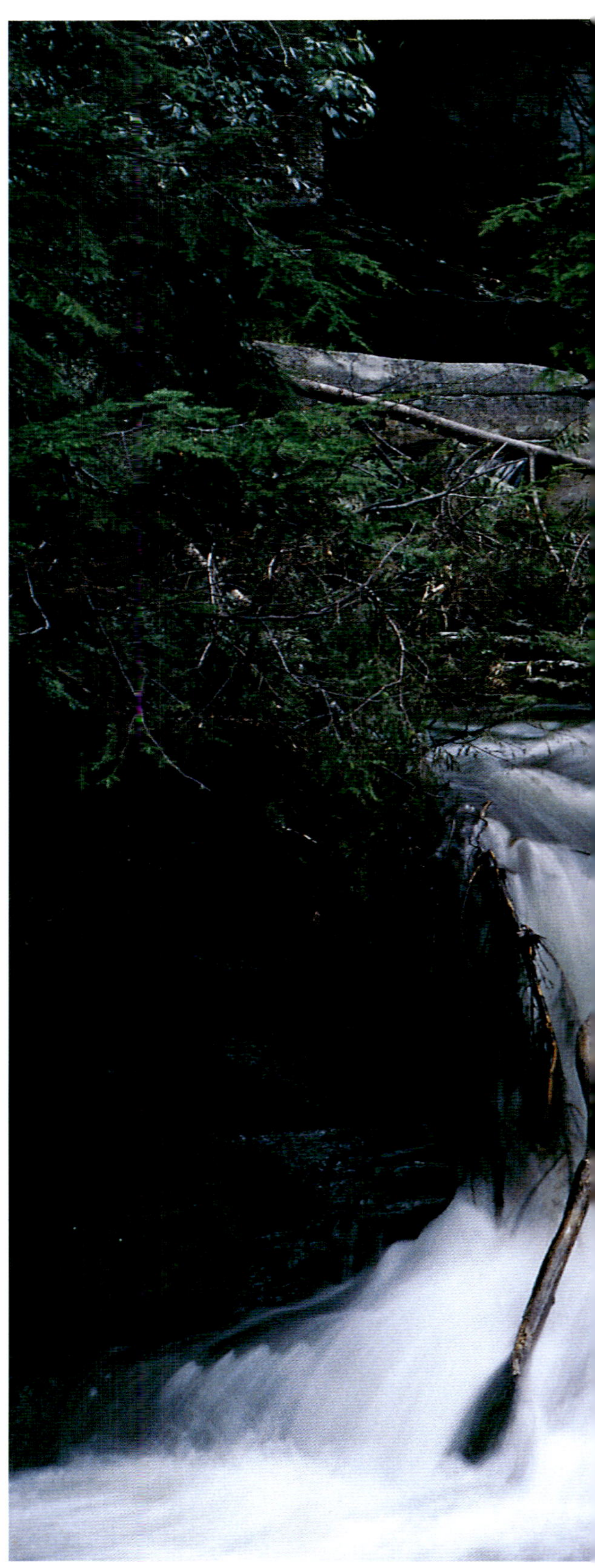

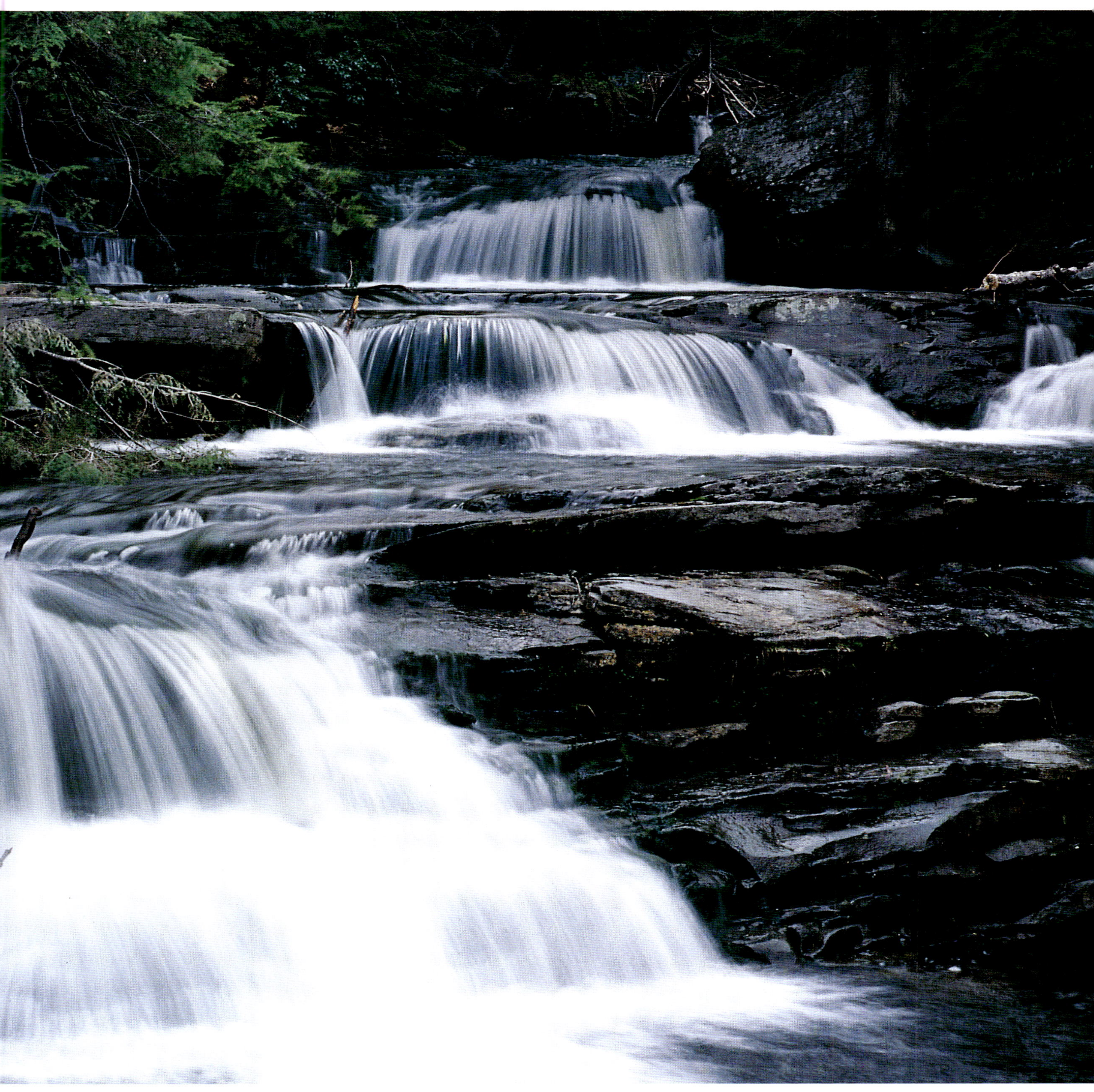

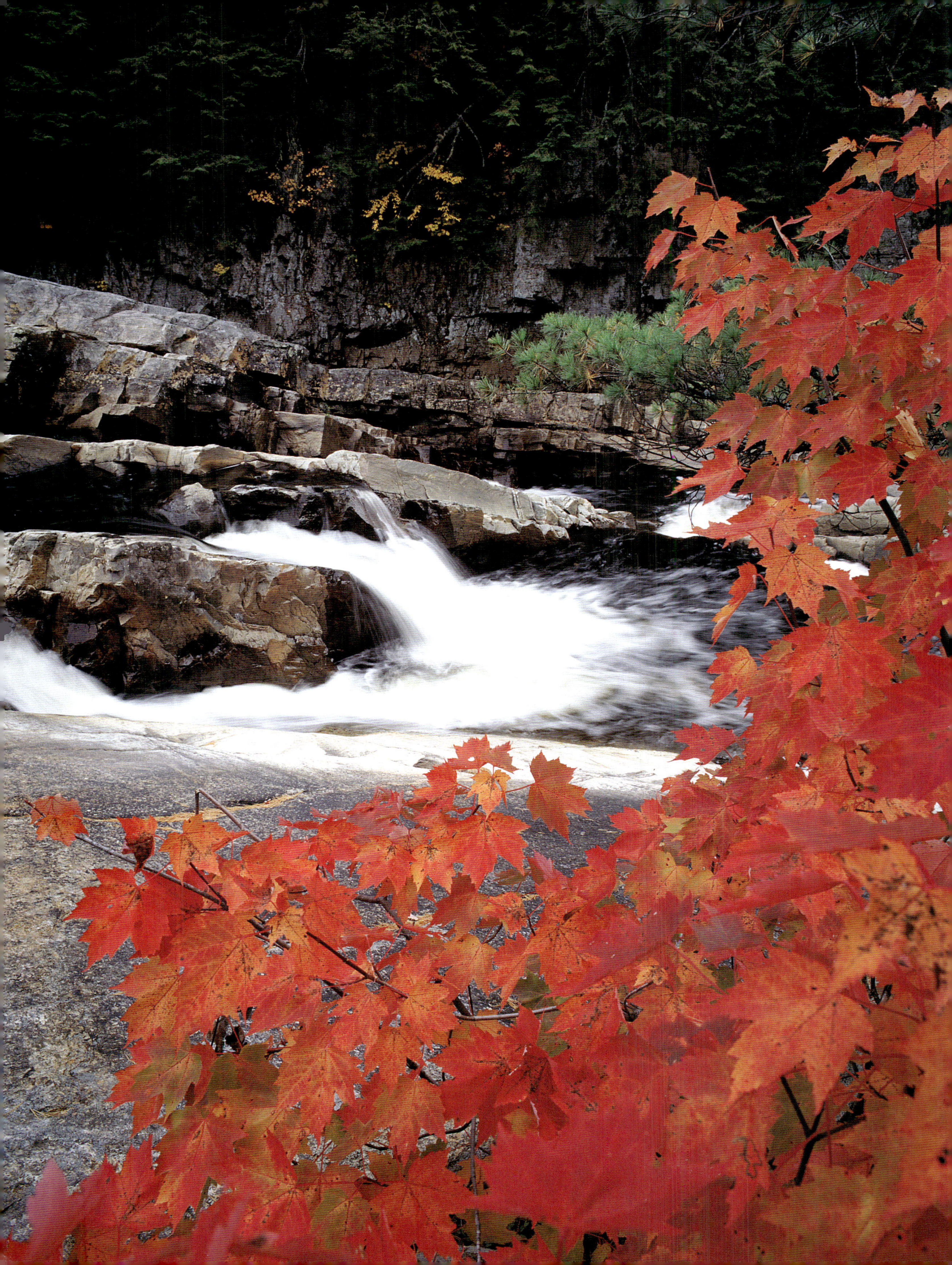

TIPS FOR PHOTOGRAPHING WATERFALLS

Keep it Simple

Don't try to include too much information in your photograph. The result may be a busy clutter of elements, each competing for the viewer's attention. Compose with a simple, strong point of interest (just the waterfall), or a primary and a secondary point of interest—say, the waterfall and a nearby tree with lots of character.

Add Depth

Foreground interest can add a three-dimensional feeling to photographs of waterfalls. Depending on the season and the amount of water flowing, effective foreground elements might include:

- Overhanging tree branches
- A stream "leading" your eye to the waterfall
- Nearby ferns, flowers, a weathered log
- A scattering of recently fallen autumn leaves
- Exposed tree roots
- Stepping stones, curious-shaped boulders
- Ice formations from repeated freezing of spray coming off a waterfall

A wide-angle lens helps add a feeling of depth to any scenic photograph by exaggerating perspective. It can dramatize the scene by making the foreground appear larger and the background (waterfall) seem farther away.

When including the foreground for depth and interest, the image will generally be most effective if both near and far subjects are in sharp focus. With wide-angle lenses, focusing for simultaneous near and far sharpness is quite easy because these lenses have excellent depth of field, even at wide-open apertures. Stopping down a lens to f/16 or f/22, however, insures even greater sharpness over the entire range of subjects within the scene. Our favorite lens focal length was 24mm, although sometimes we used an even wider, 20mm lens when we wanted to include an attractive foreground element that was only a foot or two away.

Besides providing the appearance of greater depth, wide-angle lenses often helped us capture an entire waterfall in confined locations. Without a 20mm, super-wide lens, for example, our shots of Rainbow Falls in the Adirondacks would not have shown both its base and top in a single image. If we had used a normal or slightly wide-angle lens, we would have had to back away considerably. That would have placed our viewpoint too far downstream and too low to show the boulder base of the falls.

Watch the Light

Overcast days usually give the best lighting for waterfalls—especially the ones which lie in deep gorge and forest locations. Too often, cameras are left behind on days when the sun doesn't shine. In the minds of many photo hobbyists, dreary weather promises dull colors and unexciting scenes. But photographers who are sensitive to detail and the delicate subtleties of tone and color can turn a bad day for a suntan into a great day for picture-taking. Overcast days produce nearly shadowless, even lighting—the opportunity for excellent exposures in both highlit and shaded areas.

Overcast days also mean a featureless, gray-white sky which can be very distracting in a photograph. To reduce the sky's dominant brightness, mask it with a foreground frame such as tree branches. Better yet, compose the scene to exclude the sky entirely.

Create a Mood

Blur the water for a smoke effect. Use a tripod and slow shutter speed such as 1/8 second or slower. The movement of water in the scene, during the time the shutter is open, will record as a blur on the film. This gives moving water the soft appearance of smoke or cotton, which is often more attractive than trying to "stop" the flow with a fast shutter speed.

Camera Equipment

Just about any point-and-shoot camera, even the inexpensive single-use models, will deliver good record shots of waterfalls. They're simple, lightweight, dependable and, in the case of the disposables, expendable—features that make them adequate for documenting most waterfall settings, most of the time.

So why did we set off on every waterfall trek burdened down with four or five complex cameras between us? And why did our array of lenses, filters, meters, tripods, gadget bags, and backpacks nearly fill the entire six-foot cargo area of a Ford Explorer?

Part of the answer relates to a variation of Murphy's Law: The amount of photo gear you pack expands to fill the space available, regardless of need.

The other part of the answer is the famous motto of the Boy Scouts of America: BE PREPARED. Scouts are taught to prepare for whatever comes along so they will always be ready to meet life's challenges.

As we headed for most waterfalls, we knew there would be plenty of challenges. But we had little idea of what the situations would be like in advance. Would we be able to get close enough? Could we successfully deal with obstacles where we needed to position our cameras? Would the temperature be too cold for our batteries and shutters? Would the rain hold off until after we made our shots? Would we have enough daylight to find our way back? To conquer the unexpected and bring home the pictures—as well as ourselves—we needed good gear and plenty of it.

At each location we visited, we tried to make photographs that would represent more than just straightforward records. We wanted our images to convey some of the feelings we had experienced at the time and in a particular place: The jarring power of water—tons of it—crashing down on unyielding granite boulders. The vertigo in standing at the precipice of a gorge, its floor two hundred feet below. The ethereal, smoky character of tumbling water dissipating into a quiet, ink-black pool. The still forest around us. The magic of twilight along the homeward path.

To help convey these and other evocative feelings in photographs, the camera must have a few special features—adjustable shutter speeds including a time-exposure setting; a tripod socket; the capacity to accept interchangeable lenses. The camera also must be easy to use so that it can become an almost-natural extension of the photographer's eye. We cannot overstate the importance of seeing through the viewfinder the same image the film will record. Depth of field, selective focus, filtering, image compression, deliberate distortion—all can be readily seen only through a single-lens-reflex (SLR) camera's viewing system.

Our standard cameras were 35 mm Nikon SLR models, with lenses ranging from super-wide 20 mm to a robust 300 mm telephoto. The very portable 35 mm camera

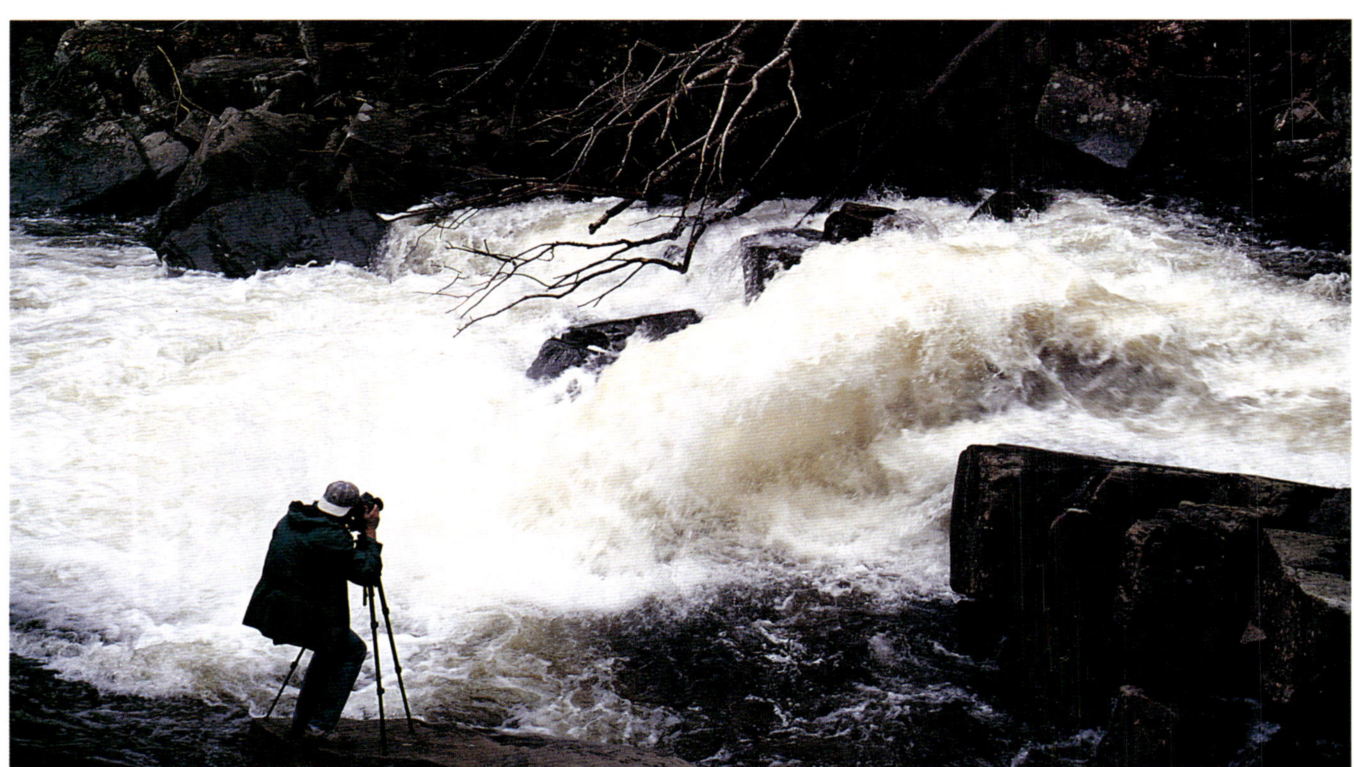

format made it easy for us to move around for dramatic viewpoints as well as take extreme close-ups. The 35mm cameras can also hold 36-shot rolls, especially convenient and economical when bracketing exposures (a photographer's practice of shooting at one stop above and one stop below the light meter's averaging exposure or a selected exposure to allow for light variables in the scene and inevitable mistakes) on slide film. On long hikes, we always favored these cameras because, like the tripods we used with them, they are light in weight and relatively compact.

We also used medium- and large-format cameras, particularly where subjects had the potential for full-page blowups. While most of today's 35mm films enlarge very well, maximum sharpness can be achieved from images made on larger film formats. The downside of working with larger cameras, though, is their weight and bulk. The bigger the format, the heavier the camera and its accessories.

The Large-Format Camera—Friend and Foe

Whenever a waterfall was nearby (within two or three miles of our vehicle), and the weather was reasonably calm and dry, my first choice was always a 4x5 field camera. It's slow to set up. It's heavy and cumbersome. It does not have a viewfinder so composing and focusing must be done under a dark cloth while studying an upside-down image on a plate of ground glass in the camera. It uses film holders which are bulky and hard to keep clean. And by the time I decided what to shoot, got set up and focused the camera, and measured the light for correct exposure, Derek had usually finished half a roll and moved on in search of other subjects.

But the color transparencies produced by a 4x5 camera are awesome. Big, sharp transparencies that show every detail in a scene. Rich colors that jump off the light box and, hopefully, impress the picture editor.

The other reason I like working with 4x5 is the discipline. Because of its design, the camera takes at least several minutes to lock in on a chosen subject and composition. This forces me to take special care in selecting lens focal length and composing an image. Then, like a meticulous chess player who is finally ready to make a move, I ask myself, "Is this the best composition possible given the current circumstances?"

By the end of the day, the number of photographs I have made is often small, but the percentage of success is usually quite high. And even if my images don't make the grade, wrestling with all that heavy camera equipment gives me a good workout.

KEITH BOAS

The Best Safety/Survival Gear and Advice for Day Trips to Waterfalls

Take a buddy with similar interests, gear, and stamina.

Start with a full tank of gas in the car.

Leave word of your route with someone you can trust.

Bring:

- A pocket knife
- A hiking map of the region
- A compass with an emergency whistle
- At least 50 feet of heavy-duty rope
- A small flashlight
- Full water bottle (16 oz.)
- Energy food—granola bars, gorp, beef jerky, fruit
- Emergency space blanket

Wear proper foot gear for the season:

- Sneakers with good tread
- Comfortable, insulated hiking shoes with good tread, laces, and water-repellency
- Polypropylene inner and heavy wool outer socks for comfort, warmth, and protection against blisters
- Snowshoes or cross-country skis for deep snow conditions
- Instep crampons for ice

Carry a basic first aid kit, including several bandages and sterile gauze dressings plus tape, elastic bandage, moleskin, antibiotic ointment, anti-bacterial towelettes, and acetaminophen tablets.

Use a day pack, fanny pack, or photo vest for hands-free climbing.

Dress well:

- Warm hat
- Insulated, water-resistant gloves

Carry rain gear and extra dry shoes, socks, sweater, pants.

THE ADIRONDACK REGION

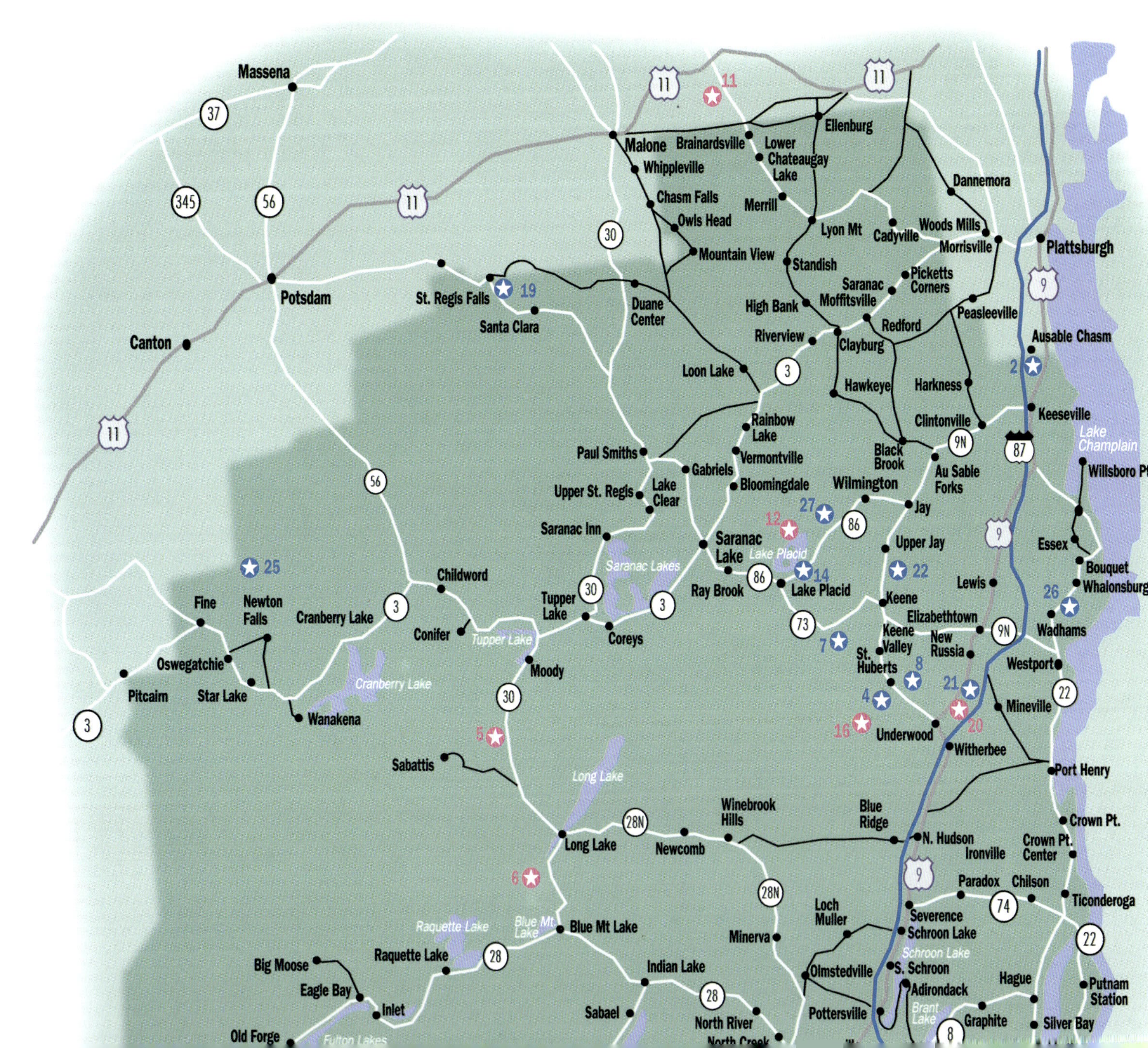

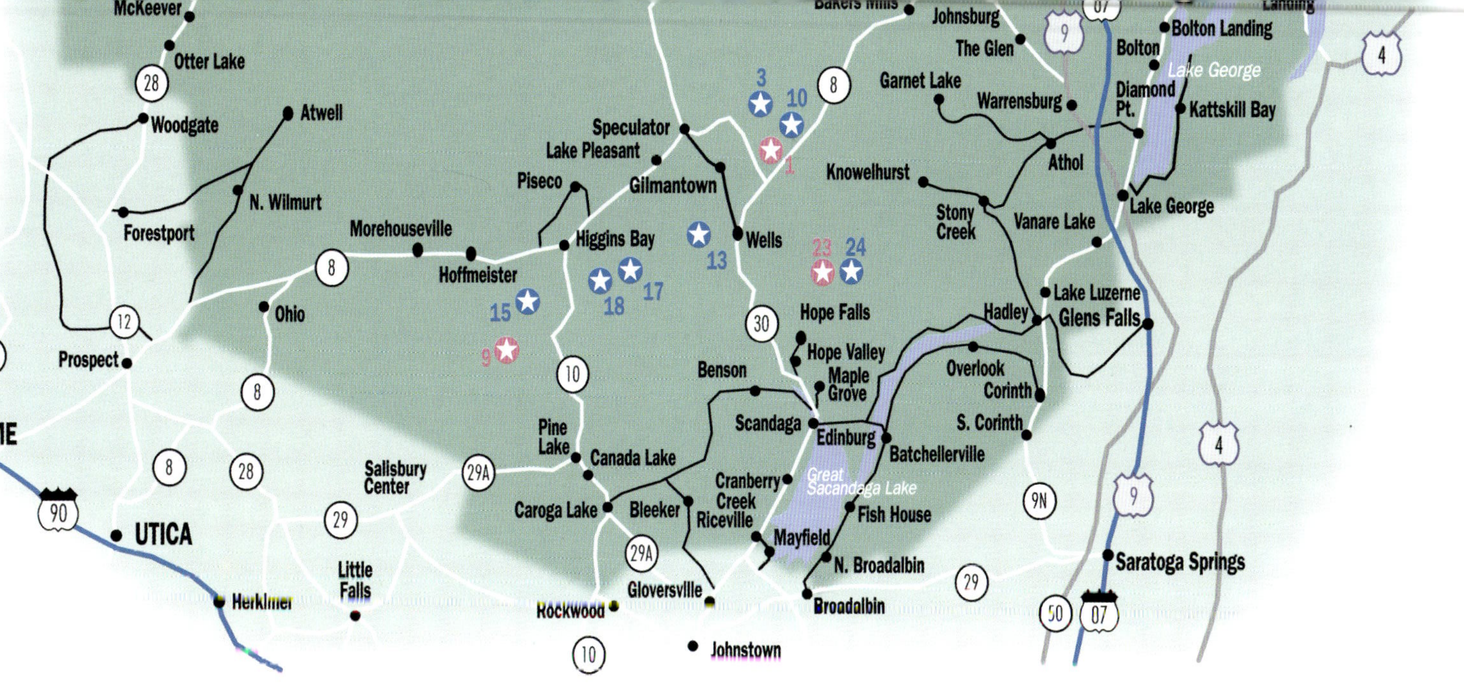

Map Key

✪	**1**	***Auger Falls***
	2	Ausable Chasm, *Rainbow Falls*
	3	Austin Falls
✪	**4**	***Beaver Meadow Falls***
✪	**5**	***Bog River Falls***
✪	**6**	***Buttermilk Falls***
	7	Cascade Falls
	8	Flume Falls, Route 73
✪	**9**	***Goldminer Falls***
	10	Griffin Falls
✪	**11**	***High Falls***
✪	**12**	***High Falls Gorge***
	13	Jimmy Creek Falls
	14	Monument Falls
	15	Potholers
✪	**16**	***Rainbow Falls,*** *Lower Ausable Lake*
	17	Lower Sacandaga Falls
	18	Upper Sacandaga Falls
	19	St. Regis Falls
✪	**20**	***Split Rock Falls***
	21	Lower Split Rock Falls
	22	Styles Brook Falls
✪	**23**	***Middle Tenant Falls***
	24	Upper Tenant Falls
	25	Twin Falls
	26	Wadhams Falls
	27	Wilmington Notch

✪ *Some falls to visit, see pages 120–122*

THE CATSKILL REGION

Map Key

1 Anonymous, *near Buttermilk Falls*
2 Artist's Grotto
3 *Ashley Falls*
4 Awosting Falls
5 Backyard Waterfall
6 *Bastion Falls*
7 Buttermilk Falls
8 Dog's Hole
9 Fawn's Leap Falls
10 Ferndale Falls
11 Frost Valley Cascade
12 Glen Falls
13 High Falls
14 *Kaaterskill Falls*
15 Manor Kill Falls
16 Plattekill Road Tributary
17 Sawmill Falls
18 *Shinglekill Falls*
19 TOMSCO Falls
20 *Vernooy Falls*

Some falls to visit, see pages 122–123

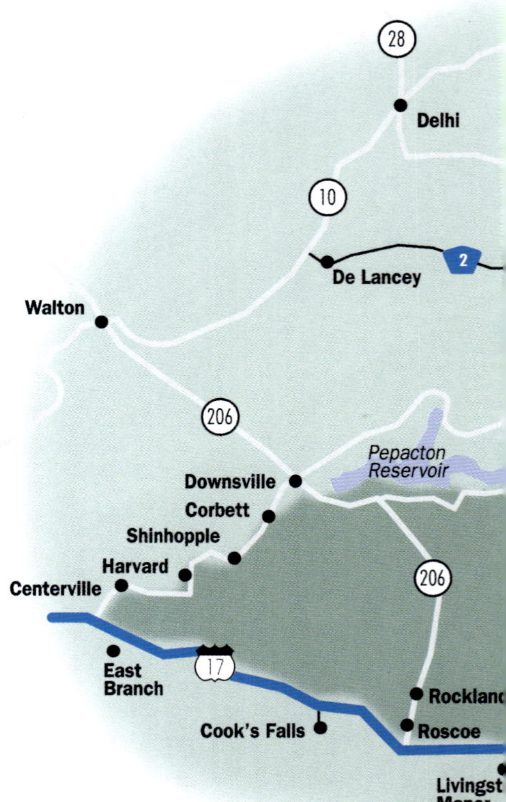

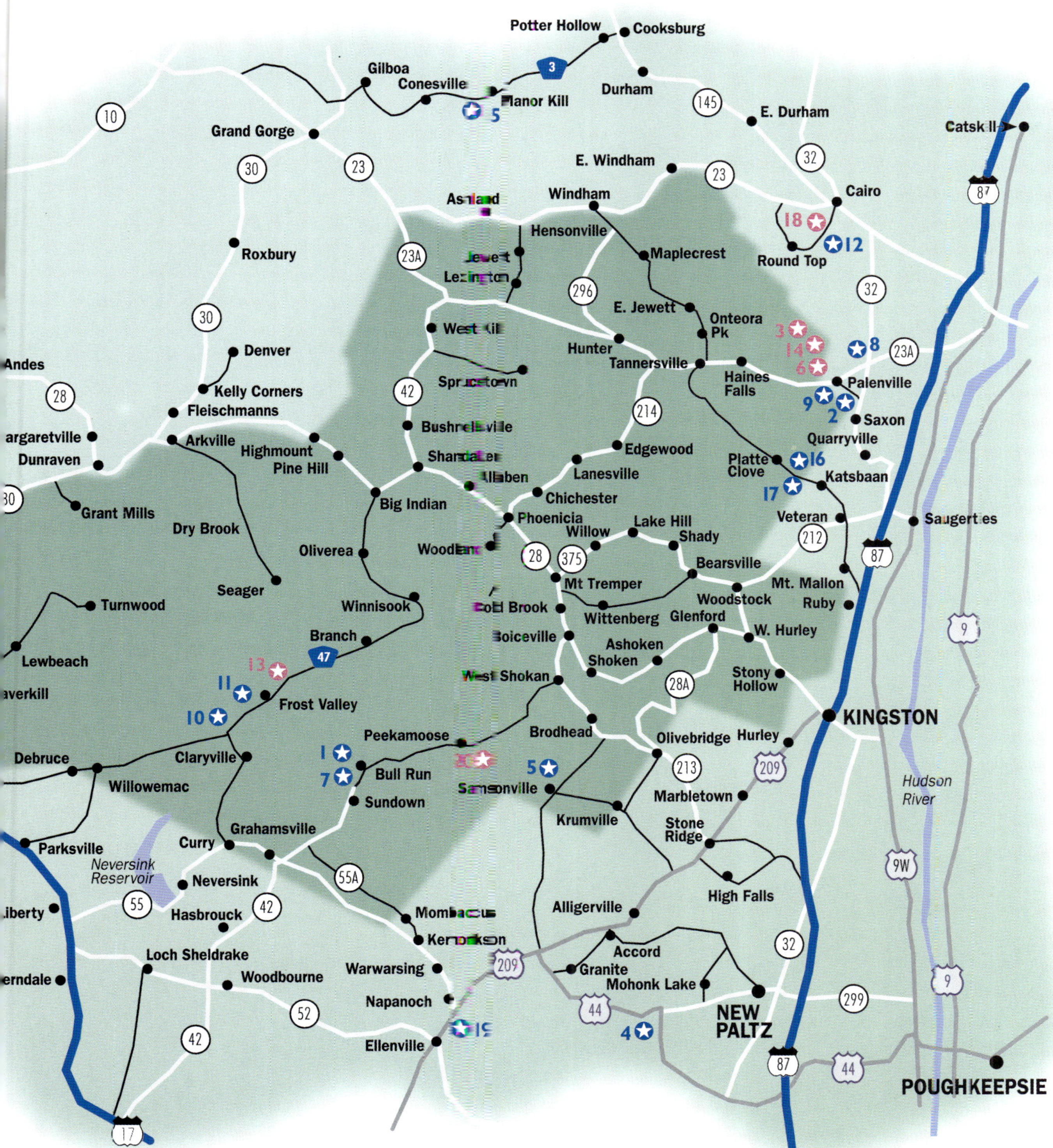

Potter Hollow
Cooksburg
Gilboa
Conesville
Durham
E. Durham
Grand Gorge
E. Windham
Cairo
Windham
Hensonville
Roxbury
Maplecrest
Round Top
E. Jewett
Onteora Pk
Hunter
Tannersville
Haines Falls
Palenville
Saxon
Quarryville
Denver
Andes
Kelly Corners
Fleischmanns
Arkville
Highmount
Pine Hill
Dunraven
Big Indian
Edgewood
Lanesville
Chichester
Phoenicia
Platte Clove
Katsbaan
Veteran
Saugerties
Grant Mills
Dry Brook
Oliverea
Willow
Lake Hill
Shady
Bearsville
Mt Tremper
Mt. Mallon
Ruby
Seager
Turnwood
Winnisook
Wittenberg
Woodstock
Glenford
W. Hurley
Branch
Ashokan
Shokan
Stony Hollow
Lewbeach
Frost Valley
KINGSTON
Peekamoose
Brodhead
Olivebridge
Hurley
Debruce
Claryville
Willowemac
Bull Run
Sundown
Marbletown
Hudson River
Krumville
Stone Ridge
Grahamsville
Curry
Parksville
Neversink Reservoir
Neversink
High Falls
Hasbrouck
Alligerville
Loch Sheldrake
Accord
Granite
Mohonk Lake
Woodbourne
Warwarsing
Napanoch
NEW PALTZ
Ellenville
POUGHKEEPSIE

SOME WATERFALLS TO VISIT

Numbers correspond to maps

IN THE ADIRONDACKS

NEAR THE ROADSIDE

Bog River Falls, Tupper Lake **5**

ACCESSIBILITY: Easy.

DIRECTIONS: At the southern tip of Tupper Lake, turn off Route 30 onto Route 421. Within a mile, you cross the small bridge which spans the mouth of Bog River. Immediately after the bridge, there is a small, roadside picnic area where you can park your car.

HIKING TIME: At roadside.

HIGHLIGHTS: State-owned. A panorama of gentle cataracts that you can see best directly from the bridge. Upstream, behind the picnic area, the river splits, with part flowing to the right around some rocky terrain. It then returns to the main flow at a sharp angle, taking on the appearance of a tributary.

Buttermilk Falls, Deerland 

ACCESSIBILITY: Easy.

DIRECTIONS: From the village of Long Lake, go about three miles south on Routes 28N/30 to North Point Road at Deerland. Turn right. After approximately two miles, watch on the right for the trailhead sign for the falls. Park along the widened shoulder of the road by the sign. The falls are about 200 feet north, along a gentle, mostly level trail.

HIKING TIME: Five minutes.

HIGHLIGHTS: State-owned. Attractive riverside setting with huge, rounded boulders and picturesque evergreens. Flowing through here, the Raquette River first descends as raging rapids, then suddenly plunges straight down into an inviting, natural swimming pool at the base. This is a popular location for family picnics in the summer.

High Falls Gorge, Lake Placid **12**

ACCESSIBILITY: Easy.

DIRECTIONS: From Wilmington, go west on Route 86 for five miles. You will find the parking area well marked on the right. Enter through the gift shop in the main building.

HIKING TIME: 45 minutes, round trip.

HIGHLIGHTS: Admission fee. There are four waterfalls along a deep, narrow gorge cut by the West Branch of the Ausable River. Several vantage points from catwalks and observation decks offer safe picture-taking opportunities. Save enough film for Climax Falls at the farthest point of the walk. The best view of this 50-foot plunge is from the foot bridge below the falls.

Rainbow Falls, Ausable Chasm **16**

ACCESSIBILITY: Easy.

DIRECTIONS: Ausable Chasm is located 12 miles south of Plattsburgh on Route 9. If coming from the south on the Northway (Interstate 87), get off at Exit 34. From there, take Route 9 northeast through Keeseville, and continue for another two miles.

HIKING TIME: At roadside.

A few of the sites pictured in this book are on private property.
Please inquire before visiting and respect the rights and wishes of property owners.

HIGHLIGHTS: Since the last glacier, the plunging waters of the Ausable River have been carving through a fault here in sandstone bedrock. The result is a deep chasm commencing with a majestic display of waterfalls. Since it is a commercial attraction, admission is charged for the two-mile water tour through the chasm. But parking is free by the Route 9 bridge, from which you see the best view of the falls.

Split Rock Falls, New Russia 20

ACCESSIBILITY: Easy, but be careful. The drop-off is extreme, and there are no railings.

DIRECTIONS: From the intersection of Routes 73 and 9, go north on Route 9 for about two miles. Just after going over a small bridge, you will come upon the parking area for the falls on the right.

HIKING TIME: Two minutes.

HIGHLIGHTS: Recently acquired by the state. A three-tier, staggered group of falls with a total drop of 30 feet. You can see the entire setting well from the cliff about 50 feet downstream from the parking area. This area has not been developed. Hiking along the edge of the cliff is dangerous.

Hiking Destinations

Auger Falls, Wells 1

ACCESSIBILITY: Easy.

DIRECTIONS: Going north from Wells on Route 30: About one and one-half miles past the bridge where Route 8 joins Route 30, watch for a driveway on the right. There is no sign. The driveway leads to the parking area for a picnic site belonging to the International Paper Company. Just before the parking area, only a few feet from the highway, turn right onto a narrow dirt road which parallels the highway. (Depending on conditions, you may want to leave your car in the parking area and walk along this pothole-laden road.) After 1/10 mile, you will come to a sign on the left marking the trailhead. From there, it is about 2/10 mile on foot to the falls.

HIKING TIME: 30 minutes, round trip.

HIGHLIGHTS: State-owned. The falls and adjoining flume rush below the bouldered, tree-framed hillside. Areas along the edge are extremely steep. Water spray and perpetual dampness near the falls make footing treacherous. Watch your step.

Beaver Meadow Falls, Rainbow Falls, and Artist's Falls, Keene 

ACCESSIBILITY: Moderate, mostly because of the distance.

DIRECTIONS: At the southern edge of Saint Huberts, turn west off Route 73 on the road to the Ausable Club. The trailhead is located near the tennis courts. But unless you are a member, you are not allowed to park on club grounds. Follow the road around until you exit the golf course property. Partway down the hill and back on public land, you come upon several opportunities for public parking. Park safely off the road anywhere you can and hike the half-mile or more back up to the trailhead. Carry a good trail map that identifies the locations of each of these falls. A good hike plan would make a loop, going first to Beaver Meadow Falls, then Rainbow Falls, and finally Artis'ts Falls on the way back.

HIKING TIME: 6 hours (about 10.5 miles), round trip.

HIGHLIGHTS: Private. Each of these falls has its own distinctive personality, with Artist's Falls cozy and small, Beaver Meadow Falls fresh and vigorous, and Rainbow Falls high and majestic. Rainbow Falls is also the farthest from your vehicle. If you get a late start, you may want to consider turning back after visiting Beaver Meadow Falls, saving Rainbow and Artist's for another day.

Goldminer Falls, Arietta 

ACCESSIBILITY: Moderate.

DIRECTIONS: From the south side of Piseco Lake on Route 8, turn onto Route 10. Go south about two miles to Pawley Road and turn right. After about 8.5 miles, watch for an open, marshy area. Park along the road north of the small bridge which crosses the West

Branch. The unmarked trailhead, tucked into the woods, is on the west side of the road just north of the bridge.

HIKING TIME: 1 hour 30 minutes, round trip.

HIGHLIGHTS: State-owned and very picturesque. Lots of exposed bedrock with potholes and a narrow channel carrying the water below the falls. The setting is also heavily forested.

High Falls, Chateaugay 11

ACCESSIBILITY: Easy to moderate. The entire walk is on a well-maintained trail. You can choose between two routes to the bottom of the gorge: a short, steep trail containing several stairways; or a much longer walk with a gentle grade. If you have weak legs and/or become short of breath easily, descend via the steps and return along the kind-hearted, gentle grade.

DIRECTIONS: Go east from Malone on Route 11 for about 10 miles. After Thayer Corners, where East and Selkirk Roads meet, take the next right which is two miles further east. From there, follow the signs to High Falls.

HIKING TIME: 45 minutes, round trip.

HIGHLIGHTS: Admission fee. A spectacular, narrow fall with a vertical drop of 120 feet. The base is flat and open, providing sharp contrast to the rugged cliffs and plunging water.

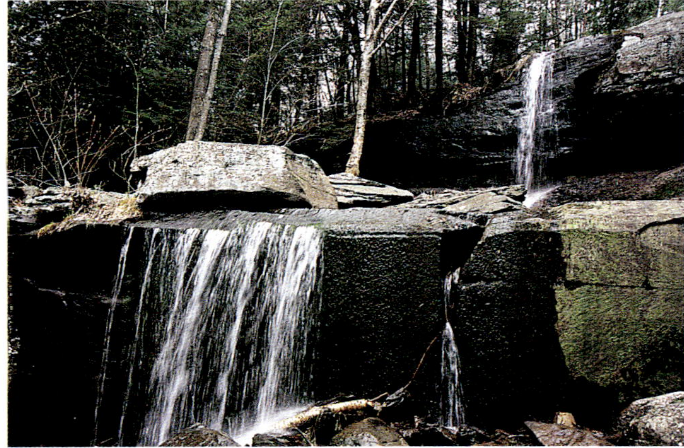

Tenant Falls, Hope 23

ACCESSIBILITY: Easy, then moderate.

DIRECTIONS: From Northville, take Reed Street to Old State Highway. After about three miles, turn right. Once you pass the hamlet of Hope Falls, drive another four miles to the trailhead at the end of the road. Walk a short distance to Tenant Creek, then turn right (east) and follow the trail upstream.

Note: In winter, the last 1.5 miles of road to the trailhead are closed to vehicles except snowmobiles.

HIKING TIME: Spring-Autumn: 1 hour 30 minutes, round trip from the trailhead.

HIGHLIGHTS: State-owned. There are three separate falls along a three-mile stretch of Tenant Creek. The first cascade is easy to reach. It has a wide, calm pool at its base, making it a popular picnic spot for families with young children. The next two falls, while more picturesque, are harder to reach because of the rugged condition of the trail.

IN THE CATSKILLS

Near the Roadside

Bastion Falls, Palenville 6

ACCESSIBILITY: Moderate.

DIRECTIONS: Take Route 23A, either east from Haines Falls or west from Palenville. Park in the Molly Smith parking area about 500 feet southwest of (above) the hairpin curve and bridge. Then walk down to the bridge, facing traffic, along Rt. 23A. Be careful walking here; the shoulder is extremely narrow.

HIKING TIME: 20 minutes, round trip from the parking area.

HIGHLIGHTS: State-owned. The falls cascade in three interesting steps. You can get a good view of the lower falls from the road by the bridge. Hike about 1/10 mile upstream, along a steep trail, to view the next two waterfalls which are smaller.

Shinglekill Falls, Purling 18

ACCESSIBILITY: Easy.

DIRECTIONS: From the south on Interstate 87, take Exit 20. Then go north on Route 32 to Silver Spur Road where you turn left. Go two miles to Country Route 24. Turn left and go 200 feet.

HIKING TIME: At roadside.

HIGHLIGHTS: Private. There are two excellent locations for viewing the falls: from halfway down the driveway which leads to the charming Tumblin' Falls House (bed and breakfast); and, on the opposite side of the stream, through the old mill (antique store) and down to the base of the falls.

Hiking Destinations

Ashley Falls, Mary's Glen, North/South Lakes 3

ACCESSIBILITY: Easy.

DIRECTIONS: From Route 23A at the village of Haines Falls, drive east on Route 18 up to the North/South Lake Campground. After passing through the toll gate, bear left at the fork in the road. The trailhead for Mary's Glen, and the spur trail to the falls, is on the left. From this point, the walk is about a quarter-mile to the falls.

HIKING TIME: 30 minutes, round trip.

HIGHLIGHTS: State-owned. Although the trail along the west side of Ashley Creek is fairly level, it is often wet. It also is frequently interrupted with exposed tree roots and stepping stones. To get really close to the falls, you need to climb over a few large, slanting boulders. But the in-your-face effect is worth it.

Kaaterskill Falls, Palenville 14

ACCESSIBILITY: Difficult. After passing the upper section of Bastion Falls, the unimproved trail continues to climb. Boulders and exposed roots make the footing precarious at some points, particularly in wet weather.

DIRECTIONS: (Follow directions to Bastion Falls.) Then continue along the trail for another 4/10 mile.

HIKING TIME: 1 hour 30 minutes, round trip from the parking area.

HIGHLIGHTS: State-owned. The highest falls in New York State, calculated upon a combined drop of 260 feet in two majestic tiers. The picturesque scene from the base of the lower falls has attracted tourists and artists for more than 150 years.

Vernooy Falls, Peekamoose 20

ACCESSIBILITY: Easy.

DIRECTIONS: On Route 209 going northeast from Ellenville, turn left on County Road 3. After driving 3.4 miles, you come to an intersection. Turn left. Then keep left at each fork until you come to Cherrytown. Turn right on Upper Cherrytown Road. About three miles later, you reach the trailhead.

HIKING TIME: 1 hour 15 minutes, 3.6 miles round trip.

HIGHLIGHTS: State-owned. There are four cascades, with a combined vertical drop of about 30 feet. A wide pool at the base of the falls provides an attractive, pastoral foreground, especially in the soft light of early evening.

GLOSSARY
TERMS, NAMES, ACRONYMS, AND LANDMARKS

Adirondacks See "Great Northern Wilderness" and "Hadirondaks."

Adirondack Dome A circular uplift in northeastern New York State, measuring 160 miles wide and one mile high. This geological uplift occurred approximately five million years ago, although it consists of rocks which are more than 1,000 million years old.

Adirondack Park Established by New York State in 1892. Largest state park system in the United States. More than five million acres, including 3,200,000 acres in private property. The park contains nearly 30,000 miles of brooks and streams which form 1,000 miles of rivers. Also see "Blue Line."

ADK Adirondack Mountain Club.

Ausable French word for sandstone.

Ausable Chasm Commercial tourist attraction in the Adirondacks, opened in 1870.

Blaze A trail marker, usually a brush stroke of paint at, or above, eye level on a tree trunk.

Blue Line Reference to map outline identifying boundary of the Adirondack Park. First drawn in 1892 by the New York State legislature, it encircled approximately 2,800,000 acres. Over the years, the scope of the Blue Line has been enlarged several times. It now includes more than five million acres —a fifth of New York State.

Buddy System Traveling/hiking with another. person, preferably one with similar interests and abilities, for safety.

Bushwhack (Noun) A route where there is no trail. (Verb) To pick your way through unmarked, unimproved, and usually heavily wooded terrain without aid of a trail. Usually requires a map, compass, and attire sufficient to handle extremes of weather and footing.

Cascade Water plunging over steep rocks; a waterfall.

Cataract A waterfall.

Chasm A cleft in the earth's surface; a gorge or ravine.

Chute A narrow channel of rapidly moving water.

Cirque A bowl-shaped amphitheater carved on the side of a mountain by a glacier.

Clove A narrow valley.

Confluence Where rivers, tributaries, or streams flow together to form one body of water.

DEC New York State Department of Environmental Conservation.

Erratic A rock deposited by a glacier. Erratics are often seen scattered in fields, stream beds, and along hiking trails.

Escarpment A steep slope or drop in the terrain.

Flume A steep-sided trench carrying fast-moving water.

Fracture Block A boulder that has broken off from the ledge rock of a waterfall.

Glen A small, secluded valley.

Gorp See "Trail Mix."

Great Northern Wilderness A term used by some big-city journalists in the nineteenth century to describe the Adirondack Mountains.

Hadirondaks (Mohawk) Bark-eaters. The unflattering name the Mohawks gave to members of the Algonquin tribe who had to exist partially on tree bark during harsh winters. The name is often considered to be the origin of the word "Adirondacks." Another theory, offered a few decades ago by the Smithsonian Institution, suggested that the word "Adirondacks" came from another tribe who lived along the St. Lawrence River in the early 16th century. To them, the word meant "They of the Great Rocks."

High Peaks The 46 mountains in the Adirondacks that are more than 4,000 feet above sea level.

Hollow A small valley.

Homer, Winslow (1836–1910) Famous artist who often painted scenes of the Adirondack forest and its woodsmen.

Howe, John Discovered Ausable Chasm. Made first descent suspended from ropes.

Hypothermia A general cooling that occurs when the human body can no longer produce enough heat to maintain a normal temperature. Signals include shivering; slow, irregular pulse; numbness; and decreasing levels of consciousness. A major danger to hikers and nature photographers who are unprepared for sudden weather changes or wet conditions.

Irving, Washington (1783–1859) Author of *Rip Van Winkle,* a classic in American literature, set in the Catskill Mountains.

Kill Dutch for a stream or river.

Ledge Rock Horizontal rock across a stream which creates a waterfall.

Moraine Jumble of rock, sand, and pebbles left behind by a glacier's retreat.

Mouth The point where a stream or river flows into another body of water.

North Country The area of New York State above the Mohawk River, including the Adirondack Mountains.

Outcrop Exposed rock or rock strata above the ground.

Portage To carry [a canoe] from one body of water to another, or around a waterfall; also, the place over which the craft must be carried.

Precipice A high, overhanging rock or the brink of a cliff.

Raquette French for snowshoes. Name of a river and a lake in the Adirondacks, chosen for the many snowshoes which were discovered (abandoned by Sir John Johnson, his family, and servants as they fled to Canada) on the shore of that lake during the Revolutionary War.

Ravine A deep gorge, usually worn by a flow of water.

Riffle Area in a stream where flowing water mixes with air, charging the stream with oxygen. Slight rapids.

Rivulet A tiny brook; a streamlet.

Shale Rock rich in clay.

Shatter Zone A valley, pulled open by stresses from the uplift of the earth over time. Subsequent stress produces closely spaced joint blocks, many of which collapse under the action of water and ice.

SLR Single-lens-reflex camera

Smoke Effect In photography, the visual effect achieved on film when making a time exposure (1/8 second or longer) of waterfalls and rapids. The longer the exposure time, the greater the effect. Also called "cotton-candy" effect.

Snag A still-standing dead tree, killed by a permanent rise in water level which drowned its roots. Snags often provide popular habitats for birds.

Space Blanket Lightweight emergency blanket. Silver side reflects body heat for warmth. Also can be used as a windbreaker or ground cloth.

Switchback A trail that zig-zags up/down steep terrain. Although making the route longer, it reduces the strain on the hiker. A switchback trail also minimizes erosion during rainstorms and spring thaws by diverting water runoff.

Thoreau, Henry David (1817–1862) An American writer and naturalist.

Topographic Map A map indicating changes in elevation.

Trailhead The point where a trail begins.

Trail Mix High-energy snack for hikers. Often consists of some or all of the following: mixed nuts, raisins, dried apples, dates, sesame seeds, sunflower seeds, and granola. Also called "gorp."

Watershed Geographic drainage area from which a large body of water, such as a river, is fed.

Weir A shallow dam in a stream, usually constructed to divert water to a mill or irrigation ditch.

Wisconsin Glacier Covered much of New York State until slightly less than 10,000 years ago. Considered by most geologists to be responsible for depositing erratics and sculpting most of the current features of the Adirondack Mountains.

BIBLIOGRAPHY

The authors would especially like to acknowledge two series of hiking guides which proved invaluable. Barbara McMartin's series of books (from Countryman Press) thoroughly cover the Adirondacks and offer directions to many waterfalls. The series of hiking guides published by the Adirondack Mountain Club is excellent. Both series are meticulously prepared and provide accurate directions to trail heads and trail hikes.

Hochschild, H. K. (1962). *Lumberjacks and Rivermen in the Central Adirondacks: 1850-1950.* Blue Mountain Lake, New York: Adirondack Museum.

Isachsen, Y.W. et al. (1991). *Geology of New York: A Simplified Account.* Albany: New York State Museum Geological Survey, State Education Department. University of New York Educational Leaflet No. 28.

Jaffe, E. and Jaffe, H. (1986). *Geology of the Adirondack High Peaks Region, A Hiker's Guide.* Lake George, New York: The Adirondack Mountain Club.

Lamb, W. (1956).*The Historical Atlas of New York State.* Phoenix, New York: Frank E. Richards.

McMartin, B. and Kick, P. (1985). *Fifty Hikes in the Hudson Valley.* Woodstock, Vermont: Backcountry Publications.

Newhall, Beaumont (1949). *The History of Photography from 1839 to the Present Day.* New York, New York: The Museum of Modern Art.

Raymo, C. and M.E. Raymo (1989). *Written in Stone: A Geological History of the Northeastern United States.* Chester, Connecticut: The Globe Pequot Press.

Schneider, P. (1997). *The Adirondacks, A History of America's First Wilderness.* New York, New York: Henry Holt and Company.

Titus, Robert (1993). *The Catskills: A Geological Guide.* Fleischmanns, New York: Purple Mountain Press, Limited.

——— (1996). *The Catskills in the Ice Age.* Fleischmanns, New York: Purple Mountain Press, Limited.

Van Andel, T.H. (1985). *New Views of an Old Planet. Continental Drift and the History of the Earth.* Cambridge, England: Cambridge University Press.

Van Diver, B. (1985). *Roadside Geology of New York.* Missoula, Montana: Mountain Press Publishing Company.

White, W. C. (1967). *Adirondack Country.* New York, New York: Alfred A. Knopf, Inc.

INDEX OF PHOTOGRAPHS

ADIRONDACKS

CATSKILLS

ABOUT THE AUTHORS

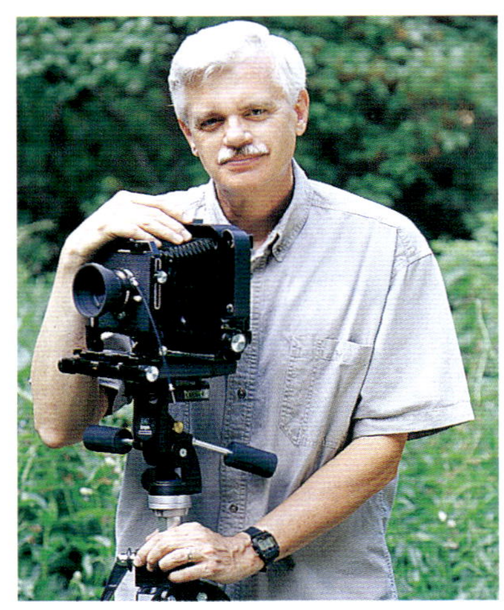

KEITH BOAS has been photographing the scenery of New York State since college when he worked summers as a postcard photographer in the Adirondacks. After receiving a degree in photography from Rochester Institute of Technology, he joined Kodak where, for 35 years, he produced travelogues, photo how-to books, and a variety of marketing materials to help launch new products.

Now retired from Kodak, he does freelance photography and contract writing. Most of his photographic work focuses on the landscape and landmarks of the northeastern United States. Keith's wife, Carol, often keeps him company on his photo expeditions.

When not hunting for interesting subjects with his camera, Keith generally can be found in his backyard garden, tending his bonsai collection and his homemade, recirculating waterfall.

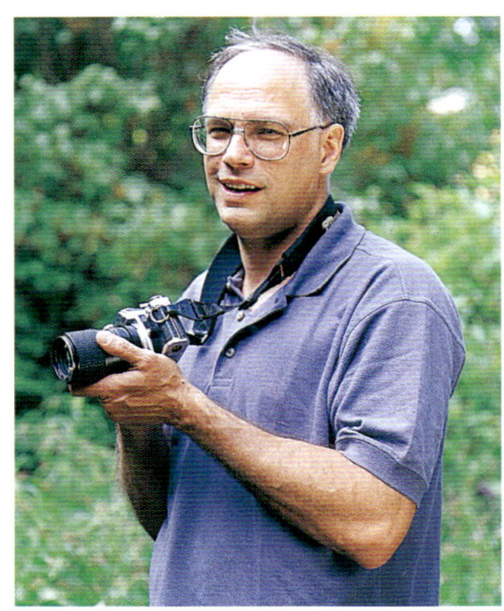

DEREK DOEFFINGER, author of *Waterfalls and Gorges of the Finger Lakes* (McBooks Press, 1997), works in marketing at the Rochester headquarters of Kodak, where he has also written some photography books. His wife, daughter, and their two dogs sometimes accompany him on his waterfall outings. When he's not sloshing up a creek, he's huffing and puffing as he tries to keep up with his daughter while they jog on the Erie Canal towpath.